Also by Jane M. Healy, Ph.D.

*Endangered Minds: Why Children Don't
Think—and What We Can Do About It*

*Your Child's Growing Mind: A Guide
to Brain Development and Learning
from Birth to Adolescence*

*How to Have Intelligent and Creative
Conversations With Your Kids*

Failure to Connect

*How Computers Affect
Our Children's Minds—and
What We Can Do About It*

Jane M. Healy, Ph.D.

A Touchstone Book

Published by SIMON & SCHUSTER

⼂⼋

TOUCHSTONE
Rockefeller Center
1230 Avenue of the Americas
New York, NY 10020

First Touchstone Edition 1999

TOUCHSTONE and colophon are registered trademarks
of Simon & Schuster Inc.

Designed by Jeanette Olender
Manufactured in the United States of America

1 3 5 7 9 10 8 6 4 2

Library of Congress Cataloging-in-Publication Data
Healy, Jane M.
Failure to connect : how computers affect our children's minds—
and what we can do about it/ Jane M. Healy.
p.   cm.
Includes bibliographical references (p. 323) and index.
1. Computers and children.   2. Computer-aided instruction.   I. Title.
QA76.9.C659H43   1998
371.33'4—dc 21   98-24971   CIP
ISBN 0-684-83136-8
0-684-85539-9 (Pbk)

*This book is dedicated to my mother, who
understood nothing about computers but a lot about
living successfully as a human being . . .*

৯৬

*. . . and to my grandchildren, who, I hope,
will understand both.*

Contents

Preface

A popular story in the education business concerns a young girl who was asked to write a report on a book about penguins. Her report, in total, read, "This book told me more about penguins than I really wanted to know." After the past last twenty-four months, I feel a bit the same way about digital technology. This intense adventure, climaxing twenty-five years of enthusiasm over the possibilities of computers in learning, has taken me into scores of classrooms and homes to observe children interacting with their new electronic companions and teachers. As always when one is around children, I have learned, laughed, and cried. I have found myself horrified and thrilled, but rarely bored. I have talked with parents, teachers, and other experts, and from each I have continued to learn. It is impossible to name them all here, but you will meet them in this book and realize how much I owe to their generous sharing of time and thought.

Several individuals—human and digital—were particularly instrumental in helping with this book. First, my agent and friend, Angela Miller, whose not-so-subtle prods ("I'm not going to buy you another lunch until you give me a new book proposal") and ongoing enthusiasm finally got me back into the writer's chair. I was immensely fortunate to work again with editor Bob Bender, whose calm reassurance and faith that "This is the right book at the right time" kept the chapters rolling in, and with Johanna Li, always responsive and helpful. Trudi Youngquist often bent her life out of shape to help me with typing, and the reference staff at the Vail Public Library helped me find numerous books and articles. Friends and colleagues listened, sympathized, and, I hope, overlooked my increasingly distracted behavior as the months rolled on. My children, as always, shared interest and support; now that they are parents themselves their insightful comments are more valuable than ever. I am most grateful, as always, to my husband, Tom, who offered timely suggestions and practical support while waiting patiently for his human wife to reemerge at last from the virtual world.

My deepest gratitude and occasional frustration is due to my dear Macintosh and Microsoft Word, to the telephone, the Internet and the fax machine, and to a handy laptop that enabled me to keep working on location. I thank them for not crashing too often, and for teaching me to be a "bricoleur" (an explorer in pushing mystery buttons) instead of a linear thinker in need of precise directions. It is never too late to adopt a new learning style, it seems.

Finally, I would like to express gratitude to all those parents and educators who have attended my lectures and lent their stories, suggestions, questions, and encouragement to this effort. Anyone who thinks that today's adults do not care deeply about their children and their children's future is sorely mistaken. But we all need guidance, and that's what I hope this book will provide.

Failure to Connect

PART ONE

Digital Dreams Meet Reality

Chapter One

Blundering Into the Future:
Hype and Hope

"Computing is not about computers any more. It is about living."
Nicholas Negroponte [1]

"Computers? The more the better. I want my kids to be prepared for the real world out there."
Suburban father, Atlanta, Georgia

"Technology! I feel as if we're being swept down this enormous river—we don't know where we're going, or why, but we're caught in the current. I think we should stop and take a look before it's too late."
Assistant Superintendent of Schools, Long Island, New York

Technology shapes the growing mind. The younger the mind, the more malleable it is. The younger the technology, the more unproven it is. We enthusiastically expose our youngsters to new digital teachers and play-mates, but we also express concern about the development of their brains, bodies, and spirits. Shouldn't we consider carefully the poten-tial—and irrevocable—effects of this new electronic interface with childhood?

Today's children are the subjects of a vast and optimistic experiment. It is well financed and enthusiastically supported by major corpora-tions, the public at large, and government officials around the world. If it is successful, our youngsters' minds and lives will be enriched, society will benefit, and education will be permanently changed for the better. But there is no proof—or even convincing evidence—that it will work.

The experiment, of course, involves getting kids "on computers" at school and at home in hopes that technology will improve the quality of learning and prepare our young for the future. But will it? Are the new technologies a magic bullet aimed straight at success and power? Or are we simply grasping at a technocentric "quick fix" for a multitude of problems we have failed to address?

In preparing to write this book I spent hundreds of hours in class-rooms, labs, and homes, watching kids using new technologies, picking the brains of leaders in the field, and researching both off- and on-line. As a longtime enthusiast for and user of educational computing, I found this journey sometimes shocking, often disheartening, and occa-sionally inspiring. While some very exciting and potentially valuable things are happening betweeen children and computers, we are cur-rently spending far too much money with too little thought. It is past time to pause, reflect, and ask some probing questions.

This book will present a firsthand survey of the educational comput-ing scene, raising core issues that should be addressed before we com-mit to computer-assisted education. We will consider technology use in light of brain development, stages and styles of learning, emotional-social development, and successful educational practice in school and at home. We will examine questions such as:

> ❧ When and how should children start using computers, and should they have them at home?

> ❧ How can parents and teachers support children's learning with technology?

> ❧ What kind of software applications and educational technology uses are best at different ages?

> ❧ Which ones may be harmful, and why?

> ❧ How do we balance education and entertainment?

> ❧ How should we deal with health concerns related to computer use?

> ❧ Will computers make human beings smarter—or will they erode important forms of thought? How will interacting with artificial brains influence our ideas about what constitutes "intelligence"?

  ❧ What effect will technologies have on children's creativity and their emotional, personal, and social development?

  ❧ Will, or should, emerging technologies change our concept of education?

  ❧ If schools are adopting computer technology, which priorities are most important?

And . . . the most important question of all: How can we best help the young prepare for a changing and unpredictable future?

Belief vs. Fact

"In sum, if computers make a difference, it has yet to show up in achievement."

Samuel G. Sava, Executive Director, National Association of Elementary School Principals, in a 1997 speech [2]

"The research is set up in a way to find benefits that aren't really there. Most knowledgeable people agree that most of the research isn't valid. . . . Essentially, it's just worthless."

Edward Miller, Former Editor, *Harvard Education Letter* [3]

Exaggerated Hopes and Unmet Promises

Why do we so desperately need to believe in computers? After surveying current attitudes for the nonprofit organization Learning in the Real World, William Ruckeyser told me, "The nearest thing I can draw a parallel to is a theological discussion. There's so much an element of faith here that demanding evidence is almost a sign of heresy." Witness the federal government's initiative to wire all schools for telecommunications by the year 2000, under the simplistic assumption that connecting kids to "information" will somehow make them more able to read and use it intelligently. Meanwhile, library and sometimes even school budgets are cut across the nation.

Eighty percent of people who plan to buy a personal computer soon will cite children's education as the main reason.[4] Ninety percent of voters in the United States are convinced that schools with computers can do a better job of education, and 61 percent would support a federal tax increase to speed the introduction of technology into the schools.[5] In 1995 the American Association of School Administrators published the results of a survey that asked parents, teachers, leaders from various fields, and members of the general public what skills would be important for students graduating in the twenty-first century. "Computer skills and media technology" ranked third in a list of sixteen possibilities, outvoted only by "basic skills" (reading, writing, and math) and "good work habits." Computer skills were deemed more important than "values" (e.g., honesty, tolerance) by every group but the leaders. "Good citizenship" and "curiosity and love of learning" were considerably farther down the list, and such topics as "knowledge of history and geography" and "classic works (e.g., Shakespeare, Plato)" were near the bottom (highly valued by only 29 and 21 percent of business leaders, respectively).[6]

An atmosphere of hysteria surrounds the rush to connect even preschoolers to electronic brains. Of the ten best-selling children's CD-ROM titles sold in 1996, four are marketed for children beginning at age three. Computer programs are advertised for children as young as eighteen months. In the United States, computer users under the age of six owned an average of six software titles in 1996, a number increasing every year.[7] Parents and educators in Europe and Japan are astonished as well as amused by this push toward electronic precocity.

It is less amusing to realize that research to be cited throughout this book demonstrates how computer "learning" for young children is far less brain-building than even such simple activities as spontaneous play or playing board games with an adult or older child. "Connecting" alone has yet to demonstrate academic value, and some of the most popular "educational" software may even be damaging to creativity, attention, and motivation. In 1995, a seminar of knowledgeable academics concluded that computers have *no place at all* in the lives of young children.[8] In 1997, Samuel Sava, head of the National Association of Elementary School Principals, told school leaders that computers have done little to improve student achievement and questioned the nation's spending up to $20 billion a year to fill schools with computers.[9]

Even for older children and teens, research has yet to confirm substantial benefits from most computer-related learning products at school or at home. Analyzing home computer use, Julian Sefton-Green and David Buckingham from the University of London found "not much to be excited about." They learned that parents tended to greatly overestimate the power of computer hardware to help their youngsters' learning and "secure their educational future." A major problem was that few knew how to support their child's use of the technology and allowed children unlimited and unsupervised computer use. Most were not worried about kids having open access to the Internet. The one thing parents did fear was too much time with computer games; some of the youngsters had incorporated schemes by which they could quickly punch some keys to substitute a page of text when a parent walked through the room.

Although Sefton-Green and Buckingham began the study expecting to find highly imaginative and stimulating computer use, they discovered that youngsters used the computer mainly for solitary "messing around," with little creative or academic outcome. "The sheer availability of home computers did not itself make children use them for educational purposes," they conclude. Moreover, "It has been assumed that the computer will simply facilitate children's 'natural' imagination by somehow bypassing the need for them to develop technical skills. . . . Yet if anything we have found the reverse to be true. . . . Indeed, we suspect that the idea of a 'naturally' computer-literate child is more of a social construct than an empirical reality." These authors conclude that children and teens need close adult mentoring and well-defined educational projects to make their technology use constructive.[10]

Needed: Accountability and Common Sense

In an era when mechanistic and scientific remedies are sought more often than humanistic or personal ones, such faith that technology can accomplish what mere mortals have failed to do is not surprising. Currently, school districts are lining up to spend scarce education dollars on equipment that stands a good chance of being outdated in two or three years. These funds, as well as the considerable space needed for the computers, are often drawn from more developmentally important areas such as physical education, art, music, drama, traditional library resources, and textbook purchases. Much of the glitzy new machinery is either misused or underused once it arrives at school; not only do machines sit idle because of lack of technical support or teacher preparation, but poor implementation of software turns learning time into trivial game-playing.

We lack both substantive research and guidelines on how to use new technology in the most constructive way for children—or, in fact, for learners of any age. Pressing issues of developmental readiness for computer use have barely been explored. What is right for a fourteen-year-old may not be right—and may be outright damaging—for a four-year-old. Questions about emotional, social, personal, and health hazards have barely been asked, much less answered.

The few studies showing positive results for educational technology have been largely funded by computer corporations or conducted by educators who are (or would like to become) consultants for the technology business. Even glowing anecdotal reports from classrooms often turn out to have been written by "teacher-techies" who are bucking for jobs in the industry. In the next chapter we will review the major studies, but the fact is that we still await objective validation of benefits from educational computing.

Nevertheless, beyond naive excitement there are still exciting prospects. Not all learning is easily measured, and the majority of educational computer use to date has been poorly managed and badly executed. Throughout this book you will find both positive and negative examples. I believe success is possible, but it is not automatic, inexpensive, or attained without a great deal of thought and effort.

If you are a parent, a teacher, or a citizen interested in the upcoming generation, you need to consider these questions seriously. This technology is expensive not only in terms of money but also in the use of developmental time—that precious interval when brain, body, and spirit are still at their most formative stages. We need a critical and objective analysis and clear, practical guidelines for classroom and home.

From Techno-Pusher to Critic: A Journey of Puzzlement

My own experience with educational computing is typical of those of many educators who have reluctantly moved from bedazzled advocacy to troubled skepticism. It is also instructive in several respects, not the least of which is shaking up some simplistic pedagogical assumptions.

Certainly, it has been a long and interesting odyssey since my initial honeymoon with machine intelligence back in 1979. Fired with enthusiasm from using computers in graduate work, I wangled funding to buy the first Apple computer for the elementary school of which I was then principal. For an educational psychologist eternally fascinated by questions about why and how children learn, the potential of this left-hemisphere extension (some might say contraction) of the human brain was irresistible. Soon a dedicated tenderfoot programmer in Applesoft Basic, I was even willing to forgive the machine's choleric disposition and struggled excitedly on while it superciliously spat out its favorite phrase: "syntax error." (Those were the days when a "user-friendly" machine would have been spurned by aspiring "digerati.") I was eager to observe firsthand the computer's potential with kids, so I selected a half-dozen of our best fourth-grade math students for an "enrichment" mini-course.

Since accessible educational software had yet to be invented, our project was to learn how to write a simple program. "Learn" is the operative word here, for teacher and students were about equally innocent. Nevertheless, to my great pride (which, as you know, always goes before a fall!) we finally managed after ten class sessions to make the computer display a simple multiplication problem and ask for a reply; the user would then type in an answer and receive either a congratulatory message ("Good job!") or a prompt ("Try again.").

I was ecstatic and, I'm afraid, a bit obnoxious in touting the potential of this amazing gadget. The students appeared to enjoy the exercise, or possibly they welcomed a change from their classroom routines, but I believed they were learning important skills of logic and sequencing ("if/then" statements, for example), if not a great deal of math. In fact, I immodestly concluded that this was probably close to a perfect lesson with teacher and students exploring and learning together—while having a lot of fun. I was well on my way as a born-again techie.

Years later, with only some of my original enthusiasm dimmed, I returned to the same district as a visitor observing technology use and sat down in the high-school computer lab to do some word processing. By chance, the young lady at the machine next to me was one of those original fourth-graders, now a charming junior, who greeted me cheerfully.

"Well, Charmayne!" I beamed. "What an amazing coincidence! Here we are together in the computer lab, and I'm sure you remember that your very first computer experience was with *me!*"

Charmayne smiled, politely, but blankly. "I'm sorry, Dr. Healy, I don't remember that at all," she said.

One of my best lessons? As my pedagogical ego withered, she added, "But I do remember my fifth-grade computer teacher."

The death blow had been struck. What had this person done that I failed to do?

"His dandruff was so bad that every time he shook his head it fell all over the keyboard!"

Moral: Kids are always learning, but they're not always learning what we think they're learning—even with the help of technology! It is all too easy to become so seduced by the glitz and novelty of this wondrous equipment that we make optimistic assumptions about what it is doing for their brains. Experience suggests we should temper our enchantment with a critical look at whether anything educational is really being accomplished.

Playing With Powerful Ideas

It wasn't long before I discovered Seymour Papert's seminal book, *Mindstorms: Children, Computers, and Powerful Ideas,* first published in 1980.[11] In it he describes his innovative programming language, LOGO, through which even five-year-olds might discover fundamental principles of mathematics while learning to write simple computer programs. A true advocate of "constructivism" in education, Papert holds that all learners absorb and remember best when they themselves "construct" or figure out the underlying principles of the lesson rather than having the teacher "spoon-feed" it to them. Needless to say, considerable disagreement surrounds this "learner-centered" approach to education, which stands in direct contrast to more traditional methods. In the next chapter we will return to this point, since "constructivism" has become a fulcrum of controversy in educational politics. For now, here's the basic principle of LOGO: The student develops his own learning by exploring and programming a computer. Also called "turtle geometry," LOGO invites the child/programmer to input commands to a small turtle icon on the screen, which then "walks" a certain number of steps either in a straight line or at an angle, drawing a line as it goes. For example, in programming the turtle to draw a square, the child will ultimately figure out that he must walk straight for a certain distance, turn 90 degrees, then repeat the action three more times. The programs have subsequently been updated and expanded, although research has never consistently substantiated the expected educational gains.[12] (We will consider possible reasons as we view some current LOGO applications in Chapter 8.)

Back in the early 1980s, however, *Mindstorms* got me so excited about dynamic new electronic teaching that I began running around the country searching for schools to observe, wrote a grant request, and obtained funding to buy two more computers for our school (I think we may now have been up to Apple IIEs), to pay a part-time teacher willing to learn to be a computer consultant, and to purchase a floor "turtle" for the kindergarten. The latter, a space-age-looking object which only vaguely resembled any real-life amphibian, beeped, walked and turned on typed command from the child at the keyboard, theoretically making the experience more accessible for the young programmers.

The outcome? Although we tried to build into the study reliable pre- and post-tests of math and visual-spatial reasoning, we were not very confident of the tests, and we did not find any statistically significant improvements even at the end of three years—results typifying the problems and outcomes associated with measuring intellectual gains from computer use. Nevertheless, I was convinced we were doing something good for children's minds, and especially for the girls, who may tend to avoid activities of this sort in favor of more pencil-and-paper work, to the probable detriment of their future mathematical rea-

student who had never used a computer before arriving at college. All agreed they primarily wanted students who could read, communicate, and think; computer use was far down the list of priorities. Moreover, here are the three estimates of how long it would take for a complete neophyte to get up to speed once on campus: (a) one month; (b) one semester; (c) one week (in a course required of all freshmen, regardless of past experience).

These experiences, and others, caused me to question many of my own assumptions. Just because children—particularly young ones—are performing tasks that look technologically sophisticated does not mean they are learning anything important. Moreover, the activity inevitably takes time and attention away from other types of learning. Today's software is far more powerful, far more compelling, and, as you will discover in later chapters, far more dangerous than anything we conceived of back in the early days. The brain undergoes certain "critical" or "sensitive" periods in both childhood and adolescence when learning environments exert special kinds of effects and when certain types of activities and stimulation are most appropriate and necessary to maximize mental potential. By providing the proper kind of experience at different ages, we help shape not only the intelligence of brains, but also children's "habits of mind" for a lifetime. If we waste or subvert these developmental windows, the losses may be irrecoverable. I hope we will ultimately learn to harness electronic media to assist learning without compromising other important aspects of development. At present, however, we are still figuring out how to do this, and it is a mistake to make guinea pigs out of children who have better ways to spend their time.

Challenging Change

Rather than mindlessly accepting "change" as important and necessary for our children, we should begin by pausing and reflecting on the long-range personal and cultural implications of our new technologies. Neil Postman, who can always be counted on to raise probing questions about any form of mechanization, is profoundly skeptical of the American search for a "technological fix." He also objects to the overwhelming desire to fit our children for "success" in the marketplace. Schooling, he maintains, should not be so much about making a living as about making a life. His book *Technopoly* presents a strong case that change, per se, does not necessarily represent an advance.

"Stated in the most dramatic terms, the accusation can be made that the uncontrolled growth of technology destroys the vital sources of our humanity. It creates a culture without a moral foundation. It undermines certain mental processes and social relationships that make human life worth living." In addition to considering what technology can do, he suggests, we should also examine what it may undo.[13]

At 10:30 one mellow Saturday night in October, 1996, I happened to be out walking on the upper east side of Manhattan. Few people were strolling at that hour, but I noticed one brightly lit store which contained a veritable bustle of activity. It was one of those all-hour work centers where computers, copying machines, FAX, and other time-saving appurtenances of modern office life are available for short-term use. There crowded at least two dozen sharp-looking twenty- or thirty-somethings, energetically going about their business as if it were 10:00 A.M. on a Monday morning.

As a parent and a grandparent, I find such experiences unsettling. Most of us love these electronic conveniences—but at 10:30 on Saturday night? Is this what we now call living? Is this the purpose for which we are educating our children—so they can work, work, work, until the work itself substitutes for life and becomes the central purpose of their days? Are we programming our children, and thereby turning them into analogues of the machines they so efficiently utilize?

Cello Lessons or Video Games?

Surveying expert opinion on the question of how computers will ultimately affect our children's lives yields a provocative range of ideas. Patricia Greenfield, a cultural psychologist at UCLA who specializes in analyzing tool use and art forms, points out that as a culture we increasingly esteem technological intelligence and devalue the social and emotional. Thus we expose our children to computer games, programmed learning software, and computer camps, all of which have children working with external symbols (pictures on a screen) rather than with internal ones (language, mental images). Although parents tend to be skeptical about video games, many overcome their concerns with the hope that their children are learning mental skills somehow valuable for the future. (Greenfield, in fact, terms these games the "training wheels for the computer age.")[14] Many educators find this emphasis troubling. Linda Pogue, of York University in Toronto, observes, "This machine is so cognitive, we're forgetting the affective [emotional and social development]. I find children and university students too much in their heads—they're not experiencing life, they're thinking about life."[15]

Software magnate Bill Gates paints a much rosier picture: "I think this is a wonderful time to be alive. There have never been so many opportunities to do things that were impossible before. It's also the best time ever to start new companies, advance sciences such as medicine that improve quality of life, and stay in touch with friends and relatives." Gates adds, however, "It's important that both the good and bad points of the technological advances be discussed broadly so that society as a whole, rather than just technologists, can guide their direction."[16]

Douglas Rushkoff, author of *Playing the Future*,[17] represents a new cadre of thinkers who are pushing hard on old value systems. He sees traditional educational priorities based on linear thought (as in written text, planning ahead, writing or reading music, or cause-and-effect reasoning), dying off in favor of the holistic flow of living in the moment. He thinks today's youngsters, whom he terms "screenagers," represent an evolutionary leap in human consciousness because they aren't bound by old-fashioned ideas of order but rather thrive in the state of chaos found on the Internet.

Physicist Fritjof Capra disagrees. He sees the information technologies as totalitarian, demanding ever more of our time and priorities, distorting people's relationships to the world and to each other, and eliminating alternative views of reality. Capra, a committed skeptic regarding children's computer use, believes we are far too worried about our youngsters' store of information; we should be more concerned with the kind of thinking, caring, aesthetically sensitive humans they are becoming. "Increasingly, all forms of culture are being subordinated to technology, and technological innovation, rather than the increase in human well-being, has become synonymous with progress," he asserts.[18]

"We need a large technical class that is well trained to do work that is mind-numbingly boring," stated Eric Roberts of Stanford University's computer science program in commenting on an escalating demand for computer science majors with programming skills.[19] While many programmers disagree, Roberts's remarks should at least make us pause to consider the future prospects of children propelled into toddler-to-teen technology.

As I watch solitary youngsters sitting at home mesmerized by their latest video game or software, I am reminded of Bill McKibben's observations in *The Age of Missing Information,* as he laments our children's separation from nature and real-life lessons such as patience and limits learned from interacting with the physical world.[20] The global consciousness of an information society, he worries, is separating us from local, regional, and personal consciousness in which our actions have direct and observable effects on other living things. McKibben contends there is as much important "information" and a great deal more depth inherent in studying natural phenomena in real (snail-paced!) time than in cruising nature videos. For a child, reflectively examining a leaf or a pebble would be far more valuable than any published CD-ROM.

Philosophical arguments aside, what we really need to think about is how to prepare our children for life in an information-loaded but depersonalized landscape. Is it by connecting them to computers, or by spending comparable time on giving them an early grounding in humanity? As one thoughtful scientist and father mused, "Should I spend the money on cello lessons or video games?" Not enough people are asking these questions. I keep recalling Thoreau's warning that if we aren't careful, we could all become "tools of our tools."

Technology and Power

Throughout history, new technologies have altered the existing social order, economy, and power structure. "Technology" is any tool or medium that helps people accomplish tasks or produce products more efficiently, and computers are only the latest in a long line of innovations—going back to axes and fire—that have changed the way humans interact with the world and each other. Computers, like all technologies that introduce new information or alter the format of information, are changing the balance of power in schools. Increasingly, the "techies," rather than the educators, hold the power to make educational decisions.

"When these computers first came out, they were simple enough that any of us could deal with them. Now hardware and software have gotten so complicated, as they've added all this new gadgetry—most of which we don't even need—you have to have an 'expert' just to keep it running. I'm really disillusioned. The whole field is being taken over by techno-nerds—they know basically nothing about education but they're starting to run the show instead of the teachers," one teacher remarked bitterly.

"The whole movement has been driven by techies, the 'priests and priestesses,' from the beginning of mainframes, and now it's getting worse because everyone on campus is networked," agrees Al Rudnitsky, a technology enthusiast teaching a popular course on "Information, Technology, and Learning" at Smith College. "We can't manipulate our own equipment because we might mess up the whole system. Most troubling," he feels, "is that most teachers have no underlying conception of what they ought to be doing with these things. They are overwhelmed by their regular duties; they don't have enough time to prepare first-rate instructional programs for a whole new medium."[21]

Educators are worried that education is becoming an adjunct to the technology business, a sort of training school for the high-tech world. We parents want to see our children succeed, but the foundations for true success—even future technology "guru" status—rest on skills that will not become obsolete with the changing of a microprocessor. Most successful technology innovators did not grow up with computers, but rather with rich, internal imaginations. Many were divergent thinkers who failed to flourish in the traditional world of school.

In ensuing chapters we will see how the adult-child balance of power may also change as a function of computerized learning. For now, let's introduce a final theme, which concerns the changes in mental skills that will inevitably accompany the increased use of so-called digital tools along with the erosion of abilities that could result from using too much of today's inferior software.

Changing Technology, Changing Brains

"Reading books is boring and it takes too long. Searching the Web is faster and more fun because we can get sound recordings, like of a dolphin's sounds, or a video of the discovery of the bow of the Ti-tanic."

Eleven-year-old student, Glenview, Illinois

In addition to altering society, new technologies also have a disconcerting habit of changing the mental skills and even the brain organization of people using them. Historically, one of the most profound examples of this neurological reorganization accompanied the advent of language, which furthered the size and power of left-hemisphere systems for logical, analytical thought. More recently, scientists have observed that even differences between pictorial languages (one form of Japanese writing, for example) and alphabetic scripts of European languages cause physical alterations during brain development.[22] Fast-paced, nonlinguistic, and visually distracting television may literally have changed children's minds, making sustained attention to verbal input, such as reading or listening, far less appealing than faster-paced visual stimuli. (This thesis is explored in depth in my book *Endangered Minds*.) One of my most pressing curiosities in writing this book has been how computer use will change the developing brain, and how we can maximize its positive effects without neglecting aptitudes we value, such as reading, reflection, original thought, or internally driven motivation and sustained analysis.

"But It's Only a Tool . . ."

"It's so cool to be an animator, and you can really mess with people's heads."

David J. Masher, Animator for "Carmen Sandiego"[23]

In almost every conversation I have with either parents or educators about technology, this phrase arises: "But it's *only* a tool." This dismissal is, of course, a comforting demystification. Tools are subordinate to humans, like crayons or hammers. Surely, nothing to worry about so far as our kids' minds are concerned.

I disagree. Whatever your attitude toward computer technology, neither this machine itself, nor the software it uses, is *only* a tool. First, studies demonstrate that people react to and treat computers, no matter what their software, as more "human" than machine.[24] Second, the minute we add software, we are subject to the objectives, knowledge base, interests, and the biases—recognized or not—of the programmers.

Even utilitarian, tool-like software, such as word-processing programs and computer-aided design, imposes subtle attitudes. For example, students using word-processing software instead of pencil and paper tend to be motivated to write more but may regard the printout as finished before it is carefully edited because the first draft already looks so neat. Teachers are confronting the need to reevaluate their customary criteria in grading papers when masses of information can be downloaded, complete with graphics, spruced up with elaborate formats and typefaces, and presented as the result of "research." The very availability of spell-check programs and calculators calls into question how much time to spend teaching "basic skills" such as spelling and arithmetic, as well as how actually to go about it. (More about all this later.) Drawing or designing by computer likewise changes the task demands—and the mental skills required—from doing the same work by hand, and may even alter our definitions of creativity.

Many of us who have struggled with "upgraded" versions of a familiar software package may agree with Clifford Stoll, a disillusioned pioneer of the Internet, who comments, "The computer requires almost no physical interaction or dexterity, beyond the ability to type . . . and demands rote memorization of nonobvious rules. You subjugate your own thinking patterns to those of the computer. Using this 'tool' alters our thinking processes."[25] Pointing out that the handwritten note is qualitatively different from an e-mail greeting, Stoll also worries that by learning to depend on a computer when confronted with a problem, we will limit our ability to recognize other solutions, and ultimately degrade our own thinking powers.

Others, of course, are convinced the computer enhances our mental

powers by enabling us to farm out low-level skills and mechanical operations and focus on the "big picture" reasoning which only humans can
(thus far) do. Computerized interventions have repeatedly shown their
value in helping the learning disabled and physically handicapped bypass difficulties and exercise their true intelligence. Yet as computer
power and our dependence on it expands, this "tool" may be sliding ever
so quietly into the driver's seat.

THE STATE OF CHILDREN'S SOFTWARE: HARDLY A "TOOL" FOR LEARNING

Unfortunately, the state of most software "tools" for either entertainment or learning is disappointing at best and abysmal at worst. George
Burns, director of computer use at the highly regarded Bank Street
College of Education in New York City, is one of numerous thoughtful
educators who believe that approximately 90 percent of current "educational" software is not worth buying.[26] Currently, most is programmed
by "techies" ("market droids" in the words of one Apple executive I
spoke to) who have little if any knowledge—or interest—in child development or educational philosophy. Many are described in the trade
as "classic computer nerds" who take their work very seriously but primarily enjoy seeing if they can make a program do something—for the
pure excitement of making it work. Thus much "educational" software
is crowded with extraneous and time-consuming effects that accomplish little beyond distracting children and distancing them from real
learning. Moreover, many programmers are more interested in technical than human interfaces and are forced by speed-of-light production
scheduling to subvert personal and social concerns to almost inhuman
working hours. "Speed is God. And time is the devil," one computer executive stated recently as he exhorted his employees toward ever
higher-speed product development.[27]

Are these the values we want influencing and teaching our children?
More responsible companies are employing educational consultants,
but as has happened in television, their counsel may not be heeded
when "bottom-line" issues are at stake. The market moves quickly, and
when it does, most software firms will worry less about educational
goals than amusing special effects.

In the next chapter we will look closely at some examples and consider how software decisions both reflect and influence our ideas about how children should be taught. I hope we will put to rest the notion that a computer is *only* a tool.

The Plan of This Book

To probe the effects of any technology on young people's minds, we should first understand the fundamental processes of mental growth and brain maturation. I have approached the topics in the following pages from my perspective as a developmental and educational psychologist, presenting important background information about ages and stages of cognitive development and what adults can do to optimize their children's mental growth. Thus, this book incorporates a practical guide on how to help children develop their minds right alongside the when, where, how, and why of using—or not using—technology to assist in the process.

I must also mention that, although I have been invited by several software developers to consult on products, I have no business association with or particular allegiance to anyone in the computer industry.

The book is divided into three parts. In the next two chapters we will visit the current scene in schools, homes, and home schools, review the basics of educational computing, and offer guidelines for technology choices. Part Two will treat with personal issues in technology use: physical health, intellectual and brain development, and the social, emotional, and other personal aspects of children and teens using computers. Part Three describes practical applications that illustrate appropriate and inappropriate ways to use new learning technologies with different age groups. Finally, I will tackle some observations about the future, which will inevitably present our young people with challenges not yet envisioned. With thought, planning, and our own good sense, we should be able to develop young minds that are able to deal not only with these challenges, but also with anything else that the digital revolution has up its hard drive.

Chapter Two

Computing Basics for School and Home

"The potential of computers for improving education is greater than that of any prior invention, including books and writing."
Derrick Walker, educational researcher (1984)[1]

"The tacit and achingly optimistic American belief that wonderful technologies will make things better has run into rough water."
Jan Hawkins, Director, Center for Children and Technology (1996)[2]

The "computer revolution" in education involves far more than simply finding new ways to help kids learn. It challenges some of our most deeply held beliefs about how children should be raised and educated. Much of the abysmal state of today's educational technology results from failure to confront three basic issues: (1) technology's potential to alter the adult-child balance of power and change schooling as we have known it; (2) the implications of software choices; (3) appropriate planning for computer use at home and school.

In this chapter we will approach these issues, as I did, by visiting real classrooms and homes to observe what is really being done to our children in the name of "computer learning."

The Balance of Power: Who's in Charge Here?

Mr. Smith's classroom carries the faint scent of computer dust mingling with adolescent angst. Twenty-two computers are arranged around the periphery, with chairs facing the center of the room. As we await the arrival of his students, he explains that I am to see a seventh-grade class starting an eight-week cycle of "computer literacy," including technical information and word processing. This is their second class; in the first they watched a video explaining how a computer works. Mr. Smith, a former industrial arts teacher, sees 125 students a day and also oversees all technology planning and support for the building. We are in a suburban school district noted for its forward-thinking philosophy and strong history of educational excellence.

As the students file in they somberly take their places with their backs to the machines.

"Wear your clothes properly in my class," barks Mr. Smith at one young man with his hat pulled over his eyes. A hostile glance from the student earns him an immediate "time-out" in the hallway.

"Get out of here until you're ready to follow my rules."

Class begins. Half the students take notes and the rest gaze at the floor as Mr. Smith lectures and questions them. He expects precise answers. Students who have parents in the computer business seem to be the only ones who know the material, and I find much that is unfamiliar to me as I try to follow a technical discussion of differences between Macintosh and IBM engineering and fine points of MIPS (millions of instructions per second). Five out of the twenty-two students participate in the discussion; Mr. Smith airs his expertise while the rest avert their eyes and glance at the clock.

"I don't know the name, but . . ." One earnest girl struggles to answer a question.

"Don't give me that," snaps their teacher. "I want a name."

Finally one boy ventures hesitantly, "When can we get started working on the computer?"

"When you learn all about it." Before they can turn their chairs around and touch the keys, each student will have to pass a test on the content of Mr. Smith's lectures.

Three blocks away another seventh-grade computer class is meeting, this one a part of the math curriculum. Here I see a similar set of computers, but the chairs face the machines and each chair holds an intense young body. A hum of energy pervades the room as the teacher circulates, quietly asking questions or responding to requests for guidance. Although MIPS may not be on their minds, these youngsters have little difficulty making the machines do their bidding.

This class is preparing a statistical analysis of data it has collected in a survey on the habits of middle schoolers, such as amount of time spent on homework. Each student is preparing a written report summarizing the findings, and they enthusiastically describe their projects upon request. I am impressed by their mastery of both the technology and the mathematical subject matter.

I stop behind one girl's chair. "Did you find any correlations between these variables?" I ask, clearly recalling my own struggle with these concepts during college years.

"Oh, we can't with this data set," she replies. "These are not continuous variables."

Oh.

Changing Power for a New Generation

> *"I want my son to learn history, not spend his time at school playing computer games!"*
>
> Media Executive, Connecticut suburb

> *"The most interactive experience you ever had with your computer is less interactive than the most meaningless experience you ever had with your cat! Watching the computer industry hop aboard the words 'progressive education' to its own advantage but not to the advantage of teachers or kids makes me uncomfortable."*
>
> Tom Snyder, educational software designer

Computers won't make bad teachers into good ones, but choices in technology use reflect important philosophical differences and may change not only what we teach but also how we teach it. In fact, decisions about technology use are intensifying tensions that have long existed between so-called traditional and progressive educators. On the one hand, computers may reinforce what is sometimes termed the "factory model" of education: a teacher (or a software program) firmly in charge, dispensing a well-defined body of knowledge, and preparing a work force accustomed to lining up, doing what they are told, and not asking too many questions. Far out on the other end of the continuum is the "learner-centered" approach, in which the teacher acts as more of a "coach" and students are expected to ask questions and actively pursue learning because it is important or interesting to them.

For example, in a booklet published by a telecommunications company, computer teacher Peggy Wyns-Madison, from PS 131 in Brooklyn, New York, describes what happened when she switched from traditional whole-class instruction to small-group work with students using open-ended computer software. "My students took control over their learning while having fun too," she comments. "My role as a teacher in the traditional sense vanished."[3]

Many educators think that traditional roles must change because today's students are increasingly difficult to teach. Their learning habits have been shaped by fast-paced media that reduce attention, listening, and problem-solving skills as they habituate the brain to rapid-fire visual input. Moreover, children's media access to the adult world of information has undermined the authority of adults who used to control both the curriculum and the means (e.g., teaching reading) to access it. Faced with wandering attention and even outright rebellion, we search for more positive ways to approach a generation that has become cynical before it has learned to think critically.

Jack McGarvey, middle-school computer teacher in Westport, Connecticut, believes computers will "force a change in the way we all do school." He teaches twelve-year-olds to create multimedia reports using art, animation, photographs, sound, text, and film clips to study Greek mythology. "I have become more of a coach than a dispenser of knowledge," states Mr. McGarvey. "The joy of all this is that these children have rediscovered intuition, a virtue that is not honored in most of today's schools, which still cling, incredibly, to chalk-and-talk as the predominant mode of teaching."

"Empowering" youngsters to "construct" knowledge rather than having adults decide when and how to funnel it into their brains has long been an objective of many future-oriented (some say "progressive") educators. In fact, such constructivist methods long predate the computer, and we lack substantive proof that children gain anything more than fun from adding multimedia. Research by Judi Harris at the University of Texas indicates that having computers in the classroom does not, by itself, change either teachers' belief systems or their teaching. She found they will either select software that reinforces what they have always been doing or simply ignore the computers.[4]

Mr. McGarvey acknowledges that not all of the faculty share his enthusiasm, insisting that more traditional written demonstrations of knowledge require more subject matter understanding than knowing how to scan photos into a report.[5] Other skeptics claim that many glowing reports of computer use are pie-in-the-sky hype promulgated by those more interested in peddling or teaching computer than in teaching subject matter. They worry that new technology is being used as a Trojan horse to smuggle untested—and even radical—theories and lowered standards into the schools.

Power Shifts at Home

"It's really hard to know how to set limits these days."
Parent of a twelve-year-old

On the home front, I constantly hear from parents confronting the issue of how much power to yield to the demands of their media-saturated children. As it becomes difficult to control what comes into the family living room, traditional lines of family authority are constantly tested.[6] Moreover, many intelligent adults who believe themselves technologically challenged cave in too easily to their youngsters' demands for techno-stimulation. They tend to believe software can do a better job of teaching than they could themselves and may even assume that "machine-smarts" are better than "real-world smarts."

I have heard far too often, "These kids are so much smarter than we were. Look how they manage these computers!" Nonsense!! It's not that difficult, and even if your child is using a computer, she still needs your involvement. Your kid may be teaching you about the machine, but you are still in charge of teaching things that are far more important!

In short, computers are a new way to stir up old questions of how best to raise and educate our young. As we begin now to consider the important topics of choosing and using software (defined here as programs or applications, including CD-ROMs) we will discover that these decisions reflect attitudes that may profoundly affect the quality of children's learning.

Software at Work: For Better or Worse

It is 9:30 in the morning as I approach the forbidding hulk of an elementary school in an urban neighborhood noted mainly for the density of its housing projects and the too-often unfulfilled aspirations of the generations they have sheltered. Seeking "best examples" of computer use, I hope to see motivated students, reenergized teachers, new paradigms for learning. This school, noted within the district for the magnitude of its technology expenditures, represents my first stop.

Ascending the stone steps worn concave by yearly echelons of small feet, I check in at the desk of the armed security guard. The building's halls are wide, clean, and empty, suggesting order, purpose, and respect for authority. I glimpse teachers in classrooms with many rows of children earnestly going about the business of school. This is the real world: Whether or not these children are asking questions and "constructing" knowledge is deemed far less important than whether they are on task, attentive, and able to pass the competency test. When released later, the youngsters will march wordlessly through the halls, arranged by height from tallest to shortest, as did the generations before them.

When I locate the computer room—distinguished by a huge banner that reads, "COMPUTERS ARE OUR FUTURE!!!"—I find thirty-two nine- and ten-year-olds lined up at two rows of machines. Each head is adorned with large black earphones, conveying the impression that I am calling on a colony of extraterrestrial gnomes. Each child pursues a solitary task while one teacher and an aide circulate. The teacher—who is actually a paraprofessional employed as chatelaine of this electronic castle (and with an enormous ring of keys to prove it)—explains that this group comes four times a week to practice reading and math skills. Many, she indicates, rolling her eyes down the rows of plugged-in heads, are below grade level in basic skills.

I randomly select a position behind Raoul, who is engaged in a math activity. The director reminds the students to enter the program at the correct level for their ability, but I begin to suspect something is amiss when Raoul effortlessly solves a few simple addition problems and then happily accepts his reward—a series of smash-and-blast games in which he manages to demolish a sizable number of aliens before he is electronically corralled into another series of computations. Groaning slightly, he quickly solves the problems and segues expertly into the next space battle. By the time I move on, Raoul has spent many more minutes zapping aliens than he has doing math. My teacher's soul cringes at the thought of important learning time squandered. I also wonder if what we are really teaching Raoul is that he should choose easy problems so he can play longer, or that the only reason to use his brain even slightly is to be granted—by an automaton over which he has no personal control—some mindless fun as a reward. I wonder who selected this software, which seems so incongruous in the no-nonsense atmosphere of the school. Is there any plan here—or are these machines window-dressing for a struggling district?

Dareesha, on the other side of the room, has been assigned practice in reading skills. According to the aide, she has one of the lowest reading levels in the class and should be getting remedial help in language expression and understanding. Dareesha watches as a page with a few lines of storybook text appears, embellished by a colorful illustration. She examines the pictures as the cursor highlights and a voice reads each phrase of the text. This takes approximately twenty seconds; now Dareesha's face breaks into a broad grin as she seizes the mouse and for several enchanted minutes clicks skillfully on the objects in the illustration. In response, each picture animates and performs a clever act: a mailbox opens and waves its flag, flowers bend in a rhythmic dance, vegetables turn jet-propelled and zoom across the screen. Dareesha, mesmerized, laughs aloud, unfortunately attracting the attention of the aide who materializes over her shoulder. "Read me that story!" she demands. Dareesha wilts and begins futilely to attempt sounding out the words on the screen.

"You'd better try harder or you'll never pass this grade," comments the aide, moving on. Dareesha sighs, looks over her shoulder, makes a few limp passes at the words, which are clearly too difficult for her, and begins once again clicking on the pictures.

As the class files silently out ("You've grown!" exclaims the aide, propelling one child two places ahead in the row), I have a chance to chat with the director of the lab.

"No, I don't have nearly enough time to give attention to each kid," she sighs. "Actually, I'm not really a trained teacher. They drafted me because I was pretty good with these machines. So I get the kids started on the programs, then I can go about my business—a lot of paperwork and there are always a few of these darn things that need fixing."

"Who selects the educational software?" I wonder.

"Oh, I do, mostly. Occasionally we get something from the central office, but the kids like these better. I get all these samples from manufacturers, so I take them home and let my eleven-year-old daughter try them out and pick the ones she likes best. Then we get several copies. I have a budget for ordering new stuff. Some of the CD-ROMs *are real cute.*"

Wincing, I express my thanks and take my leave. The guard is still in place as I sign out of the building.

"Good visit?" she inquires with a smile.

"I guess so," I reply. "I learned a lot."

■ ■ ■

Across town, in a neighborhood of elegant townhomes and modestly shuttered boutiques, I locate the discreet placque of one of the city's most exclusive private schools. A waiting room with Williamsburg decor and gleaming antiques serves as a genteel holding pen for an anxious couple awaiting the admissions director. One of their reasons for choosing this school, they tell me hopefully, is its computer program. "We want our daughter to have a head start," they beam. "That's what kids need these days—everything's so competitive." She will be four in September.

The technical coordinator of the lower school is delighted to show off her lab: twenty sparkling machines and a dazzling array of the latest software. Although the coordinator has no training in teaching or child development—in fact, she "came over" from business—she also serves as computer consultant for software selection to other schools. Among her criteria for choosing new programs, "cute" once again ranks high.

Eighteen small first-grade bodies take seats around the room. "Class" today consists of exploring software, and the level of enthusiasm is high. The director has asked them to pair up ("So they learn to cooperate"), and most of the pairs get on well—mainly by letting the more dominant member handle the mouse. A few altercations break out when the subordinate partner becomes discontented and tries to grab the controls. I am reminded of a comment by a wise preschool teacher: "Automatically teaches cooperation? Ha! What they do is fight." In this case the difficulty is dealt with by promising each his own turn the next time, but a couple of sulky faces remain.

I am looking hard for learning, but I am having trouble finding it. Since every one of these students has access to a computer at home and they choose familiar programs to play with, they are all adept at the controls. The most popular choice is a graphics program that allows them to draw and color pictures on the screen, using the mouse as a drawing implement with a number of "tools" such as different colors and patterns of "paint," wide or narrow lines, etc. They may also add "clip-art" (predrawn images), stamps (stars, dots, letters, etc.), or text. Although currrent educational wisdom suggests this type of program is most valuable when directly linked to some teaching objective, such as illustrating a story the child has written or exploring patterns for a math unit, no such goal is apparent. The fad today involves exploding the pictures with a ticking bomb, which produces a gratifying noise as it instantly annihilates the drawings.

Mindful of many early childhood teachers' reservations about computer drawing programs (see Chapters 5 and 7), I poll the class.

"Would you rather draw with a computer or with crayons and markers?"

All the boys and all but two of the girls vote unequivocally for computers. Why?

"It's easier." (The majority.)

"It's funner."

"It's prettier."

"I can blow it up—that's cool."

The popularity of this type of program guarantees I will have plenty of opportunities in my travels to contemplate whether it is worth the money and the time for children of this age to be delving into this new "multimedia" instead of—or even in addition to—more traditional forms of multimedia such as fingerpaints and mud pies.

One pair of nonartists chooses a "problem-solving" game, making their way through a "virtual" building—vividly depicted in realistic graphics—in a quest to solve a mystery, noticing clues as they go along and making inferences about how each relates to the goal. Trying to get kids to reason and draw conclusions is important, but the way these youngsters (and even older ones I have watched) go about playing the game obviates the purpose, since they approach the problem purely as a "guess-and-test" challenge. That is, one player watches and makes cryptic comments while the mouse-handler runs through the brightly colored scenarios as quickly as possible, clicking randomly until something works. Having learned, purely by trial and error, how to get to level one, they randomly click again until they master level two, and so on. Thus, they eventually build up a seemingly impressive repertoire of the right moves to make without having had to reason about anything. This particular game has a secondary goal of getting the player to make a "mental map" of the building so he doesn't crash repeatedly into the same walls and can navigate intelligently between rooms. Again, this objective is obliterated by the children's guess-and-test strategy.

I am discouraged by my estimate of what they are learning, namely: Don't stop to think, don't work the problem through, don't read the few text screens (even if they could), just jump in and try something—if it doesn't work you can blow it up, start again, or switch programs. I am vividly reminded of the legions of experienced teachers who have plaintively told me, "I can't get these kids to concentrate on anything for more than a few seconds. If the answer doesn't come right away they have no patience and no strategies for problem-solving."

I am also frustrated by my observer role, since I am sure that as a teacher, with only these two students, I could encourage thought and learning from this game. Of course, even with a small class, this option is not possible for the director, who has all she can do to keep everything running and is currently busy rebooting a machine that has rebelled against its overly enthusiastic user. So I gently interrupt the players only to ask them to explain to me what is happening.

"Can you tell me what you're supposed to be doing?"

"Just get to the end," the mouse-handler replies through clenched teeth, as he clicks yet again into the same blind alley and finds himself standing once more outside of the virtual building as the bell rings. Frankly, had he spent this period outside the real building on the playground, he would have engaged in more meaningful problem-solving. As I leave the building, I pass the admissions office where the parent applicants are concluding their interview. I wish I could tell them they should ask some serious questions before picking a school just because it "has computers."

In 1987 Diane Ravitch warned about the danger of letting the "glamour and gimmickry of educational technology" erode the humanistic side of the curriculum, the search for meaning, and the ability to analyze materials that do not produce instant gratification. She quoted a comment by the editor of the technology section of *Forbes* magazine: "In the end it is the poor who will be chained to the computer; the rich will get teachers."[7]

■ ■ ■

It is 5:00 in the afternoon and Suzanne is tired. Running a consulting business at home with two preschoolers underfoot is a challenge, and today has been particularly difficult because she has tried to enforce the "no TV" rule. Suzanne cares a lot about her children's development, and the toys and projects strewn about the living room when I arrive are obviously chosen for their educational value. She glances apologetically at the untidy kitchen, where two-year-old Amy has removed all her clothes and is standing on a chair, blissfully pouring water into containers in the sink. Four-year-old Jeff is sulking on the couch, whining to watch TV. "How about your computer programs?" inquires Suzanne. "Jane wants to see how you can do them."

"Thank goodness we've got the computer," she confides to me. "At least he'll be learning something. This kid would watch something on TV twenty-four hours a day if I'd let him!"

Wordlessly, Jeff runs down to the basement office and climbs into the chair in front of the computer.

"I'll put in the alphabet program . . . you like that one." Suzanne inserts a CD and hastily runs upstairs to check on Amy. Jeff, already mesmerized, seizes the mouse as a display of letter *A* appears. He clicks on the pictures, each of which animates, performs a routine, and recites an alliterative sentence: "The aching alligator avoids the ape." It is a "cute" program, with charming and amusing graphics, and Jeff is riveted to the screen, his mouth hanging slack and silent. "Interaction" consists of pressing the key and looking at the show. At one point I try to initiate a conversation about something on the screen, but Jeff has beamed up beyond my space, oblivious to my voice.

Given Suzanne's choices at this moment, it is understandable why she has seized upon this alternative, but if she thinks her son is "learning" anything more than he would from TV or a children's video, she is probably mistaken. Simply selecting and *watching* a screen is a pallid substitute for real mental activity. Moreover, reading and writing are not primarily built on alphabet knowledge, but on language ability—including the power to listen carefully, understand what others are saying, and express ideas effectively. If Suzanne could spare the energy at this taxing time of day to read to her children and discuss the story or let Jeff play in the kitchen and talk with her while she prepares dinner, she would be doing something far more educational (and "interactive"). Or had Jeff not already been seduced by the hypnotic power of a screen, he might even spend this time playing independently and actively using his brain. But he is a child of the media and perhaps he has already lost touch with the quiet intelligence of his own thoughts.

One of the most troubling aspects of this situation is that most people don't seem to think there's anything wrong with what I've observed. "Don't you love to see these kids learning so much!" is the general attitude. There's no question that one's initial reaction to much children's software is bedazzlement; it takes a while to realize that the remarkable tricks are mostly being played by the computer, not by the child. I admit I tend to be a critical observer, but it doesn't take an educational psychologist to assess the value of computer applications—just cut through the colorful dog-and-pony shows and consider the degree of real mental stimulation. Whose brain is doing the growing—that of the programmer, or that of the child? Fortunately, better choices are slowly becoming available. Here are some practical tips for evaluating software:

Tips for Choosing Software

1. Determine what purpose you wish to accomplish, realistically considering the child's age. Avoid giving a youngster overly advanced selections.

2. Preview the program if possible, and don't always believe package claims. (If you enlist the child's help in the review process, keep in mind that youngsters tend to respond enthusiastically to any novel program—even brain-numbing ones.) Some possible sources of objective information:

Libraries (community or school) often have sample software, and librarians and media specialists are excellent sources of information.

A *trusted teacher* at your child's school or district office may be able to suggest appropriate software that fits with the school's curriculum.

A review in a reputable *magazine or journal*, preferably one that does not accept advertising from software companies, may point you in the right direction.

University libraries subscribe to professional journals in technology education that often contain software reviews. Ask the librarian for assistance.

Friends, neighbors, and other parents at your child's school may be willing to let you borrow software that they own.

Educators can seek out recommendations from reliable colleagues or professional resources.

In schools, experienced hands suggest a *minimum of three faculty evaluations* before any software is purchased. A multidisciplinary perspective is helpful.

"*Just because it's cheap or free, it isn't necessarily any good,*" say the experts.

3. Look for programs with varying levels of difficulty, clear and understandable "graphical user interfaces," i.e., the ease with which the child can navigate through the program's educational features.

4. Examine graphics and sound critically with an eye toward artistic

merit. Is this the material you want influencing your child's aesthetic sensibilities and tastes?

5. Consider whether the content is directly related to the learning or simply a thin veneer of information pasted over a "shoot-'em-up" or icon-clicking game.

6. Does the software encourage original thinking? Is anything left to the child's imagination?

7. Be alert for gender biases in characters or activities. Are both male and female characters portrayed as active problem-solvers?

8. Seek suggestions of activities that go beyond the computer. Do they relate to the program and have some inherent learning value? Are there support materials and noncomputerized activities to provide meaning and follow-up?

9. Does playing this program mean that your child will be "sold" anything—from products to ideas—of which you might not approve?

10. *"Cute" is not a valid criterion for choosing a learning activity.*

Educational Software for Thinking Skills

The best programs can extend problem-solving skills. Here are comments from those in the know about software decisions:

🐾 Josh Barbanel of the *New York Times* sets four criteria for good educational software:

1. It does more than simply transfer paper lessons to the screen. For example, if your child needs skill-building (e.g., multiplication tables, fractions, angles, irregular spelling words), look for programs that intersperse quick drills with more conceptual learning (e.g., interesting simulations that require using the skill to solve the problems).

2. It should teach (i.e., coach the child on why an answer was incorrect or clearly present new information) as well as drill.

3. It should not make them feel stupid if they don't know the answer.

4. It can't be boring.[8]

🐾 Barbanel objects to programs that "secretly scramble their minds, training them to be nonlinear, nonrational thinkers," but wants an "orderly progression of the mind" instead of programs that look like video games or fast-paced television commercials.[9]

    ❧ Software reviewer Warren Buckleitner advises that the best software lets your child "take play one step further with 'virtual' manipulatives, giving her exposure to hard-to-characterize concepts such as symmetry, time and motion" as well as plenty of time to experiment with these concepts. (Still, he points out, the learning gained will never replace that gained by caring for a pet or playing outdoors.)[10]

    ❧ Technology consultant David Thornburg believes the child should be able to "craft a personal pathway through the content" rather than being driven by the program through a set scenario.[11]

All agree that programs should give the child the pleasure of gaining mastery over a difficult problem or succeeding in a task, rather than rewarding with extra games or silliness.

No matter how good the software, children often need direction ("scaffolding") to use it effectively. For example, one California study compared learning from a problem-solving lesson for three groups of ten-year-olds as they worked in pairs on computers. One group was guided in asking good questions; another group was simply told to ask and answer questions with each other; a third group was simply told to solve the problems. The first group's performance on the task, as well as its scores on a follow-up test, was dramatically better than that of either of the other two.[12]

The Seduction of "Edutainment"

I have been asked to consult with a small elementary school, and in my "downtime" I visit the library, where four computers are grouped in one corner. Eight third-graders have been sent here by their teacher to work with a software program designed to motivate story-writing. First they create a picture by selecting one of several backgrounds and elaborate the scene with a wide choice of icons; then with their imagination presumably stimulated, they write a story.

These youngsters have used the program before, and they immediately set to work. Two boys deftly call up a landscape and add a river, a bridge, and a pagoda (although they don't know its name). They drag in icons of trees and flowers and spend a number of minutes debating their placement and experimenting with their size. They are clearly having fun, and the visuals are very compelling, but so far no writing has occurred. Conversation is limited to giggling and terse comments: "It should go there." "O.K." Other groups are similarly engaged, but they, too, have yet to do any writing. Two girls spend the entire time printing their names and changing fonts.

At this point the teacher arrives to check their progress. She is a second-year teacher with a graduate degree from a premier college of education. She scans the group.

"Aren't these great?" She asks me. "It gives them ideas what to write about. We use this program a lot."

"But the period's half over and they haven't done any writing," I point out.

She turns to the children. "I hope you're doing some writing."

At this point, one serious-looking girl becomes disgusted and moves to another area where she can use a computer with plain old word-processing and no graphics. Her partner, who is a dyslexic with a prescription for reading and writing remediation, continues to paste, resize, and erase icons.

At the teacher's urging, the two boys begin a story. "Onse there was a dintist in japan on 48th street." But now they decide the brightness level of the picture is wrong, so they begin to fuss with it and then spend ten minutes choosing some music to add. Soon they determine they don't like the story and start to erase words. At the end of the forty-minute period, they are left with one word, "japan." The group on the end has still written nothing but their names, and another pair has produced a picture and the following text:

"The next day Lila, Jass, Liz where out taking a walk in the forist when a giney apird! I well grat you all three wshis, said the giney. Lila said let me thank. OK said the giney."

Meanwhile, the motivated writer at the word processor has returned with a two-page draft. Although it is unrelated to any computer icons, it displays considerable imagination. The children return to their classroom, where the teacher says to me, "Isn't it wonderful what this technology can do!" Other than getting them out of her hair for the better part of an hour, I seriously wonder.

■ ■ ■

As a language arts specialist, I admit to being a bit hard-nosed about the development of reading and writing skills. I am also easily aroused when children in need of help are wasting valuable instructional time at a critical period of development. Some might say these youngsters are developing their visual creativity and thus are not wasting time, but I cannot agree. First of all, the activity just described doesn't strike me as very creative. Moreover, what skills are being learned? Most children will choose an entertaining visual task over a more taxing linguistic one. The children with limited language skills, who are most in need of verbal exercise, are the most vulnerable. If we don't care about reading and writing, it doesn't matter—but then why are we bothering to send them to school?

An experienced and capable teacher—with time and energy to plan and supervise—can devise numerous ways to use such software in a more constructive manner. But will that accomplish anything more than—or even as much as—crayons or markers, paper, pictures from books, and basic word-processing software (or even a pencil)? Are the kids just described above motivated to write—or to be entertained? Why use unrelated images of which they have no personal experience—either in their lives or in their own imaginations? Or are we admitting that the minds of today's children have been stripped of images unless inserted by some form of media?

"Edutainment" is a term meant to describe such electronically sugar-coated "learning." It is found most often on CD-ROMs and is mainly produced by entertainment companies, not educators. It already represents a multibillion-dollar-a-year market in the United States and Canada[13] and successful software spawns lucrative product markets: The heroine of one geography program is featured in a television series, cartoons, and board games.

At this point, let me offer a few thoughts about learning. First of all, please remember that *just because children like something does not mean it is either good for them or educational.* Doubtless many would enjoy unlimited television viewing, perhaps even mind-altering drugs, but most adults are wise enough to set limits.

Second, *learning is, indeed, fun, but it is also hard work.* In fact, working hard, surmounting challenges, and ultimately succeeding is what builds real motivation. Any gadget that turns this exciting and difficult process into an easy game is dishonest and cheats the child out of the joy of personal mastery. Encouraging children to "learn" by flitting about in a colorful multimedia world is a recipe for a disorganized and undisciplined mind.

Third, accessing or memorizing isolated information, or dabbling at an occasional skill sandwiched amidst an entire loaf of intellectual Wonder Bread, has nothing to do with *true learning,* which *requires making meaningful connections between facts and ideas.* Today's children are overpowered with data and special effects, but teachers report they have trouble following a logical train of thought or linking ideas together.

Finally, *some of the "habits of mind" fostered by this software are dangerous,* to wit: impulsivity, trial-and-error guessing over thoughtful problem-solving, disregard of consequences, and expectation of overly easy pleasure. Even so-called interactive edutainment often shares these flaws.

Roger C. Schrank, director of Northwestern University's Institute for the Learning Sciences, elaborates: "They're trying to make edutainment appealing to kids so that kids will pick it up, but it isn't providing much of anything for them to do or learn." Simply clicking to move something, choose a picture to view, or change someone's hair color is not mentally stimulating, according to Schrank. Rather than just thinking, "I pressed this and something happened," he wants the user to feel, "I was trying to figure out a problem and I had to come to some conclusions."

Simplistic and vacuous "fun" is a long way from meaningful learning. Inundating youngsters with easy and amusing trivia is more likely to make them fools than wise men. So before you spend your money on software, consider your educational goals. Then make sure it is used effectively.

Guidelines for Using Software

🐾 Accompany the child as he or she explores the program, letting the child take the lead. Take time out (stop the program briefly if necessary) to talk about it. Ask the child to tell you *what* is happening and *why* certain things occur.

❧ If your child is responding impulsively, remove the mouse (or move him away from the touch screen) and help him explain his thinking.

❧ Help your child think visually; use pencil and paper to draw the spatial layout of complex programs: maps, charts, diagrams, hand-drawn pictures may help clarify context. Ask a child using a computer drawing program to tell you about the picture *before* she draws it. Similarly, suggest that the student using a story-writing program briefly summarize the story and describe or draw the picture *before* going to the computer. This encourages planning, imagination, and imagery, but it also takes more mental effort, so don't be surprised if your child prefers the ease of *selecting rather than generating* ideas. (If the child needs the visual stimulation of pictures, you could start with family photos or magazine illustrations.)

❧ Ask the child to give a critical appraisal of the software's value. Call attention to criteria for judging the quality of a program. Help children become selective consumers.

❧ Emphasize "mastery goals" ("You tried hard, you learned something, and you finally did it!") rather than reward-driven goals ("Let's see how many you can shoot today.")

❧ Ask yourself: What is being learned? What mental habits are being encouraged? Could this same goal be met as well or better with a real-life experience? If so, you may want to go for reality, not the virtual stuff.

A *Rundown on Educational Applications and Software*

In general, current uses of computers can be divided roughly into four categories:

1. Applications software, or "tools" to accomplish routine tasks more efficiently.

2. Programs for teaching basic skills, such as multiplication tables or phonics, or for information on topics such as dinosaurs or photosynthesis.

3. Communications links, such as to the Internet and the World Wide Web, to enable faster and broader transmission of messages or access to information.

4. Laser disc or computer "environments" or simulations specifically designed to foster content knowledge, thinking, or problem-solving.

1. Applications Software: Computerized "Tools"

Applications are the closest thing we have to using the computer as a "tool." They can support either highly structured, drill-and-practice type activities (e.g., using a word-processing program to copy definitions of vocabulary) or more active learning (e.g., composing a story or poem.)

  Word processing, which basically amounts to using the computer as an "intelligent" typewriter, is the most common use. These programs automate mechanical aspects of writing and editing. They are one of the most prevalent educational computer applications.[14]

  Spell checkers, thesauri, and dictionaries are an integral part of word processing. They help students with spelling or vocabulary problems, but most educators agree they should not substitute for teaching basic skills.

  Grammar checkers are available but are still too simplistic to be of much value.

  Outlining and other organizational aids provide a framework to arrange thoughts before writing. Their utility varies considerably and may result in overly formulaic writing.

  Data base software helps create electronic filing systems that can group and regroup information according to different categories. For example, for a report on animals, a student might read about each animal and enter data on its habitat, feeding habits, size, etc. Then he could select all jungle animals who roam at night, all small herbivorous domestic animals, etc. The information could be used for a computerized chart, math lesson, report, field guide, or other purposes. Commercial data bases are also available. A student preparing a report on ancient Rome might gather data about political, cultural, or social life and draw conclusions about Roman life. Using data bases can teach categorization, making inferences, and research skills. They can, of course, also simply access facts to be memorized.

❧ *Spreadsheets* are similar to data bases and facilitate organization and/or graphing of numerical data, computations, and comparisons. Teachers use them to keep track of grades. In one elementary school students tackled a problem of trash in the lunchroom by counting and categorizing data on trash thrown away and trying approaches to reduce the amount generated.[15] Spreadsheets enable such diverse activities as simulating the stock market, studying probability, graphing trends in social studies, and learning about conservation of energy.[16] Even young students can "play" with variables, as in having the computer add 7 to or take a fractional part of every number in a category.

❧ *Classroom and school management aids* are very popular uses. They not only coordinate records and compute grades, but allow teachers to collaborate across distances, communicating lesson plans and new ideas.

❧ *Aids for the handicapped:* A complete discussion of the many ways in which technology can facilitate learning and life for those with handicaps is beyond this book's intent. We will explore just a few of these applications in upcoming chapters.

❧ *Computer-aided design* enables construction of blueprints, diagrams, and three-dimensional visual models for architectural and engineering projects. You can take a virtual "walk" through an unbuilt home by simply entering a special set of plans into a computer, and students of acoustical engineering simulate how sounds such as music will project as they manipulate different design features in a virtual auditorium.

❧ *Laser discs* enable a visual presentation of a lesson which can be quickly entered at any point. One of the most popular is a mystery story whose episodes require the students to uncover and use science and math clues to help a young detective solve the problem.

❧ *CD-ROM encyclopedias* and other reference works. Information is presented incorporating visual and auditory as well as text formats.

❧ *"Hypertext" and "hypermedia"* are terms describing nonlinear, branching programs. The user chooses the order in which she wishes to view/read/hear (and, possibly, feel) the elements of the presentation. This flexibility, called "linking," is attained by inserting links or "buttons" in the program, on which the viewer can click to move from one display to another. The buttons may be contained in key words highlighed in the text or in graphic symbols (icons) or text (e.g., a rectangle which reads, "Click here to see a microscopic view of the maple leaf."). Hypermedia is characteristic of CD-ROM and laser discs, which can store large amounts of text and graphics.

❧ *Multimedia (or hypermedia) authoring tools* combine text, sound, animation, and graphics to create teaching aids, reports, or projects. They are among the fastest-growing in home and school markets. Even small children can write a story and use computerized drawing tools. For a report on France, one high-school student wrote about French history, drew illustrations, recorded herself singing the "Marseillaise," took her "readers" through a visual tour of relevant paintings in world museums, added an animated street scene, and worked in a quiz of irregular French verbs.

Because the use of hypermedia almost inevitably puts the student in charge of developing a project and constructing both knowledge and problem-solving strategies, it is one of the applications that may most drastically change education as we know it.

2. Programs to Teach Basic Skills or Information

❧ *Drill-and-practice* programs give intensive work on specific academic skills. Because most are based on a "behaviorist" theory of learning that emphasizes stimulus, response, and reward, they tend to give the student a certain number of problems (sometimes after a pretest), offer direct feedback on whether the answer is right or wrong, and dispense a reward for correct performance. Rewards range from a verbal prompt ("Great job!") to a game which may occupy the student for longer than the actual drill. Much inferior "edutainment" software is simply drill-and-practice disguised by animations, graphics, and trivial simulations. While some drill-and-practice uses are effective, others are just expensive electronic worksheets.

❧ *Integrated learning systems.* Companies design full curricula of skill-building software graded according to students' abilities and hire out to schools to run technology programs. A pretest determines each student's level, and exercises move from easier to more difficult levels; this approach lends itself better to quantitative subjects such as math than to more conceptual ones such as literature. The program keeps records of progress for individual students and whole class achievement. A major disadvantage of integrated learning systems is the expense and total commitment required by some of the proprietary companies, who may specify that one- to two-thirds of each student's time be spent on the computer. It is also difficult to integrate prepackaged learning with a teacher's curriculum. Although advocates claim this indivualized and self-paced form of instruction increases motivation,[17] for many it soon loses its fascination.

&. *Cognitive or "intelligent" tutors* offer more sophisticated self-paced teaching. Cognitive psychologists first analyze the skill to be taught and determine a sequence of necessary steps. Then they analyze how the computer will know if the desired learning is taking place. When a student makes an error, the computer is programmed with cues to give immediate feedback and "coach" him instead of simply giving the answer. Cognitive tutors show particular promise for math or science, and some are in the works for reading.

&. *Interactive "edutainment" software* teaches through a game-type format. Their value is debatable, varying considerably among different products.

3. LINKS TO COMMUNICATION AND INFORMATION

&. *The Internet and World Wide Web* enable us to communicate instantly (if the system is "up") across national and international borders through "electronic mail," or "e-mail," to call on the resources of famous libraries, museums, or data bases, and to acquire information about commercial products, services, and practical concerns through a worldwide network of information resources referred to as the "Web." Despite the significant growing pains of this new window on the world, some believe it may enable us eventually to eliminate the traditional classroom altogether—if we want to.

&. *Distance learning* has the student in a different geographical location from the teacher or the classroom. It is especially useful for college- and university-level courses where students are motivated to work independently. It can bring students a special resource such as a noted professor. The most popular course in the Stanford University distance-education network is taught by Kosuke Ishii, described by his students as "vibrant"; $300,000 worth of communications hardware makes the linkage possible. With further advances, students in widely separated locations can engage in a "discussion" together with the professor, and possibly even see each other in the process. Although some find this form of learning "sterile," it presents numerous benefits for those who lack access to a nearby facility.

We will consider specific applications of the Internet and Web in Chapter 8.

4. Problem-Solving and Thinking Skills

❧ *Video games* remain the most popular problem-solving software. We will explore benefits and problems in Chapter 5.

❧ *Academic problem-solving* software falls into two general categories. The first is based on the belief that there are general problem-solving skills which, once learned, can be applied across several domains. For example, if a child learns to analyze a given set of facts and draw a conclusion in science, he may transfer the skill to drawing conclusions in history or algebra. Psychologists have yet to agree whether or how this transfer can occur. The second category of problem-solving software addresses thinking skills specific to a subject. In her book *Computers and Classroom Culture* Janet Schofield describes using geometry tutoring software in a traditional high school, where students generally found the structured, nongamelike nature of the instruction both effective and individually motivating. Schofield points out, however, that implementation of even such relatively straightforward programs is a complicated task and demonstrates how entrenched attitudes by educators can short-circuit positive effects of new technologies.[18]

❧ *Simulations* combine content and problem-solving by immersing students in experiences that would be difficult to duplicate in real life, as in giving pilots experience which would be too costly or dangerous to attempt firsthand. In schools, students may construct a new planet and control its ecosystem, lead a pioneer wagon train, design a boat, travel though the human circulatory system, or plan and execute the operations of a business. The effectiveness of simulations varies widely, and they should have sufficient complexity and variety to remain challenging. The advent of educational applications of virtual reality, in which the individual can feel part of the scene, increases both the power of simulations and the need for effective psychological controls.

🙏 *Systems thinking* models are a new form of simulation that mimics behavior of a complex system, letting students explore the mutual interactivity of component parts and processes. Teachers using the basic software have developed curriculum materials for osmosis, chemical reactions, earthquakes, and immunology.[19]

🙏 *Programming languages*—the commands by which the computer is made to do its "tricks"—were the original subject matter of computer courses, but most students no longer study them unless they are preparing for technical work. Exceptions are the LOGO and COCOA computer languages from the MIT media laboratory, where scientists search for ways to help youngsters "learn things in new ways."[20] For example, children program computer problem-solving environments called "microworlds" to investigate systems theory (you will find an example in Chapter 5).

🙏 Other cognitive scientists are at work to *improve the human brain by investigating how it solves problems.* If they succeed, software decisions will take on even more interesting dimensions. "We can have new learning environments based on cognitive principles," suggests psychologist J. T. Breuer in *Schools for Thought*, "but many of us—superintendents, principals, political and business leaders, parents—may have to change our representations of what classrooms and schools should look like."[21]

How Good Is Software as Teacher?

We still await research telling us how—or even whether—software can best be used to teach either subject matter or skills. Four fatal flaws characterize most research to date. First, studies cover too short a time span. Second, quality or type of software is not well controlled. Third, outcome measures—usually standardized tests—tap only a limited span of skills, and we need broader measures.[22] For example, one study of young children looked at creativity along with academic gains. It showed significant reductions in creativity after even moderate use of a popular reading software system.[23] A fourth serious problem is failure to control for "teacher variables." Since the most innovative and energetic teachers are often the ones to take up new technologies, their expertise, not computers, may account for positive gains. Conversely, one shouldn't be surprised to find negative results if computers are imposed upon a reluctant faculty. And published statistics don't always tell the whole story.

Recently I was one of five adults, including a school superintendent and a reporter for a local paper, who clustered around one little girl in a class of eight-year-olds. She had been asked to demonstrate the math work she did in the computerized learning system that had been purchased at great expense and with considerable fanfare two years previously. A so-called statistical analysis had "proven" the system's value in raising math achievement test scores, and this information had been widely publicized. In fact, someone other than the superintendent should have read the study's fine print; since the classrooms with computers had been allocated twenty minutes extra math time per child every day, it was hardly news that they produced better scores.

After the little girl flawlessly solved her daily problems, one of us inquired,

"How do you like learning math from the computer this way?"

To considerable administrative chagrin, she replied, "I don't. It really gets boring and sometimes the answers are really confusing. I used to like math, but now . . ."

Some studies indicate CAI (computer-assisted instruction) in drill-and-practice programs and learning systems can be useful for specific types of teaching.[24] But questions have also been raised about the quality of the material and feedback to students, and the accuracy in reporting progress (i.e., sometimes students who really knew the material were judged by the system as not knowing it, and vice versa).[25] Moreover, much of the positive research has been funded by the producers of these products and thus arouses skepticism.

A popular statistical method called "meta-analysis" groups a number of studies to look for general trends, although credibility naturally varies according to the quality of the individual studies. In general, meta-analyses have also shown a moderate advantage for CAI on a set of fairly limited objectives.[26] A closer look at two major studies, however, cautions against overly eager interpretation of even such lukewarm results.

James Kulik of the University of Michigan ran a meta-analysis of ninety-seven studies in elementary and high schools and found major discrepancies in the data.[27] Some computerized instruction raised achievement scores, but some significantly lowered them. Kulik also found inconsistent results for LOGO (e.g., some studies showed gains in problem-solving skills, while others did not) and "little effect" on science learning from simulation programs. Most notable, when he compared CAI with *the same amount of time spent with pencil, paper, and printed materials*, the traditional materials did as well or better. Students tutored by fellow classmates scored almost as well as those tutored by computers. We might expect that skilled teachers would produce even better results.

A more recent meta-analysis by Claire Fletcher-Flynn and Breon Gravatt of the University of Auckland synthesized 120 studies, also finding mixed results. The slight positive advantage for drill-and-practice CAI over standard instruction was eliminated *when equivalent teaching and materials were used in noncomputerized classes*. None of the newer multimedia were included in this evaluation. The authors conclude that when class sizes are large, as in a first-year university course, computers can provide time savings for teachers, and motivational and academic gains for students in certain subjects.[28]

Higher levels of motivation are often reported but are difficult to measure. How long will this new fascination hold its power? One interesting study questioned whether positive results from computer learning are due to a temporary novelty factor. Calling much of the research "simpleminded," researchers from Indiana University looked at elementary and high school youngsters' attitudes over the three years following introduction of computers.[29] Students' preference for learning from computers declined significantly, as did their impressions of how much they were learning.

In short, the research on software's effectiveness is still limited, vague, and open to question. Some computer use appears effective within a narrow set of educational objectives, and it appears to motivate children, at least to use the computer and at least temporarily. Can it actually improve learning? No one really knows. Even if it were possible to measure or equalize the quality of adult interaction, definitive "results" on complex cognitive variables are never easy to come by.

Now we turn to our final issue in computer "basics": the crucial importance of planning effectively before we even start to spend our hard-earned money.

Planning for Technology

I am visiting an urban school where the computer coordinator has been desperately trying to cope single-handedly with a large class of children. As she sinks into a well-used armchair in the teachers' lounge, she is eager to explain the difficulties in implementing a technology program that the school board mandated but failed to support. The plan called for teachers to use computers in their daily lessons.

"But I saw the computers in the classrooms," I point out, "and no one was using them."

She sighs. "A lot of the teachers think they're just another nuisance—take up their time and all that. So the computers just sit there unless the kids are playing games on them. The board forgot to include enough money to train the teachers."

This is only the first of dozens of times I will hear this same refrain. In the United States in 1997, only 15 percent of teachers had received at least nine hours of training in educational technology, and most school systems spend far less than the recommended portion of one-third to one-half of their technology budget for this purpose.[30]

"I wish the teachers would come up to the lab with their classes and see how it works, but it's their planning period—you know how it is, they're pretty overworked, too. They've got so many kids, and different languages, and so many problems."

Acutely aware of the near-impossible demands on even master teachers who must acculturate as well as teach large classes of unprepared youngsters, I understand why the teachers lack time and energy. Sighing, I prepare to leave.

"Oh, by the way, that lab of yours is a great room—where did they find all that space?"

"Well, it used to be the music room. You know we've been having these budget cuts, so they had to eliminate some of the extras in the curriculum."

■ ■ ■

At the next school I call on, I'm greeted by an aide, who is efficiently overseeing eight six-year-olds who are in variable states of concentration as they laboriously hunt-and-peck words from their reading books. Twenty-two other machines sit lifeless around the perimeter of the room, surrounded by unopened cartons of expensive software.

"Oh, didn't they tell you?" she inquires sympathetically. "I'm so sorry, our system is down. Has been since the beginning of school—over seven weeks now. I've asked for a technician so many times—but I haven't got one out here yet." She gestures to the eight working machines: "These are just leftovers from before. They're not on the network, so they still work, but they won't run the new programs—it's a different platform. But I do know how to fix them when the kids mess up."

"How about the computers in the classrooms? Are they down, too?"

She smiles ruefully. "They've never been up. This building is full of asbestos and they won't drill through the classroom walls to put in the lines—guess no one anticipated that glitch. The only reason this room is connected is that a friend and I came in here on a weekend with a couple of drills and went through the door frame." She gestures at wires draped over the molding. "But it's going to be great when we finally get up on the Internet; I'm hoping the teachers will bring their classes up here and work on projects. Only a few even want computers in their rooms—they haven't learned how to use them. I'd like to teach them to go on-line, and I'm also going to run classes on weekends for the parents—that is, if and when the central office sends me a techie."

"Is it always this hot in here?" I am becoming distinctly uncomfortable and I notice that some of the children are visibly perspiring.

"We sure need some fans," she replies. "In fact, air conditioning would be nice—ha! You know these computers generate a lot of heat, and this room gets the afternoon sun. Imagine what it'll be like when they're all working—we'll need bathing suits! Maybe I'll get the fans when I get the technical help I need to run this show—that'll be the day!"

The rows of blank screens gaze, vacant as an empty promise. Under the tables are more computers, unopened, consigned to premature retirement due to asbestos and poor planning. I find myself contemplating the proven low-tech interventions, such as Reading Recovery, that teach literacy in a motivating, effective, and cost-efficient manner. They operate with a special brand of technology called trained teachers—who don't even need electrical connections to keep them running.

Asking the Right Questions

Far too many schools are rushing into new technologies without asking the right questions. Without adequate planning and sound educational rationale, computers will be either misused or unused. Teachers are overwhelmed and resistant. Space, time, and money are appropriated from more important activities. Expedient software choices are made by noneducators, and computer time becomes mindless game-playing. When they are used for academics, computers are mainly employed for word processing, some graphic drawing programs, occasional reinforcement of basic skills, sometimes for research, and maybe a data base or two, but school essentially goes on as usual. The enormous expense is rationalized with the feeble argument that kids need to become familiar with computers before they enter the work world, even though the equipment will have changed dramatically and the poorly educated won't get the sort of job where they will even use complex technology.

The situation is not any better at home. Children spend time with inferior and possibly damaging software. Parents lack the understanding or sometimes the will to ask the critical question: How and why is this activity benefitting my child?

The technology is capable of far more, but it must be planned for and managed intelligently. If you or your district are purchasing computers, start by considering these questions:

> ⮞ How can computer technology help achieve our educational goals?

Are these goals compatible with the interests, abilities, and needs of today's students?

❧ How and why will this experience improve the quality of learning sufficiently to justify the cost and the time involved?

❧ What will it have to replace (family activities, silent reading, social playtime, art, music, gym, recess, foreign language) and is the trade-off acceptable?

❧ Who makes software decisions and on what criteria?

❧ Are we willing to loosen traditional top-down structures of education and produce students who will think—and question?

❧ What content can be taught, and how do we measure the outcomes? Are computers the best—not just the trendiest—way to do this particular job?

The mere presence of computers guarantees nothing about their educational value. This is no time to be jumping on the boat just because everyone else is—especially if we don't know where it's going.

Effective Integration of Technology in Schools

Once a legitimate educational rationale is established, implementation guidelines are necessary. These are best developed by an individual or committee well informed about educational technology. Too many administrators are still naive, and some tech coordinators have little background in teaching or curriculum. Having visited and worked with schools that received grants from the U.S. West Foundation, Lin Foa, Richard Schwab, and Michael Johnson offer these practical recommendations:[31]

1. *Support the innovators* willing to devote energy and commit to change. They may be teachers, principals, or superintendents who understand the potential of technology and can not only develop effective uses but also gain resources by grant-writing and other means.

2. *Plan for teacher education first.* Good training is expensive and ongoing. Teachers must have access to the equipment and time to practice while they are learning about it.

3. *Technical support needs to be on-site, individualized, and teacher-*

oriented. Having to phone for help and wait endlessly for needed repairs makes technology more of a nuisance than a benefit in a busy classroom.

4. *Move forward with those who are ready.* Some teachers will resist change. Allow others to become models of what can be accomplished.

5. *Expect changes in the school power structure.* Administrators and teachers may feel threatened. "Techies" may try to gain control and prescribe placement or use of computers. Sufficient training of all personnel should minimize conflicts.

6. *Successful integration of classroom technology implies changes of huge magnitude in educational philosophy, classroom management, and curricular goals.* "The common belief," state the authors, "is that if one simply teaches teachers how to use computers and telecommunications and provides the necessary equipment, classroom teaching and learning will improve automatically. Nothing could be farther from the truth. For the technologies to be used optimally, teachers must be comfortable with a constructivist or project-based, problem-solving approach to learning; they must be willing to tolerate students' progressing independently and at widely varying paces; they must trust students to sometimes know more than they do and to take on the role of expert teacher . . . and they must be flexible enough to change directions when technical glitches occur." These demands often represent a departure from professional experience and may even be at odds with core beliefs.

7. *Build learning from what is known for teachers as well as students.* Introducing teachers to new technologies is most effectively done by reducing the implicit threat of change. For example, emphasize that multimedia is not an end in itself, but rather one more means to accomplish familiar educational goals.

8. *Consider the social and emotional aspects of learning to use technologies.* Teachers need hands-on, personal encounters to understand how these programs can be of use to them, not abstruse explanations of the inner workings of the computers.

9. *Remember that change takes time.* "We are asking already overworked individuals to undergo profound belief and habit transformation."

10. *Allow students to take responsibility for teaching others.* A cadre of

classroom volunteer "experts" can help other students and troubleshoot simple problems.

11. *Use technology to link school, parents, and the wider community.* Parent technology-training sessions, interaction with senior citizen programs, and technology open houses bring the community into the school. Corporations may donate used equipment superior to what the school can afford. Students can make multimedia presentations at school board meetings, community events, and even in the legislature.

Where Shall We Put Them?

Locating computers in schools can be complicated and may be a major clue to prevailing attitudes. The "traditional" (if such a word is possible) way has been in a computer lab where groups of students come on a scheduled basis or during free time. A lab setup by itself may indicate a more didactic framework or one where technology hasn't really been integrated into the curriculum. Students who simply "take computer" once or twice a week have little opportunity to utilize its deepest potential. A developing rule of thumb, adding one classroom computer for every four students, gives everyone time at the screen and encourages group projects. This number, of course, is readily promoted by the manufacturers and is certainly not necessary; I have seen teachers work successfully with only one machine or a few old donated ones.

Some schools start with a central lab where an entire class of students can work at one time, gradually adding machines in the classrooms as funding permits. If the school can afford both, a lab with enough machines for practice on such skills as word processing is helpful but no substitute for integrating computers into daily lessons. If a class goes to the lab, the teacher should work with the computer teacher to integrate what happens there with the curriculum. A good computer teacher will be a source both of technical help and ideas to enhance learning plans.

In one example, classroom teacher and computer specialist worked together as eight-year-olds studied the geography and history of their city. First the children read multiple sources of information and used word processing to write imaginary journals from that time period, illustrated with crayons. After a field trip to the local park, they learned to chart its elevations and physical features with a computer-aided mapmaking program; at the same time they built a three-dimensional, hands-on scale model. It is probably unnecessary to add that the children were very proud of their learning. Did they really need all that technology to learn this material or feel the same satisfaction? Good question.

It is necessary to add that this unit took place in a school serving mainly children of the upper middle class. Children from lower socioeconomic groups are much more likely to be marched into a lab and given drill-type exercises.

Then What? Or Sic Transit . . .

What happens after the machines and software are in place? All too often good beginnings fizzle in the embers of equipment obsolescence or personnel change. In one model program, described in a book published by the Apple Corporation, South Philadelphia High School science teacher Tina Petrone developed a successful program to motivate low-achieving urban students with "hands-on" activities in botany. With $300,000 in technology grants, she renovated a greenhouse and purchased equipment so students could not only cultivate plants but also record data on growth, conduct simulations, and write reports. Within a year they were winning awards at plant shows and expanded the project to organize and analyze data on local water quality; they developed computer models to make neighborhood dwellings more energy-efficient. In her glowing report to Apple, Ms. Petrone enthused, "Dreams have come true. Tired, discouraged teachers are revitalized, students enjoy school, new programs have become realities. Students blossomed along with their plants."[32]

A follow-up phone interview revealed the follow-up realities. Still overflowing with enthusiasm, Ms. Petrone described the turnaround she had seen. "Those kids got so they wouldn't even go to lunch—they wanted to stay in the greenhouse. We gave them a haven, something most had never experienced at home." Unfortunately, staffing changed, the computers are now badly outdated, and Ms. Petrone is moving on. The machines themselves are only part of the necessary equipment.

Planning for Home Computing for Kids

"I'm not sure what he's doing, but at least he's not watching TV!"
Suburban mother of a seven-year-old

When I give a lecture to a parent group these days, I often hear some variation of the same anxious question: "Does she really need a computer? We have so many expenses, but, well, you feel like you want to give her the advantages and it's so much better than watching television. . . ."

This "halo effect"—faith that the computer is somehow automatically better than television—is unjustified. First of all, if your child is watching too much TV, the first thing to do is start applying some limits rather than adding yet another excuse to tune you out! Naturally, manufacturers would like to encourage parental guilt (a psychologist friend calls guilt the "maternal hormone"), but what should really make us feel uncomfortable is letting any kind of electronic device do our child-rearing and educating for us.

Even if the computer replaces TV, it is not necessarily more educational. In fact, the novel special effects make it even more engrossing and potentially mind-dulling than the tube. When a child is "watching" some of the better television programs, she may be learning from an informational context or playing creatively with only an occasional glance at the screen. With the computer, attention is easily transfixed to content unworthy of the attention it compels.

Moreover, if parents are willing to monitor and participate in quality viewing, television can provide information, exposure to ideas, and topics for family conversation. The same is true, of course, of computer use. Neither medium is automatically better, and neither should be used as a rationale for habitually idling brains.

If your family decides to invest in a computer, you also need to start by considering important questions:

1. *When might a child need a computer?* The answer, of course, varies with different children. Preschoolers and even six- to eight-year-olds in no way *need* computers (a complete explanation will be found in Chapter 7). For older children, computers may assume more importance.

2. *How should we select a computer?* Consult with the school computer coordinator for advice about which machines will be most compatible with the ones at school. If the budget is tight, youngsters can use one at school, earn money to buy a secondhand one, or share with the rest of the family. Advertisers' claims to the contrary, it doesn't have to be a costly and complicated machine.

3. *Which hardware and extra equipment are necessary?* Figure out ahead of time what the computer is to be used for. A relatively simple one can do basic functions such as word processing and spreadsheets; many of the expensive additions are used for flashy games that your child is better off without. If you want CD-ROM encyclopedias, hypermedia, or Internet connectivity, be sure to inquire whether the machine will allow it. For the Internet, you will also need a modem, an additional device connected to a telephone line that links your computer with the outside world. Purchasing a printer is usually a separate expense; you will have to decide whether to spend extra money for a color printer or one that will turn out more-professional-looking copy. Computer magazines give up-to-date information on products and pricing.

4. *What if we decide not to get a computer? Will our child lose out?* What children need most is not found in machines. If you decide to hold out, some school districts loan out computers and software if student projects require them. Local libraries have technology services such as word processing or Internet access—with the additional advantage of rubbing up against enticing books and reference materials. Purchasing a computer should not substitute for more important expenditures. Moreover, in this consumerized hi-tech world, your time and attention are still worth more to your child than any equipment, no matter how glitzy. Let's review a few realities.

What Computers Can't Do

&. Using a computer will not automatically make your child smarter.

&. Facility with a computer signifies nothing special about a child's intelligence, since even complex programs are not very hard to learn. No evidence exists that any programs by themselves will make kids better thinkers (as opposed to data processors), and they may have the opposite effect.

&. "Information" is not the be-all, end-all of learning.

&. Using a computer at home now will not prepare elementary- or middle-school children for the radically different technology and job market when they graduate.

&. Given the massive current push for technology in schools, most children will have sufficient access by graduation to become computer-literate.

&. Simple parent-child activities such as hobbies, games, and reading together have a solid research track record for improving academic skills. Using computers for these activities is both more expensive and less effective.

&. The key to positive use of any medium is the quality of the adult-child interaction.

Why, then, should anyone make this investment? In the following chapters you will find many examples of how computers can spice up learning—for adults as well as kids. The important issue is whether we use computers to avoid or to enhance relationships with our children.

Where Should We Put the Computer?

"Ever since we got Jamie that computer, he's done nothing but sit up in his room with the door closed. I just know he borrowed some of those mindless games from his friends, and I really don't want him playing them! He already has enough trouble paying atten-tion in school. But I can hardly even get him to come down for meals!"

Mother of a ten-year-old

Many parents have unhappily discovered the seductive power of the personal computer by allowing their child to have too "personal" a relationship with it. As with television, one of the easiest ways to control inappropriate or excessive use is to have the machine(s) in a central place where adults can keep a subtle supervisory eye out until the youngster has developed sufficient judgment about technology use. Psychologists agree that parents should be involved with all children's media use. Even sitting with the child and watching is better than non-involvement.

Families working or playing together can discover ways—when the child is of an appropriate age—to electronically promote good thinking, conversation, and family togetherness. One father and his young teenager became fascinated with the *Titanic* shipwreck while the boy was doing Internet research for a school project. They continued to work together in occasional spare time, broadening their new hobby into a search for information on ships, which they developed into a data base. This interest led to discussions of history and geography as well as trips to the library. In Chapter 8 you will find other ideas.

Setting Limits

By developing a habit of mutual media management early on, you can save yourself a lot of grief later. Electronic playmates should never be allowed to substitute for activities such as homework, conversation, chores, hands-on games, hobbies, or just relaxing and "hanging out" together.

Family guidelines for "screen time" vary. Tally up the time your child spends on the home computer, TV, and video per day. If the total is more than one hour for preschoolers or more than two hours for elementary age, you may want to cut back. Your example is also very important here; if you're addicted, you can't expect your child to be much different.

Help! He's Addicted!

What if the situation in your house is already out of hand? (Another frequent question from parent meetings, so you're not alone.) It is not too late! Sit down with your child and negotiate a reasonable limit on both quantity and quality of "screen time."

If the youngster seems nonnegotiable, you may have to exercise your parental prerogatives. (No, you're not an ogre. This is your duty.) In survey after survey, to most parents' astonishment, when children are given choices of activities, *time spent with parents* always heads the list. You are not stooping to bribery if you promise to share more time with your child and think up enticing alternative activities when he agrees to relinquish some of his screen time.

We must develop clear parameters regarding mindless, violent, or inappropriate content. There was a time, not so long ago, when the word "wholesome" often popped up when adults discussed their responsibilities to children and teens. While the culture has obviously changed, young people's needs have not. They really want us to negotiate and enforce reasonable limits.

Rework your guidelines as children mature. While little ones need fairly close supervision, by the time teens are in high school they should be responsible for their own choices—especially if a good groundwork has been laid. Yet even with older teens, too much time spent in inappropriate sites or activities, such as obsessive use of Multi-User Domains (MUDs), should be monitored. We will examine this issue in a later chapter.

Children vary dramatically in ability to make good media choices. One very mature eleven-year-old drew herself up in indignant surprise when I asked whether her parents supervised her choice of computer activities. "Of course not!" she exclaimed. "They trust me." And I don't doubt they have reason to.

The moral here is: *The computer is not capable of taking over your responsibility.*

In a Nutshell: Helping Children Use Technology Constructively

Here is a summary of general guidelines before we move on to specific age-related considerations in later chapters:

❧ Enlist your child's help in choosing technology for the home. Collaborate in reading trade magazines, manuals, and reviews. Let your child ask some of the questions when you talk to the computer teacher, go to the store, or phone for a mail order.

❧ Make the child responsible for upkeep of his computer. Tasks will, of course, vary according to age (e.g., keeping screen dusted, installing new hard drive).

❧ Help your child become a wise consumer of software, especially games, no matter what your budget. Help her justify product demands by locating reviews or interviewing teachers and librarians. ("Why do you need/want this product?" "How will this CD-ROM help you with schoolwork?") Once purchased, enlist your child's help in evaluating quality.

❧ Start by locating the computer(s) in a place where you can tune in and participate. Supervise materials used, especially game content.

❧ Negotiate to determine appropriate limits for computer use in your family.

❧ Unless computers are used for homework, ban them until schoolwork is completed.

❧ Keep a close watch on how your child is using global communications networks where sales pitches as well as questionable content and activities are available.

Home Schooling and Unschooling

With upward of 700,000 children in the United States being taught at home,[33] the home-schooling market is a succulent one. Software for everything from assessment to drill and practice to enhancement of thinking skills and simulations are peddled at home schoolers' conferences.

As with all education, careful sifting of materials and methodology can winnow the useful from the frivolous. Some of the most popular home-schooling uses of computers are found on the Internet, where chat lines dispense information and practical tips for parents, children get in touch with other students, and distance education offers advanced topics. Thirteen-year-old Saul, of Spring Glen, New York, has been home-schooled since age seven and spends about one-third of his six-hour home-school day on the computer. He uses mainly Internet and CD-ROM encyclopedias to do research, to communicate with other youngsters, and to take credit courses under teachers' supervision. One college student who was completely home-schooled used the Internet throughout his teens to gather information and start a "zine" (on-line magazine) with over 200 subscribers.

Many home-schooling parents have taken to computers because they believe the technology jibes with their values, especially independence and self-reliance. Others stoutly maintain that natural learning is the way to go. Among the computer users, two very different philosophies tend to prevail. Those who choose home schooling because they believe the public schools are too lax are more likely to espouse a "back-to-basics" orientation, with software emphasizing drill and practice and regular testing to measure progress. At the other end of the spectrum, the "unschoolers" eschew public education because they believe it is too rigid. When they use educational software at all, it is more likely for imaginative, exploratory, or creative uses.

Susan Beatty of the California Christian Home Educators' Association is one of many who are wary of computers because she places primary importance on the emotional parent-child bond. Whatever you do, don't let computers disrupt the connection that's at the heart of home schooling, she warns. For many people, it is, after all, the reason they chose home schooling in the first place.[34]

If you are a home-schooler, you should give software decisions particular attention, and I hope you will consider both the family guidelines and the educational issues raised throughout this book. Preview software and give careful and critical thought to every purchase to ensure it enhances your child's educational objectives. If you are using the Internet, bear in mind the possible personal hazards of excessive use.

Finally, look over assessment tools carefully and analyze individual test items to make sure they are testing what you think your child should be learning. If you wish to promote higher-level thinking and critical problem-solving, be wary of low-level questions (e.g., "What color was John's wagon?") which tend to focus attention on details rather than more conceptual issues ("How did John's new wagon affect his relationships with his friends and family?") Please remember, too, that the best way to test a child's conceptual understanding is to ask him to *formulate* an answer, i.e., summarize, draw, dramatize, or otherwise display his ability to express the ideas in some new way.

Several parents have recently asked me about the use of new, computerized testing formats which purport to measure a child's intelligence. Professionals are skeptical of these instruments, not only because they tend toward superficial assessment of complex abilities, but also because they overemphasize—in both the child's and parents' minds—the wrong attributes, such as a single IQ score. The most highly motivated and best students believe ability is something that can be changed by hard work and effort, not something that can be measured in a one-shot test. Overemphasizing "smarts" at the expense of mental habits is an insidious recipe for long-term failure.

The State of Technology in Learning

"Optimistic" is probably the kindest word to describe the current status of educational computing in the United States. The good examples in this book weren't always easy to find and were far outnumbered by the bad ones. Data from Europe and Asia echo the same uncertainties, although in Europe and Japan, at least, there appears to be more faith in customary educational practice and a more skeptical attitude about the "magic" of machinery.

Use of computers by children at home is also disappointing. Studies from both London and New York conclude: (1) Families are relatively unaware of the inevitable changes that will occur in the home's "social envelope" when a child's computer is introduced. (2) Even sophisticated computer users need help in using the technology effectively. (3) Schools need to revamp their relationships with families if they are to be successful "linking agents" for positive technology use.[35]

Clearly, effective implementation doesn't come with the warranty. Technology choices represent value judgments about what is important in children's lives and learning. In the next chapter we will consider what all this expensive gadgetry is costing and what it is displacing, not only in economic but also in human terms.

Chapter Three

The Bottom Line

"I really object to the guilt-ridden ads geared at parents buying computers for their kids. It's getting so you're frowned upon if you even question it!"
Father of a preschooler, New Jersey

"Penetration of the education market with computer-based technology has depended more on effective conditioning of the market through a barrage of advertising and ideology than on the effectiveness of the technologies themselves."
Douglas Noble, author of *The Classroom Arsenal* [1]

I am attending the fourteenth annual meeting of the Midwestern Technology in Education Conference in St. Louis. The most striking thing so far is the magnitude of the "gee whiz" factor—"Wow, look what the computers can do"—compared with the lack of discussion about good reasons to do it. In three days of back-to-back sessions, I have heard only three presenters discuss the "why" of the technology. It is probably no accident these three are all classroom teachers, a fairly rare commodity in this crowd of product peddlers and tech consultants.

The exhibit hall teems with eager consumers who munch free popcorn with soft drinks dispensed by a major hardware manufacturer and line up at booths for demonstration software. I am surrounded by unquestioning acceptance that technology is now the way to do everything, from playing games with children at home to teaching reading.

I approach one particularly prominent display. This glittering multimedia package promises to automate the teaching of both reading and writing—all in one iridescent package with countless components and a huge price tag. A youthful salesman welcomes me and boots up the introduction to a "lesson." It resembles nothing more than a loud, gaudy Saturday morning cartoon.

"You interested in our great new system here?" he booms heartily.

"I'm not sure. Can you give me a couple of reasons why I should use this instead of regular materials—you know, books, pencils, teachers?"

His eyes widen, and he stares at me as if I had just landed from outer space or, more likely, should be sporting a hoop skirt, bonnet, and bustle.

"Well, I don't really have an answer for that," he fumbles through his promotional flyers. "No one ever asked me that before."

"How long have you been selling this product?" I inquire.

"About two years."

"So how many educators have you shown it to?"

"Oh, I don't know . . . probably several thousand."

"And I'm the first one who ever asked you why it is better than traditional methods?"

"Yup. What do you do, anyway?"

■　■　■

If you yearn to make a fortune, you should probably become involved with the children's computing market. School expenditures on technology in the United States during the 1996–1997 school year hit a record $4.34 billion, and meeting the Department of Education's suggestion of one computer for every five students would require an annual investment of somewhere between $10 and $20 billion for an unspecified period of time.[2] Manufacturers offer giveaways and sharp discounts as they vie to establish brand loyalty and dependence on their products and services. Software sales to schools are booming, and telecommunications companies line up to connect schools to the Internet.

Hardware and software manufacturers have also targeted the home market. "Edutainment" for home use is one of the fastest-growing portions of the United States consumer market, with 20 to 30 percent growth per year.[3] An increasing proportion of these products are targeted at parents of preschoolers—termed, with unconscious irony, the new "growth industry." "Some parents are worried, and many more ought to be," warns Seymour Papert, "about the fact that the profit-driven barons of the software industry can have as much influence as they do on the minds and the culture of children."[4]

The business world can hardly be faulted for legitimate attempts to sell its wares. What is surprising is the lack of resistance or even basic skepticism by unsophisticated parents and educators.

Doubtless it is our irrational obsession with hi-tech solutions that makes us such willing victims of advertising that promises to make kids smarter faster and to cure education problems. Carefully crafted ads play directly into a growing competition to speed up the messy, inconvenient, and demanding processes of childhood and to mechanize learning by substituting virtual for real experience (e.g., electronic "fingerpaints," math software instead of blocks, virtual field trips).

"Competitive technophilia"[5] feeds upon itself. Not only is it highly unfashionable to criticize technology, but grant funding often depends on a technological component. The presence of computers imparts a rosy luster to any proposal to a foundation or government agency. In the United States, Canada, and the U.K. policymakers and politicians naively tout the benefits of Internet connectivity for equalizing educational opportunity. Meanwhile, worthy but nontrendy calls for needed services and equipment are washed aside in a wasteful flood of pseudo-innovation: Too much, too fast, and too ill-considered.

In this chapter we will touch on some of the bottom-line issues of what technology is costing—in every sense. First, we will address the cynical on-line exploitation of the young and then confront the question of what computers are replacing or devaluing in education. As we then consider whether new technologies can "level the playing field" for children of differing socioeconomic backgrounds, we will suggest qualities needed to equip any child for success in a technological future. Finally we will examine the growing tension among intellectual, entertainment, and business interests.

Marketing to the New Generation

"This year we will see a lot of dollars chasing kids on line."
Advertising executive

An on-line (Internet) children's service recently published results from a survey that asked children which they trusted more—their parents or their computers. The majority of respondents said they put more trust in their computers.[6] This finding, part of an eye-opening report by Kathryn Montgomery and Shelley Pasnick of the watchdog Center for Media Education in Washington, D.C., suggests that advertisers have gotten carried away by the enormous spending power either controlled or influenced ("But, Mom, I *need*...") by children. In the United States, this figure is estimated at a mind-boggling $485 billion a year.[7] No wonder the advertising industry devotes time and resources to identify specific ways to—in its own words—"exploit young computer users more effectively." "Marketers are pursuing children with a no-holds barred approach," stated Montgomery at a Washington press conference. "Never before has there been a medium with this kind of power to invade the privacy of children and families."[8] One of the most insidious practices is that of building personal, interactive relationships with children on-line in order to (1) directly sell them products and (2) gain personalized information for future target marketing. Cultural anthropologists and hired-gun psychologists meet with groups of children and identify compelling themes of childhood to guide advertising tactics. Some guaranteed to appeal to young audiences are attachment/separation, attainment of power, social interaction, and mastery learning. These themes are then used to immerse kids in wish-fulfilling fantasies enabled, of course, only through purchase of the selected product: Do you want to be popular, strong, and smart like these heroes? Just buy this and watch your dreams come true!

Of course, marketing to children is a well-established practice, but because many parents have abdicated computer control to the youngsters, advertisers have an unprecedented crack at their young audience. Special concerns arise because of the age of the "targets" (as young as four) and the compelling, personal, and potentially intrusive nature of the advertising. Urging controls on such practices, the American Psychological Association stated, "Until age seven, children cannot discern the intent of persuasive advertisements. After age seven, children and adolescents are still particularly vulnerable to peer and status appeals. Lengthy exposure to advertising may result in several potentially damaging effects on children, including increased parent-child conflict, lowered self-perceptions of physical attractiveness, and/or lowered self-esteem, and experimentation with products that may be detrimental, such as cigarettes and alcohol."[9]

Insidious Practices

The Center for Media Education report identifies two types of practices that should be curtailed: (1) invasion of privacy through solicitation of detailed personal information and tracking of on-line computer use, and (2) exploitation of vulnerable young computer users through new manipulative forms of advertising. It also reveals some of the means by which children are pursued on-line:

New electronic data-gathering and monitoring make it possible to access formerly private infomation. Marketers may entice children to fill out on-line surveys or provide information to win prizes or play games. They may offer prizes to those who reveal e-mail addresses of their friends. Because young children tend to put intense trust in the computer and respond uncritically to offers of rewards, they are likely to type in whatever information is requested, such as the child's age and sex, preferences in films, TV shows, toys, and foods, as well as data about purchasing habits of other family members. Even more subtle is tracking a user's on-line interactions, known as "clickstream" data or "mouse droppings." Thus, marketers "microtarget" the individual preferences or perceived needs of potential customers. ("How would you like to have an action figure of the hero of the movie you saw Saturday afternoon? Guess what! We have one for sale.") Once a child visits an advertising site, she may receive unsolicited e-mail messages promising exciting gifts and new activities if she returns.

"If something isn't done, your child is going to turn on the computer and receive fifteen unsolicited advertisements," warned Shelley Pasnik in a recent interview. "Even research isn't safe from ads, since the search engines (the means by which information is gathered) are beholden to advertising revenue and are allowing advertisers to purchase key words."[10] For example, if your child is trying to find research on apples, the first few references she gets may be to web pages selling certain brands of the fruit, apple-themed snacks, movies, or even X-rated adult entertainment. All she has to do is click the mouse to be transported from the world of content to the world of the hard sell.

The second category of Internet manipulation of children is the use of personalized advertising practices more compelling than those in other media. Electronic "environments" entice children to spend hours playing with popular product spokescharacters, such as talking animal or hero figures. Children feel a more personal relationship to these characters; at younger ages they fail to distinguish the fantasy and may take very seriously exhortations to use particular products. In a twisted update of the Santa Claus myth, companies even encourage children to e-mail messages to the characters, implying the reply they receive is actually written by the icon itself.

At this writing efforts are under way to limit these practices. The Center for Media Education recommends five principles for control:

1. Personal information should not be collected from children.

2. Advertising and promotions targeted at children should be clearly labeled.

3. Children's content areas should not be directly linked to advertising sites.

4. There should be no direct interaction between children and product "spokescharacters."

5. There should be no on-line microtargeting of children and no direct-response marketing.

Even if advertisers adopted these guidelines, parents would still need to keep an eagle eye out for creative new practices designed to manipulate their children. It's never too early in a child's life for frank talk about what you will or will not permit.

Computers at School: They Cost More Than You Thought

"We're up against a massive marketing campaign—they have everyone convinced that if you're not up with technology, you're really out of it. Every time I write a proposal, I must answer the question: What is the computer component? Gee, I thought we wanted them to read books!"

School superintendent, Connecticut

"My school district could be IBM—you name it, we have it as far as technology is concerned. But I don't have enough textbooks; my kids have to share math books and I couldn't get money to buy a classroom literature set. When I tried to get a small stipend to attend a workshop on student problem-solving, I had to pay for it myself. The district had spent it all on computers!"

Elementary school teacher, Wyoming

Upgrading schools to technological competence is more expensive than most people realize. In addition to initial purchases of quality hardware and software, the following issues need attention:

Upgrading Hardware, Internet Access, and Infrastructure

🐾 Computers already in place must be upgraded before they can access the Internet or run new multimedia tools.

🐾 Infrastructure presents a serious problem. Some schools need additional power to run current machines; others need to be rewired internally.

🐾 Internet access requires a telephone line, a modem, and ongoing telephone access. The U.S. General Accounting Office recently estimated that half the country's schools have wiring too outdated to support Internet use. Few classrooms have telephone lines, and wires must be put in wall-mounted tubes or woven through concrete-block walls. If the school has asbestos insulation, the problems multiply.

🐾 Traditional school designs are now obsolete and new schools will cost more to build. More space is needed for workstations and projects; thus, effective deployment of computers in schools takes up to 25 percent

85

more space than is usually available in traditional classrooms. Building designs for more flexible use of space are also needed.

Guarding Against Theft

☜ Computer security is a hidden cost. More than $150,000 worth of computers were stolen from Sacramento County's San Juan district in one school year. One high school was broken in to nine times. Money that could have been spent on instruction has been used to install $2,000 alarm systems and security grates on windows in a number of districts.[11]

Expecting the Unexpected

☜ With any new technology, unpredicted glitches occur. One is the "year 2000 compliance problem" which will affect organizations using computers for personnel records. This costly and universal problem is a splendid example of the fact that we really don't understand many of the ramifications of what we're so eagerly rushing into.

Technical Support

☜ Budgeting for adequate technical support has usually been left out of technology packages. Teachers cannot be expected to teach and to re-pair machines. In a demonstration project in New York City, one teacher with twelve students, each with a laptop computer, has a full-time tech-nical support person in the classroom at all times. When I inquired if she really needed so much tech support, she replied, "Absolutely. These com-puters are always going down. Kids aren't afraid to push buttons, and they crash them regularly."[12] Most classrooms or labs I have visited contain several currently unusable machines; in some cases, whole networks are down for extended periods of time because someone forgot to budget for technical support.

Teacher Education

☜ Teacher education is the most critical component and also one of the most neglected. Experts agree that a minimum of one-third of any technical budget should be allocated for teaching teachers to use com-puters effectively.

☜ A recent article in *Education Week* summarized the situation thus: "We expect teachers to be far more independently capable of drawing on a vast repertoire of knowledge and skill than ever in the past, and new de-mands will continue to appear for the foreseeable future. The teacher of today and tomorrow no longer finds a curriculum in a textbook or classroom activities in a teacher's manual. . . . One or two workshops on how to access the Internet are not the answer to the far more complex question of how to enhance student learning."[13]

🕸 A great majority of practicing teachers are still technologically illiterate, and even new ones coming out of teacher preparation programs often have little or no understanding of classroom computer use.

🕸 Training, and time off (e.g., hiring substitutes) for teachers to take it, are expensive. Case in point: One of the most successful pioneering efforts in multimedia teaching, "The Voyage of the MIMI," was developed in the early 1980s at Bank Street College in New York. Students used videodisc, print, and hands-on experience in a simulation of a scientific exploration. When asked what advice they would offer developers, one of the program's authors had a ready reply. "Put half your development budget into teacher training." Why? Because the MIMI developers found that the program was only as good as the teacher facilitating it.[14]

🕸 A proven way for teachers to get comfortable with computers is for them to own one; buying computers outright for teachers, sharing purchase cost, and using payroll deductions are some alternatives.

🕸 Using technology's power often requires radical shifts in a teacher's methods and philosophy. Even highly motivated teachers with access to state-of-the-art equipment take approximately five or six years to change old habits to make full use of machines.

Funding for Courseware Development and Ongoing Research

🕸 Funding for development of high-quality courseware and more effective software to teach problem-solving is important if we are ever to justify the costs of computers in education. If it is true, as pundits estimate, that 85 percent of teachers can teach any given topic better than 85 percent of the available educational software, we have an expensive challenge, since good software development is a costly process.

🕸 Even more fundamentally, if technology is to earn a place in education we must understand better what human intelligence is all about and how to enhance people's potential. A new interdisciplinary initiative, "Learning and Intelligent Systems," proposes to upgrade the state of the art by offering significant funding (grants totaling $20 million in 1997) for researchers to study technology to improve intelligence. But first someone must fund projects to learn how the human mind learns and creates as well as how natural and artificial intelligence can work to-gether.[15]

In short, it is possible to surmount numerous obstacles, but educationally valuable computer use involves significant ongoing expense. "It seems a lot easier to buy 'stuff' than to support teachers," observed Kathleen Fulton, who directed an authoritative study of teaching and technology for the Office of Technology Assessment.[16]

The Real Bottom Line

The real task is figuring out how to provide more children, both at home and at school, with meaningful and valid learning experiences. In the long run, many of our decisions about technology come down to the real bottom line, which is not money but values.

Winners and Losers

One might naturally assume that wealthier schools and districts have plunged most quickly into technology implementation, but this is not always the case. Irrespective of financial wherewithall, not all educators choose educational computing, and many poor schools boast elaborate computer facilities. Nor does a large budget—in either a school or a home—say anything about the quality of use. The brutal truth, despite all the hype to the contrary, is that children without computers and with a good education are far more likely to succeed than children walled in by technological fads.

■ ■ ■

On a lush hillside rising above Waikiki Beach, Punahou School in Honolulu, Hawaii, has prided itself for 150 years on its ability to produce winners in the game of life. As one of the best-endowed private schools in the United States, its multicultural mix of 3,600 talented youngsters is guided by a thoughtful faculty with high academic standards. As I begin a visit to this famous campus, I suspect this is the closest I will come to a school with its choice of technologies to prepare students for success.

Somewhat to my surprise, the school looks much as it did ten years ago. While innovations such as Internet use, multimedia, foreign language teaching, and video conferencing are being judiciously integrated at higher grade levels, much of the gadgetry present in other schools I have visited is conspicuously missing. New technologies are used only as teachers determine their utility for curriculum. In the lower school, most of the computers are old ones donated by parents or businesses. Comparatively speaking, Punahou still—by conscious choice—relies primarily on the traditional technologies of learning, not the least of which is close teacher-student interaction.

"You can do technology poorly just as you can do anything else poorly," technology director Norm Cox tells me. "We don't need bells and whistles to provide a good education, and we don't believe in imposing new demands on professional teachers who are already doing a great job. We're considering several interesting possibilities, but there are a lot of issues to work out before we're sure they're worth doing." Posted around campus and visible outside a room where I watch middle-school students learning to construct web pages are reminders of core values: respect, responsibility, compassion, faith, commitment, love, and wisdom. "Information," I note, didn't make the list.

Such "old-fashioned" attitudes are echoed in many successful schools, both public and private. Yet political leaders mouth the new platitude: Adopting technology will somehow "level the playing field," giving students from less privileged schools the same competitive set of skills as those higher up on the socioeconomic ladder. Would that it were so simple!

A Question of Values: Who Really Wins?

One of our main goals as parents and teachers, irrespective of economic status, is to help our children become successful in the areas of life we value. These days, "winning" is increasingly defined as significant financial success. Researchers at UCLA published results of a recent survey of 350,000 U.S. college freshmen. The students chose as their top goal "being very well off financially." Unlike previous decades, when aspirations such as "developing a meaningful philosophy of life" were ranked as number-one priorities, 70 percent of these youngsters appear to be predicating life plans on consumer values rather than on personal or social ideals. Fewer than one-third of these young voters think keeping up with political issues is important.[17]

Parents and teachers tell me they see early computer experience as a key to winning the race to financial success. Yet notwithstanding the fallacy of defining "success" by such limited criteria, precocious technological expertise guarantees nothing. The rungs to the top will be built from a range of uniquely human abilities, not the least of which is creativity, notably lacking in the computer mentality. Too much money and emphasis placed on technology is detracting attention from more pressing concerns and depriving children of the education they really need for any measure of success.

Unsolved Problems

> *"Computers in class: A waste of $50 billion? Skeptics say students need more real-world learning and less high-tech flash."*
> USA Weekend headline

> *Estimated cost of developing and upgrading programs to meet the needs of all preschool children in the United States is somewhere between $50 and $80 billion.*
> The Future of Children[18]

Serious unsolved problems—not lack of access to the Internet—are the obstacles on our merry march into the future.

Overall Spending on Education

🍃 A record number of children are enrolling in schools, with more to come. Class and school sizes are growing, even though research demonstrates conclusively that smaller is better.

🍃 Overcrowding even now forces schools to hold classes in former lavatories and gym in the lunchroom. In many cities split sessions are necessary.

ﻼ In 1995 educational researcher Gerald W. Bracey reported on per capita educational spending in industrialized nations and found the United States came in ninth out of nineteen. Even these figures are misleading since U.S. schools use much larger proportions of their budgets for nonacademic services, such as cafeterias and busing. We are the only major country in which fewer than 50 percent of school employees are classroom teachers. Debunking the "myth" that money doesn't matter, Bracey cites research demonstrating significant positive effects if we

1. Reduce class size to below twenty-four students
2. Spend more money on well-trained teachers
3. Offer well-qualified and timely special help for children with learning difficulties (e.g., special tutoring, language therapy)[19]

Early Childhood Programs

ﻼ Early educational experiences, particularly between ages two and four, profoundly influence success in school and life. Even intellectually impoverished home environments can be counteracted by good preschool care. Successful students will most predictably be productive workers and citizens; unsuccessful ones are all too likely to drop out and become costly and dangerous problems. Waiting to intervene until ages five or six is too late.

ﻼ *Well-run* and *well-staffed* Head Start preschool programs have proven their effectiveness also. A long-term study of High Scope, one successful model, demonstrates positive payoff by following former students until age twenty-seven. The program *returns seven dollars for every dollar originally invested.* By spending $12,000 per participant, taxpayers could save over $80,000 in reduced costs of crime, special schooling, and various forms of assistance.[20] Unfortunately, most programs are far below this "high-quality" benchmark; salaries are near the bottom of the wage scale, turnover is high, and hiring standards are far from optimal. Most come too late (around age four) to have maximum impact. Effective early childhood programs are cost-efficient by every measure.

ﻼ The estimated cost of developing and upgrading programs to meet the needs of all preschool children in the United States is somewhere be-

tween $50 and $80 billion on top of current expenditures.[21] Coinciden-
tally, this figure represents one recent estimate of the cost of connecting
every one of the nation's classrooms to the Internet.[22] One might reason-
ably argue that funds committed to vague Internet hype be earmarked
instead for this purpose, but even though cutting off problems upstream
is far cheaper in the long run, such a proposal doesn't attract the same
corporate and political enthusiasm.

Teacher Salaries and Expertise

*"Every dollar spent on improving teacher quality resulted in im-
proved school performance."*

Linda Darling Hammond, Teachers College, Columbia University

*"What's most important in a classroom? A good teacher, interact-
ing with motivated students. Anything that separates them—
filmstrips, instructional videos, multimedia displays, e-mail, TV
sets, interactive computers—is of questionable value."*

Clifford Stoll[23]

Although the United States is a relatively big spender on nonteaching educational costs, the proportion spent on teacher salaries is
smaller than that of twenty-two other major nations.[24]

An alarming number of teachers have not studied the subjects they
teach or have otherwise failed to meet already lax licensing requirements.[25]

Physical Plant

More than three years after the 1994 Los Angeles earthquake, students in some districts were still in portable classrooms. "We have all new
computers, although our walls are still cracked," reported the office manager of one elementary school.[26]

Approximately 60 percent of U.S. schools need repair. The District
of Columbia is in the most desperate shape; at least 91 percent of schools
there report a significant need. Also needed nationally: money to comply
with federal mandates to correct environmental hazards and provide access for the disabled. Overall, it would cost $112 billion to bring the na-
tion's schools up to safe and suitable standards.[27]

Music, Art, Drama, Debate, and Physical Education

  Even in the face of massive technology expenditures, overall school budgets are being cut, and the humanities are the first to go. Even though experiences in the arts and physical education motivate students, increase overall brain power, and support curriculum, art and music rooms are being morphed into computer labs, teachers' supply budgets are cut, and PE classes are sliced away in the name of economy.

Do we have our priorities properly sorted out? According to Robert W. Mendenhall, manager of IBM's K–12 education marketing, "Most of the dollars [educators] have spent have, in my point of view, been wasted. What you get is a whole bunch of computers in the classroom, teachers who resist technology, and computers being used at recess and study hall." In a recent government study, while 68 percent of teachers surveyed had access to computers, only 42 percent used them as part of the curriculum.[28]

Technology, by itself, cannot level the playing field. I have seen too many examples of wasteful fiascoes grafted onto failing schools. When technology works in disadvantaged areas, the important factors are already in place: careful planning, vision, curriculum, training, and close supervision.

■ ■ ■

Seven-year-old Maiesha bends eagerly over the keyboard which she holds in her lap. The small student desk can't accommodate both the computer and a keyboard, so the keyboard is stored where books and papers used to be kept. The two desks that comprise the "computer center" barely fit into a back corner of this busy classroom, but Maiesha doesn't notice these inconveniences—she is engrossed in the challenge of inventing an imaginary animal, writing a story, and drawing a picture of it. As she painstakingly searches out the letters to spell a sentence, her classmate Rainell offers advice.

When the writing is completed, the two children begin drawing the illustration, using the mouse as drawing tool and experimenting with different colors and backgrounds. As stripes, polka dots, and a brilliant but wobbly rainbow are added to the screen, they giggle delightedly, but soon their time is up. In this classroom twenty-five children share the two computers. Despite this inconvenience, the computer center bubbles with enthusiasm, as children compose, edit, and practice reading their completed work.

"The kids teach each other and they take it seriously," says their teacher, who only recently dared allow children to work in pairs in the computer corner. "They don't misbehave because they want to learn this way. Children who have trouble writing a sentence will actually write and correct their work."

Such enthusiasm didn't result, however, from simply placing computers in this classroom. Instead, a long process of training and professional coaching has helped this teacher redefine her ideas about how to teach. The district's recent cap on first-grade class size has helped, too. With fewer children, she can dare to let more learning happen spontaneously, and this change has improved overall achievement.

Spinning Straw Into Gold

I am observing these youngsters—who, by the way, are engaged in one of the few educationally valid computer activities I found for first-graders—in one of the poorest sections of Queens, in New York City. In this school the vast majority of students fall below the poverty line. I am accompanied by a redoubtable dynamo named Dr. Sandra Cooper, a former second-grade teacher whose early fascination with computers propelled her into the post of district technology director. A no-nonsense administrator, Sandy is spinning a remarkable amount of gold out of the straw of budget shortages, aging buildings, entrenched classroom management styles, and students who start school without adequate preparation.

Sandy has an educationally based philosophy of computer use, clear objectives, realistic views of what technology can be expected to accomplish, and the ingenuity to make goals into reality. Scraping together available dollars and seeking funding wherever possible, she has managed to obtain hardware, wire every school office ("even with the old black phones!"), implement internal file servers so multiple classrooms can share software, and get Internet access into half the classrooms. She and her colleagues personally train interested teachers in ongoing after-school sessions, and parents are invited to courses where they learn first-hand about the equipment.

Sandy has clear ideas about the way she wants learning to look and firmly communicates her rules.

* No "edutainment" software. ("If they bring it in, I ask them to remove it.") Only applications with a strong contribution to the theme-based curriculum: word processing, multimedia authoring tools, data bases, spreadsheets, research tools. Children using drawing programs must make original drawings, rather than using the canned images of "clip art."

* Clear objectives (which are part of each teacher's lesson plans and are posted daily in the computer corner) for all students using the computer. "They always have a task to accomplish," she says. "I don't want them wasting instructional time."

* A growing cadre of informed teachers who are willing to venture away from traditional top-down delivery of instruction. "It's important that they learn the whole world won't fall apart if a few children are out of their seats or are talking to each other about their work. But they're frightened, they're so afraid of loss of control."

* Peer tutors. In these classes (which number around thirty-five students after first grade), appointed student "experts" take turns troubleshooting and helping classmates.

* Emphasis on thinking and problem-solving as well as acquisition of information.

* "Computer contests." Each year teachers enter their innovative projects, and the winners gain extra computers for their classrooms. One sixth-grade teacher we visited had eight computers and a thoroughly energized class doing research on ancient Egypt.

* Encouragement of hands-on projects and experiential learning.

* Use teachers rather than nonteaching "techies" as computer educators and mentors for other teachers.

Sandy is optimistic about the potential of technology to enhance and change education. But she is also realistic.

"Parents are under the assumption that computers are going to change everything about their child," she comments. "Even over there," she gestures across the bay to a wealthy community, "good readers are wasting their time on some simple little reading game, but the child comes home and says, 'I was on computers,' and the parents just assume it's wonderful. We really need to get these parents to understand the issues and ask the critical questions."

Unfortunately, people like Sandy Cooper are the exception in a climate where little thought is given to the philosophy of computer use, particularly for disadvantaged children. Not long after my observation in Queens, I visited a school with a similar population in a southern state. Through a new state mandate, this district had actually spent far more money per pupil on technology than the Queens district had, but with no appreciable effect on educational quality. In each classroom, several computers stared vacantly ahead, while the teacher lectured at a crowd of listless children, or one student read orally while the rest of the class fidgeted and gazed out the window.

An Equal Chance at the Future—or Reinforcing Inertias?

Although computers can be found in schools at all socioeconomic levels, affluent schools are more likely to have the freedom and staffing to use them well. An analysis in the *Wall Street Journal* reported on two contrasting examples. Exurban Plainfield, Indiana, High School boasts three computer labs, a sound plan for integrating technology into the curriculum, sufficient technical support, well-trained teachers with machines in all classrooms with Internet connectivity, and laptops available to students for overnight loan. Here, they say, technology is used "all the time," including students and teachers dialing into the library to access reference materials. In contrast, an urban high school in a lower-income section of nearby Indianapolis has more computer labs (nine) but no networking for research capability, repetitious drill-and-practice software, and little encouragement for teachers to use computers. Technology use is minimal and actually fosters discipline problems, as teachers without aides are unable to manage the questions and inevitable program glitches of an entire class.[29]

It has been suggested that one way of subsidizing lower-income areas and equalizing availability of information resources is by simply improving libraries' and schools' access to the Internet, at a cost of as much as $2.5 billion annually for five years.[30] To make effective use of information, however, students must have developed critical thinking, concentration, reading, and research skills. If they had these, they might not need the computers! In fact, in one inner-city New Jersey middle school the vaunted improvements in morale and test scores were attributed by politicians to the installation of technology, when in actuality they had occurred beforehand. Fundamental changes were responsible: longer class periods, new books, after-school programs, and greater emphasis on student-generated projects.

"Using computers to improve education is a big, difficult problem, but in the public discourse it's dealt with as superficial hype," reflected Professor Robbie McClintock in his office at Columbia University Teachers College the day after he learned his project proposal for restructuring inner-city schools had been awarded a multimillion-dollar government grant. Long recognized for his work with disadvantaged students, he believes such expenditures must change the educational status quo if they are to be justified. Smaller classes, better curriculum and teaching, and more student-centered, humanistic environments are essential to his plans. "We really need to be able to shape an educational system that is quite different," he told me, "but we will be well into the twenty-first century before we see whether technology is a step forward or a step backward, whether it's really positive or a reinforcement of the worst inertias in our culture. If so, we've put an awful lot of capital behind making bad decisions."[31]

GLIMPSING POSSIBILITIES

One of McClintock's projects is located at Ralph Bunche Elementary School in Harlem. A computer mini-school-within-a-school, led by teacher-dynamo Paul Reese, occupies one corner of a massive post–World War I brick building serving 750 students, 90 to 95 percent of whom come from families below the poverty line. The 250 students in the mini-school are randomly drawn from a pool of fourth- to sixth-graders. Students in both the standard program and the mini-school have access to similar computer labs, but the mini-school students score at least 20 percent higher on standardized tests. It didn't take me long to find out why.

As I arrived, a fourth-grade class was entering the lab accompanied by its teacher, an enduring local legend named Ellen Clare. Ms. Clare, a tall, willowy lady with cropped hair, awesome earrings, and huge spectacles, is the kind of teacher who simply doesn't have discipline problems—no one would dare! Yet her class of twenty-two (as opposed to thirty-some in the standard classroom) neatly uniformed children wriggle with enthusiasm as they seat themselves at the computers and immediately set to work. Each is writing a story or poem on a personal topic; once the text is written, they create illustrations. Quality and individuality are impressive, as are the children's personal involvement and eagerness to help each other. A thoughtful buzz of conversation hangs over the room, indicating—far more than would an artificially quiet classroom—that young brains are productively at work. Still, it takes the full efforts of Mr. Reese, Ms. Clare, and an aide to coach the students, answer questions, and keep everyone's machine operating. Like the others in the mini-school, their classroom also contains one computer used as part of everyday learning activities.

In the corner, one sixth-grader who has stayed home from a field trip works industriously to update the school page on the World Wide Web. She also demonstrates how she communicates on an Internet chat line with students in another state and shows off the student-published newspaper.

Meanwhile, Ms. Clare vibrates around the room, offering suggestions, asking questions, keeping order. I am astonished to learn that part of her mystique is that she claims to be a confirmed technophobe. "Never touch the things," she curls her lip. "But I wouldn't be without them. The kids really improve their writing and research skills, and you can see how much they enjoy the work." (Mystique to the contrary, she obviously knows her way around the technology.)

As the students file out, I compliment Paul Reese on the constructive energy in the class. He explains that this is only one example of teaching with technology at Ralph Bunche. In past years Reese has organized projects from installing a weather station on the school's roof and having students analyze weather data by computer, to developing a computer home-loan program, to students using the computer to write about and mediate interpersonal problems.

"We've actually managed to do all this without spending huge amounts of money," Reese told me. Because this school is a model project, much of the equipment has been donated. Reese has been the mastermind and change engine, and also provides tech support. When I inquired about the last item, he rolled his eyes ruefully.

"Funny you should ask—that call just now [which had interrupted the class] was a secretary who can't get her printer to work. Basically, I'm it! If this were a business application, we'd have at least four full-time techies on staff, for repair, software applications, troubleshooting. Tell the grantors about this end of the business, because they haven't figured it out yet."

(Another creative teacher I interviewed, whose school also enjoyed unusually high levels of support from university and corporate sources, echoed these concerns. "It's a whole new career on top of the other one," she confessed ruefully. "It's really not fair to expect people to do all that—I even have to install all the upgrades. Most teachers simply won't or can't do it.")

How much credit should the technology get for the obvious improvements, not only in test scores, but in motivation, morale, and quality of education at the computer mini-school, I asked Paul Reese.

"It's really not about computers," he replied at once. "It's about good teaching, and smaller classes, and the kids' involvement in what they're learning. They have higher motivation because they feel a sense of ownership. Clearly the kids who leave here have an excellent grasp of technology, but that's not what accounts for our success." It would be interesting to find out whether a program similar in administrative energy, excellence in teaching, smaller classes, and stimulating curriculum *without the computers* would result in similar gains. My guess is that it would.

Paul Reese represents a critical factor I found in every successful program: one energetic and visionary educator who knew what teaching should look like and had the energy and dedication to make it happen. No matter what the neighborhood, wealthy or poor, people like this make a difference.

As I start back down the hall, a little girl from the fourth grade shyly slips me a copy of her poem, which I had admired.

I Wish
by Ayeesha

I wish . . .
my grandfather wasn't merdered and my gramma
   didn't die of cancer
they would both met in Heaven and get there wings
my uncle didn't steal
Miss Clare was my momma
all the world had peace
some schools had better teachers
I could fly
I had long hair
I had a pony
there weren't slavery.
The End

LIFE AT THE OTHER END

At the other end of the United States in many respects, the Gold River Discovery School outside Sacramento, California, stands as an example of what can be accomplished if money, planning, and educational expertise are applied in a judicious mixture. Only four years old, this low, rambling set of buildings surrounding a central courtyard was designed to showcase educational technology. No one worries here about drilling through walls, since the school was built with extra electrical power, wiring for phones and modems in each room, an open and flexible floor plan that provides space for at least four computers per classroom and central common spaces with computer mini-labs for different types of activities. Software selection is integrated with curriculum planning. Technical support is readily available. A thick "Technology Use Plan" outlines goals for each grade level, including means by which progress may be evaluated.

As we approach the school through the neatly manicured, affluent subdivision from which most of Gold River's students are drawn, I observe that the houses are exactly alike, even down to the height of the hedges.

I ask my guide, Elementary Coordinator Linda Winthers, whether we will find expensive cookie-cutter kids to go with these expensive cookie-cutter houses.

She chuckles. "Wait until we get to the school," she replies. "I think you'll be pleasantly surprised."

Indeed, the air fairly palpitates with energy as we enter the school, and throughout our visit we hear children expressing ideas, asking questions, working together on well-articulated projects. To me, the most impressive thing I see here is not the technology use, but the integrated curriculum and the way students are continually coached on how to take responsibility and reflect on their learning. ("My plan is . . . ," "I needed to analyze the data more before I drew my conclusions.") Each child makes an action plan before starting any activity and periodically reviews both short-term and lifelong learning goals. Computers are ever-present, but the children's learning is on center stage—and there is nothing about it that even resembles a cookie-cutter! If you told these children they should be marching down a hall in silent rows arranged according to height, they would think you were joking.

The instigator of all this excitement about learning is principal Tim McCarty, who has guided into reality his constructivist vision of a school where students, teachers, and parents are important members of a learning community. Technology is used only as a means toward agreed-upon goals, and parents are welcome to come in and learn about it firsthand.

"We're really careful to use technology not just for the sake of technology. The teachers make it a seamless part of the learning process. We stress the importance of choosing the right tool for the job; sometimes it's the computer, often it isn't."

Acknowledging that his own interest in computers does not extend to expert status, he comments, "The most technically competent humans on this campus are the kids—they're so much more open-minded than the adults. They are constantly teaching us.

"Yes, it takes a lot of money. If you buy a book, it stays with you. Our computers are now four years old, and they already need to be upgraded, not to mention the constant upkeep—usually about 10 out of 140 machines are down at any one time. We have a management system to track machines from room to room, and we can also keep track of what Internet resources are accessed. We've spent a lot of time bringing the teachers up to speed, and that's an ongoing process. When teachers take courses in the summer, we pay them to learn."

In one fourth-grade class, we see an example of the children's involvement in a study of water resources. The teacher has subscribed to an international network of schoolchildren collecting data on local water quality,[32] and they communicate on-line with a "team" of twelve to fifteen other schools around the world. But hands-on learning comes first, as they visit a well to investigate local water sources and research water rights which date from the 1850 gold rush. Then they conduct science experiments to test water for chemical elements and send the results to a central "server," which collates them with data from children as far away as Russia. Finally, an adult scientist receives their data, analyzes it, and sends back a summary of her findings.

"They get so excited because it's so real-world, among other things," exclaims the teacher, whose own enthusiasm and creativity obviously have a great deal to do with the general atmosphere. "They feel as if they're really contributing to something important, and they enjoy exchanging e-mail messages with kids in other places. Sometimes I wonder if they realize how much reading, writing, and math they're doing."

In the classroom next door, students are hard at work in small groups developing printed earthquake manuals (we're in California, remember) with illustrations scanned into the computer. Using multimedia presentation software, they will also develop a slide show and oral commentary as part of a report to present to their parents. As I learn about plate techtonics from an eager group of nine-year-olds, I have to believe that something interesting is happening here. I do observe, however, that one or two of the children in each group seem to be doing most of the writing, while the nonwriters are happily distracted by the graphics. I hope the teacher will make sure each child practices each skill.

As we leave the school, we pass through a sixth-grade classroom where students are working in groups to solve math problems drawn from a mystery simulation game they have watched on laser disc. On the wall is this poster:

Lifelong Learning Standards

> complex thinking
> effective communication
> information processing
> habits of mind
> collaborative worker/community contributor

Clearly, more than one type of "basic" is valued here.

Intellect vs. Entertainment

"Our media and our culture are bought and paid for."
Bob McCannon, Director, New Mexico Media Literacy Project

Schools bursting with digital bells and whistles can impress even a skeptical visitor, but only time will demonstrate whether such changes improve learning—or are we simply pandering to our media-crazed young? Columbia's Dr. Robbie McClintock has no qualms about pointing out some worrisome trends. He believes that because computers and information technology are actually less important as learning tools than as powerful and lucrative cultural influences, they are shifting our balance from intellectual interests to the pleasures of easy entertainment.

"We're beginning to pit knowledge institutions such as schools and libraries against broadcast and entertainment institutions," McClintock pointed out. He is particularly concerned about a conflict between individual access to information, as in public libraries and the early days of the Internet, and growing control by corporations dishing out homogeneous content to mass audiences. By digitizing resources in libraries,

103

labs, and museums, he believes we can make them more generally available—but only if students use them seriously in the service of learning—not for play or simple "fun."

Even though all kids are susceptible to the saccharine blandishments of pop culture, those who come from families that value reading and academic standards are better able to discriminate the valuable from the trivial. If our schools can provide a good foundation in reasoning and critical analysis, even for those who don't have it at home, there is less threat of mind control by a virtual culture catering to the lowest common denominator. For example, McClintock suggests that children should not have Internet access until they have learned to use it judiciously. "It becomes important about age ten or eleven," he says. "Before that they must acquire basic tools of dealing with information."[33]

Could profit-oriented entertainment interests ever work with academia in the cause of improving rather than degrading the general level of intelligence? Professor Dale Mann, also of Teachers College, suggests giving companies an opportunity to both "make money and make a difference" by helping develop educationally stimulating computer environments. He points out that the entertainment industry has now replaced the U.S. defense industry as the main developer of technology, and at least half as much again is spent on entertainment as on education.[34] The industry's talent might promote innovative approaches to meaningful learning, rather than siphoning off student interest with various forms of "mind candy." Then "profit" could be toted up in terms of a more intelligent populace. Of course, more thoughtful people would be less likely to consume mindless entertainment. Don't hold your breath.

Symbolic Analysts: The "Haves" of the Future

The intellectual skill most likely to guarantee success for today's students is termed "symbolic analysis" by Daniel Burstein and David Kline in their fascinating book, *Road Warriors*.[35] Currently, only about 20 percent of the U.S. work force participates meaningfully and directly in the information sector—writers and readers of books among them. They will succeed because they can make use of symbols—the abstracted content of information, finance, and the arts. As the creation of wealth depends less on raw materials and hands-on labor and more on synthesizing information and juggling abstract numbers in financial markets, success will fall to those comfortable with multiple symbol systems: languages, math, and the arts, including new digital languages and images. The ability to read these symbols will be critical.

"While cyberspace may be filled with words, a growing portion of the American population will not be able to use, understand, or benefit from those words," state Burstein and Kline. "Some of these people may be *digitally literate*, in that they feel at home with joysticks and remote controls and are perfectly capable of absorbing the sights and sounds of multimedia entertainment. But if you are not *functionally literate*, your chances of getting a significant piece of the cyberspace pie are slim, even if you have access to it."

The new economic order will also favor those who have learned how to learn, who can respond flexibly and creatively to challenges and can master new skills. "Today, the search for innovative ideas is so intense that it has become hard to be an innovator and *not* be mightily rewarded," insist these authors.

Technology will probably widen the gap between the haves and the have-nots, but not necessarily along traditional socioeconomic dividing lines. Members of the new underclass will be less privileged not because they are computer illiterate, but because their education—be it an inner-city or a private school in the suburbs—fails to sharpen their intellectual curiosity and symbolic reasoning skills.

The Vocationalizing of Education

> "... business and its businesslike ways are becoming the dominant educating institution in our society."
> Stan Davis and Jim Botkin in *The Monster Under the Bed* [36]

One of the most disconcerting e-mails I have received came recently from a young business major who had just been hired as computer teacher for a private school. Responding to intense pressure from parents and board members, the headmaster had given her a large budget and "carte blanche" to jump headlong into technology implementation.

She wanted to debate a point I had raised in a seminar as I questioned both the validity of computer "training" for young children and too much emphasis on technology at any age. To her credit, she offered an impassioned defense of her curriculum, which involved getting children into her computer lab as soon (age four) and as often as possible. Nevertheless, she revealed in our on-line conversations an astonishing lack of understanding of either good educational practice or the most basic principles of child development. Even more worrisome, it was hard to discern from her comments any significant perspective on technology and society.

"This is the computer age," she insisted, "so what's wrong with going with the computers? After all, you can spend all that time studying history and what good is it in the long run? If they learn computer, at least they can use it to get a job." To further her argument she pointed out that many people opposed the automobile when it was first invented, but "just think, if we didn't have automobiles it would take me four days rather than four hours to go visit my mother."

To someone with this world view, it is probably useless to point out that if we lived in a world without automobiles, she would probably dwell within walking distance of her mother. Moreover, although we love our automobiles, we also recognize that lack of vision and planning created long-standing problems (e.g., pollution, misplaced freeways) which might have been avoided. But, of course, those who do not understand the mistakes of the past (maybe by studying history?) are certainly doomed to repeat them.

Do I risk being stoned in the public marketplace if I suggest that the purpose of education is not to make kids economically valuable, but rather to enable them to develop intellectual and personal worth as well as practical skills? As we become ever more instrumental in our attitudes, affixing a monetary profit and loss statement to every activity, we risk losing sight of the need to produce truly *well-educated* individuals who can adapt to the extremes of any technological climate and who have the skills (and perhaps even the wisdom) to become leaders in science, medicine, or public affairs. Some of the best jobs in the corporate and professional worlds still go to literature or history majors. Why? Because they know how to think.

PART TWO

Digital Childhood

Chapter Four

Computers and Our Children's Health

"Do we have to wait till the damage happens, then we do the research?"

Dr. Ann Barber, developmental optometrist

In a basement classroom in an aging building on Manhattan's Lower East Side an exciting new idea is reaching fruition. A dozen ten- and eleven-year-olds are hunched over laptop computers under the glare of fluorescent lights. They are writing an alternative ending to a well-known children's poem. Already proficient in keyboarding, these youngsters do much of their daily work on their personal electronic companions as a result of a special grant project to put computers into this schoolroom—one for each child.

Parents are excited and, as usual, uncritical about the program. As I converse casually with one mother after class, I can't help but wonder out loud if this intensive close work with poorly illuminated small screens has had any effects on children's vision, as I know it has with adults in the workplace.

"Well, now that you mention it," replies Mom, "her eyes do seem to be getting worse, and she is just about to have an appointment with her optometrist. I'll have to remember to ask him. I just never thought to connect it."

No one, it seems, has thought to connect it or even to question it, yet we are committing our youngsters to radically new learning environments. In every computer lab I have visited, I have asked: "Did you look at any of the research on vision before you decided how to light the room, shield the screens, size the furniture, place the computers, or how much time kids would spend on them?" The answer, with only one exception, has been a blank stare and the answer, "No." Nor has the research cited in adult occupational literature been carried out in studies of children's computer use. Not just research into obvious physical problems, such as vision, wrist and back problems, but also research on the highly controversial subject of electromagnetic radiation.

The American Academy of Pediatrics has recently expressed concern about how much time children spend in front of various types of screens. This group now recommends that for school-age children, "total screen time [TV, video, computer] should be limited to one to two hours per day, including time spent on a computer for noneducational or prosocial purposes."[1] Some physicians fear that even this amount may be too much, and many recommend less screen time for preschoolers. The academy also recommends that a "media history," including amount and type of computer, television, and video use, be taken by physicians as a routine part of a child's medical record for diagnosis of media-related problems—physical, academic, and emotional. "But you don't ask the parent how much screen time the child has, you ask the child," one pediatrician smiled wryly as he explained. "Then you watch the parent sit there and squirm as the kid tells you the truth."

If you call the United States Government Public Health Service, you will receive a weighty stack of closely typed pages documenting physical hazards of improper computer use and specifying guidelines for employers to follow if their employees are spending significant amounts of time at video display terminals. Not one of these articles addresses research on children.

It is perhaps typical of a society that seems to care more for hi-tech than for the health of our young that these issues have been so effectively swept under the carpet. Who wants to think about carpal tunnel syndrome, impaired vision, postural complaints, or even radiation emissions? Asking such questions is likely to get you labelled as a wierdo trying to block progress and hold back our ability to "get ahead." But whether our children march confidently into the next century may depend on whether they can see their way through the latest technology in bifocal lenses.

Cumulative Risks

According to numerous government reports, adult workers who use VDTs (video display terminals) during more than half their workday have significantly higher health problem rates than workers who rarely use VDTs. Most common problems involve vision (eye discomfort and eyestrain, blurring, itching, irritation, and aching, double vision, and deterioration of vision). Musculoskeletal complaints are next, among them strain in back, neck, shoulders, arms, and wrists—including carpal tunnel syndrome (numbness, tingling, and reduced sensation in the fingers). As computer use increases, more problems are reported.[2]

To date, few children other than habituated video-game players have spent enough time on the computer to warrant much concern. As more kids spend more and more time, these issues acquire greater urgency. Health effects are assumed to be cumulative—that is, something that might not hurt you in small doses can become damaging over a long period of time. With some parents starting their toddlers at computer monitors, exposure to negative effects will be long-term.

Daniel and Kimberly Updegrove of the University of Pennsylvania have examined the potential for personal risk in the adult workplace. "If, as is widely suspected, health effects are cumulative, then many of us are at risk," they report. "Unfortunately, many years will be required before epidemiological studies can provide definitive guidelines. In the interim, individuals and institutions must educate themselves about these issues and take protective measures."[3]

If something is harmful to full-grown adults, it may carry even greater risk for the developing child, as fast-growing biological systems are most vulnerable to damage. Moreover, children are not always aware of the objective condition of their bodies and may not report problems. With youth's blithe conviction that they are invulnerable, they are also less likely to observe safety guidelines. Thus, adults must consider the potential for long-lasting harm and institute steps to prevent it. First, of course, is to call for some much-needed research. Until such studies are done, however, a cautious approach to potential problems, including adopting preventive measures, is prudent for adults who supervise children using computers.

In this chapter we will examine four potential physical risks to the developing child: visual problems, postural and skeletal problems, dangers of radiation, and the displacement of normal physical activities of childhood and adolescence. We will also allude briefly to some much rarer effects on the growing brain. All these preventable health risks are unfortunately exacerbated by common physical conditions in schools: Older machines, poorly designed or nonexistent workstations, antiquated lighting, small screens, and inadequate budgets for preventive maintenance. Moreover, the appalling ignorance among most educators about computer health issues means that new installations are being made without even rudimentary guidelines. If this cavalier attitude prevailed in adult workplaces, you can be sure someone would be hearing about it!

Vision

"We are increasingly becoming an information society, and the price we are paying is our eyesight."
Dr. Jeffrey Anschel, Corporate Vision Consulting [4]

"Thanks to computers, my business is booming, I'm sorry to say. We're seeing humongous increases in the need for both vision therapy and occupational therapy because two-dimensional visual experience without related motor experience doesn't set the necessary base. Kids come in with 'the look'—I can tell right away."
Dr. John Jacobi, O.D., Traverse City, Michigan

After my son and I both became nearsighted while spending extended time at computer screens, I began to suspect a connection. It took several years, however, before I became aware of the magnitude of the developmental issues. I was speaking at a conference in Michigan soon after I started writing this book and alluded to my curiosity about computers and eye problems. At the break, a young woman who identified herself as a developmental optometrist introduced herself.

"You bet there's a connection!" she exclaimed. "You're going to be seeing lots more kids in 'learning lenses' and bifocals as a result of time on computers."

"Learning lenses," she explained, are a mildly corrective lens designed to help preadolescent children relax and focus the eyes more easily.

As a result of this conversation I interviewed several experts in eye development, all of whom assured me that computer use is indeed creating problems in children's developing visual systems. Because the screen is flat and is viewed on the horizontal plane, it does not offer different points of convergence. Moreover, children are much more likely to stare without blinking than if they were reading or engaging in other activities. "The strain is like standing with your knees locked for five to ten minutes," one specialist told me.

Visual strain is the number-one problem of frequent computer users.[5] Studies estimate that anywhere from half to 90 percent of regular computer users experience visual deterioration.[6]

After a long history of use for seeing long distances, eyes in the past hundred years have been required to adapt to "near work," including, of course, reading and writing. To do this, our species has become increasingly nearsighted.

Computer use is even more stressful than book reading in terms of the demands it places on the visual system. Instead of a white piece of paper with black print, VDTs have an illuminated screen, which continually refreshes its phosphor coating so the image doesn't fade. This refreshing must be accomplished more than sixty times a second in order to avoid a phenomenon called "flicker," often subtle and nonperceptible, which is highly stressful to both visual system and brain. Also, in reading we tend to look down at the book, whereas with a computer our eyes focus straight ahead. Not only is this more taxing, but it makes eyes more susceptible to outside sources of light, especially light coming from the ceiling. As I learned about this, I thought of the dozens of schoolrooms in which I have visited where bright (and sometimes flickering!) fluorescent lights shine. Any source of reflection or glare on the screen is a strict no-no, according to occupational experts. Actually, many schoolrooms are much too bright for optimal computer use, but dimming the lights will cause problems with other types of work. If fluorescent lamps must be used, they should probably be equipped with "diffusers," which cause the light to fall more indirectly, thus cutting down on glare, flicker, and the resulting eyestrain.

The rapid, rhythmic eye movements used when reading printed text are called "saccades," and they differ from those demanded by electronic texts, which cause a more static stare. These differences make it hard to transfer from one medium to another.[7] Whether or not children's eyes will successfully adapt to electronic text is unknown, but the new technology places more demands on the eyes at any age.

As if physical concerns aren't enough, some professionals believe too much screen time of any sort could have the potential to interrupt mental and possibly even behavioral development. According to Dr. Ann Barber, developmental optometrist of Santa Ana, California, some children who don't get enough practice integrating their visual systems with body movement in the three-dimensional real world may be shortchanged in perceptual processes important for schoolwork and even for integration of thinking skills. Balance, laterality (feeling left and right, and being able to cross the midline of the body), and body image all take lots of experience.

"Movement is so important to both visual and mental development," Dr. Barber emphasizes. "When the child is born the wiring is all there; the light hits the retina but he makes no sense of it. He needs to learn by touching, putting things in his mouth, moving around, and then he has to integrate all this with vision and the other senses to make an intelligent child that's ready for school. There are about eight or ten perceptual processes developing in the preschool years that go beyond the eyeball, and so much . . . is done with the body, manipulating objects, dropping toys to learn about distance and develop visual convergence, practicing how to catch or kick a ball, hit a target. The child also must learn to focus on what's important and make sense out of the world. How can you understand 'above, below, inside, outside' if you're not crawling into the cardboard box and seeing and feeling it? But today we see so many kids are delayed in these skills—six-, seven-, eight-year-olds who are more at a four-year-old level."

At her house Dr. Barber says her children get only one hour a day of "screen time"; after each one-half hour segment they must take a break.[8]

The actual relationship between perceptual-motor processes and learning difficulties has yet to be sorted out, and therapy programs based on visual and motor skills are controversial. Nonetheless, the question is attracting increasing attention. Several specialists have also suggested to me that improper visual-motor development may account for some cases of attention problems, either because children haven't gotten the sense that their brain can control their body, or because trying to compensate for poorly developed visual skills puts a great strain on the entire nervous system.

"They may be able to see twenty-twenty, but it takes so much energy they're not comfortable. If their focus is poor, it makes them nervous, they read inefficiently, and it makes the work too hard," explained Dr. Ida Chung of the SUNY College of Optometry in New York. Any activity that causes children to stare and not move the eyes, when the system is "frozen in space," can cause eyestrain and lead to these problems.

"Parents don't normally see the computer as the cause of their vision problems, but if you look deeper, you see it's the computer."[9]

Paradoxically, Dr. Chung and her colleagues are also using the computer for vision therapy with children. They are developing specialized video games to train the eyes for focusing and eye teaming—not just any old video games, they stress, but medically researched eye exercises in a gamelike format. Like several other therapeutic applications now under development, technology may hold the potential to ameliorate some of the problems it causes!

Keeping Eyes Healthy

&. Eliminate sources of light and glare. Be alert for direct glare from sunlight and lighting fixtures directed at the user's eyes and indirect glare due to any type of reflection on the video screen. You can assess glare most effectively when the computer is turned off; look straight at the screen and observe any reflection. Use desk lights instead of ceiling lights where possible. Place the computer at a right angle to windows and install curtains or blinds if glare persists. Try not to use computers in rooms with fluorescent lamps and eliminate all other sources of light pulsation. Be alert for "flicker" from any source; it may cause headaches, eyestrain, and even epileptic seizures in susceptible individuals. Some authorities recommend having the terminal checked every six months to be sure it is still operating within the manufacturer's specifications.

✥ Hoods may be purchased to put over screens if glare is a persistent problem (a file folder can be a handy substitute). Antiglare screens are available, but may reduce sharpness of the image.

✥ Some users find that rose-colored or reddish-brown glasses reduce eyestrain.

✥ One group of researchers wondering if screen and print color had anything to do with the accuracy with which people could proofread their writing found that light-colored type on darker backgrounds (e.g., white on blue or amber on green) was easier on the eyes and enabled more accurate proofreading.[10]

✥ Use a larger font and avoid cluttered screens.

✥ Horizontal menus may be easier to read than vertical ones.

✥ Teach children to take frequent "eye breaks"—totaling about fifteen minutes off for every hour of computer use. In addition, have them take a ten-second break every ten minutes. Use this time to rest eyes by walking around and/or shifting gaze to look at far distances. Eye doctors can prescribe exercises to relax eyes and improve focusing.

✥ Staring can strain the eyes. Remind children to blink frequently. Because computer users tend to fixate too long on the screen without blinking normally, eye lubrication is diminished and irritation may result.

✥ Computer users should view the screen at ten to twenty degrees below the horizontal plane of eye level. (Have the child look straight ahead and arrange the height of the screen and chair so she must drop her eyes slightly to view the screen.)

✥ Experiment with different colors of screen and type to see which is the easiest for your child to read.

✥ Clean the screen regularly with antistatic spray and lint-free cloth to avoid accumulation of dust from static electricity.

❧ If your child uses a computer regularly, be sure he or she has a vision checkup every year.

❧ Some authorities believe that visual stress may increase the body's need for certain nutritional elements. They especially recommend a healthy diet for computer users.

Postural and Skeletal Problems

Children look as if they could bend around any piece of furniture for any length of time and never feel the effects, but their growing bodies are not immune to injury from postural stress. Most school furniture is old, and many computer installations are far from optimal in ergonomic respects. Even new furniture may not be purchased with computer use in mind. Certainly this issue deserves your attention if you are planning for a home computer. I have seen many, many children perched on one leg on chairs far too large for their small frames, or stretching their neck to look at a computer screen because the desk was too high for them. It is also not uncommon to see youngsters hunched over keyboards they are holding in their laps. For adults, such poor posture or muscle strain results in a variety of neck and back ailments, muscle cramps, headaches, irritability, and even depression; whether these ailments will prove to be a danger for children is as yet unknown.

The only computer-related postural problem so far reported extensively in the pediatric literature is something called "video wrist," which resembles the adult carpal tunnel syndrome and includes numbness, pain, and sometimes tendinitis in wrists and hands. While these issues may not be as pressing as those regarding vision, attention to some simple design principles can help forestall future complaints.

Feeling Comfortable at the Computer

❧ Encourage children to use good posture when working at the computer, sitting straight on a well-fitting chair and resting wrists on the desk.

❧ Workstations in schools should be adjustable for different-size children. Look for chairs with adjustable seats, adjustable-height work surface or separate keyboard tray, keyboards at elbow-height, and possibly adjustable footrests.

ᴥ If your child's feet don't reach the floor, try boxes, blocks or telephone books as a footrest.

ᴥ A surface that is large enough will enable the child to use reference materials or typing copy without having to hunch over her lap. Adult word processors use document holders for text they are copying.

ᴥ A posture cushion to support the lower back can be helpful.

ᴥ Encourage your child to change positions frequently to avoid fatigue. Simply walking around the room rests both eyes and body.

ᴥ If you are going to allow your child to be "glued" to the screen for long periods, consider teaching him some deep breathing or relaxation exercises to relieve the muscular tension.

ᴥ Use the inevitable wait-times (as the computer boots up graphics or makes its little digestive sounds) to stand up, move about, get a drink of water, and relax body and eyes.

Radiation Hazards

"The heart of the controversy depends on whether you consider these emissions to be safe until proven hazardous or hazardous until proven safe."
Martin Sussman and Ernest Loewenstein in *Total Health at the Computer* [11]

Video display terminals emit both very-low-frequency (VLF) and extremely-low-frequency (ELF) electromagnetic radiation. Although newer models tend to be safer, many computers that children use regularly are a significant source of these emissions. The dangers to children of such magnetic fields, which are also found in such electrical appliances as electric blankets and refrigerators, high-tension wires and transformers, have been hotly debated for a number of years. As soon as we think we have an answer, conflicting studies confuse the issue.

According to the Updegroves (of the University of Pennsylvania), "Researchers have reported a number of ways that electromagnetic fields can affect biological functions, including changes in hormone levels, alterations in binding of ions to cell membranes, and modification of biochemical processes inside the cell."[12] Some alarming studies in

1979 and 1986 suggested a relationship between childhood leukemia and exposure to magnetic fields from electric lines, but more recent studies have questioned these results.[13] Research on adults has suggested other major health risks, including immune system effects, cataracts and cancer, but the issue remains far from resolved. The Swedish government has placed severe limits on computer emission levels, and an increasing number of hardware manufacturers throughout the world are now following their guidelines.

When I asked Dr. Raymond Neutro at the California Department of Health Services to give me some advice to pass along to parents and teachers, he confirmed the need for caution. "There's a lot of controversy about this, so how careful are you going to be?" he counseled. In fact, scientists are still arguing about what the most sensitive organ might be—retina, skin?—and theories abound. His group recommends that all new school planning include low-cost methods of avoiding potential radiation hazards. In older buildings, certain precautions make sense.

"We do know something about children's exposure nowadays, and if children are three feet away from the computer—or from the TV, for that matter—they're probably pretty safe," he concluded.[14]

Until we know the truth, it would seem prudent to monitor children's exposure, since it is thought that children are five to ten times more vulnerable to radiation than adults. Organs and systems perhaps at risk are bone, central nervous system, and thyroid gland.[15] Because of their small body weight, children may receive a higher amount of radiation per pound of body weight than adults from the same amount of radiation.

A less incendiary problem is the computer's tendency to generate static electricity. It can cause discomfort by bombarding the user with ions that attract dust particles, leading to eye and skin irritations. If these problems are present, increasing room humidity and investing in anti-static pads are said to be effective.

Laptop computers do not generate the same emissions as desk-type models.

Prudent Planning

ஐ Current recommended practice is for computer users to maintain a distance of about 30 to 36 inches from the screen and four feet or more from the sides and backs of video display terminals. Turning rectangular worktables sideways may achieve the required distance, or place the computer on a shelf about four feet deep. Magnetic field strength diminishes rapidly with distance. Using a detachable keyboard may help. Increase font size for the child to see the screen without sitting too close to it.

ॐ The backs and sides of computers and other electrical appliances generate most of the hazardous emissions. Allow adequate distance between computers. Never line up computers back-to-back, as it places children too close to the backs of the opposite machines. If your child is within four feet of someone else's machine at school, you should request changes. Better safe than sorry.

ॐ Magnetic fields can penetrate walls. Some observers advise not putting a child's bed, for example, on the other side of a wall from the back of a computer (or a refrigerator!) and advise considering this issue when locating computers in schoolrooms.

ॐ When buying a computer, select one with low electromagnetic field (EMF) radiation. Newer models generally are safer than older ones, and some LCDs (liquid crystal displays) have eliminated or shielded potentially harmful emissions. Check for manufacturer's compliance with Swedish Trade Council (TCO) emission standards.

ॐ Turn off computers when not in use, or put in "sleep" or power-down mode.

Shouldn't They Be Playing?

One of the early advertisements for a major hardware manufacturer ran in a number of educational publications and showed an empty schoolroom with a large bank of computers lined up against one wall. On the adjacent wall were several large windows through which could be seen peering, from the outside, a number of elementary-age children, eyeing the computers with their noses pressed wistfully on the glass. The caption read, "[Brand name] computers are making recess obsolete."

Presumably the company heard from enough irate individuals like me because the ad was eventually withdrawn. Nevertheless, it certainly reveals a great deal not only about marketing zeal and changing attitudes, but also about the electronic community's appalling ignorance about the fundamental needs of growing children.

Many parents earnestly believe that children are learning more when they are at the computer than they would be if they were in gym class or playing in the backyard. But health experts join developmental psychologists in expressing grave concern about this dangerous trend. Not only is physical activity—preferably outdoors—vital for health, good sleep patterns, dissipation of excess energy, and socialization, but the subtle learning and problem-solving that take place in spontaneous play are important for mental development as well.

In the United States, children are getting less fit by the year, and obesity rates among the young are increasing even more rapidly than among their parents.[16] Teachers report they find many of today's children overly stressed and anxious, and they blame lack of physical exercise for some cases of hyperactive behavior. Rushed lifestyles, pressure to do well in school, too many "lessons," organized competitive sports, and scheduled activities add their share of stress.

For some time, researchers have been examining provocative links between brain functioning and the positive effects of physical activity. Regular exercise increases the blood supply to the brain, thus giving it a greater oxygen and energy supply—for better mental abilities. In addition, chemicals secreted by the brain during and after exercise enable it to deal better with stress and anxiety, counteract the effects of depression, and help children learn more efficiently by harnessing the positive power of emotions for learning and memory. Scientists also suggest that the type of exercise most likely to achieve these positive effects is "unforced," the type of spontaneous play in which children just naturally engage.[17]

"Exercise is about as close to a panacea as you can get, and I don't believe in panaceas," says Jerry May, Ph.D., sports psychologist and psychiatry professor. "It is a health inducer, a stress reducer and a self-confidence booster."[18] Working outdoors is also an important source of learning about nature, oneself, and responsibility.

Victor Davis Hanson of California State University complains that lack of such experiences is shortchanging our children in the human domain. "We send our children to computer camps so that they may learn how to gain access to information instantaneously, but most of us would never give our children a shovel and gloves and send them to dig weeds for a month so that they develp a sense of what it is to get dirty and tired for someone else," he comments.[19]

A relatively new field of neurophysiology elaborates on the need for body movement (and I don't mean pushing the mouse or the touch screen) to build different forms of intelligence. Teachers have long re-marked that children who have trouble keeping a rhythm seem to have learning difficulties with reading, writing, and other skills. Now brain research suggests that children who have difficulty organizing stimuli at a sensory level may have problems organizing other types of input, as in reading comprehension or making sense of a math problem. Musical intuition and the sense of musical form are also grounded in the brain's experience of the body during development.[20] Thus, if you want your child to be a good student or participate in the arts, as either creator or appreciator, you are better advised to dance spontaneously to tapes or send her outdoors to play than to spend a lot of money on so-called musical software.

For some time, studies have indicated that many physically handi-capped children who are unable to play spontaneously or investigate the world with hands and bodies have difficulty in developing seemingly unrelated mental abilities, such as understanding abstract verbal con-cepts. One root of such higher-level abilities is sequencing. As a child learns to put movements in order, brain areas are primed to put words and ideas into a logical sequence. For example, some seemingly simple task such as hammering—a natural activity for young children—teaches complex scheduling of the exact sequence of activation for dozens of neurons and muscles; throwing and catching are even more complicated because they require more timing and more control—brain training for skills of planning ahead, anticipating consequences, and other important abilities.

A child sorting groceries in the kitchen is developing skills of catego-rization and grasping abstract concepts (the difference between fruits and vegetables, household products and food, the many different ways to sort these items, etc.). This three-dimensionsal, physical experience is qualitatively different from that of a child who is playing a categorization game on a computer. While both may be helpful, too much substitution of icons for touch-and-feel physical learning leaves something essential out of the developmental equation.

A recent article in *Scientific American* summarized this line of research as follows: "Human intelligence first solves movement problems and only later graduates to pondering more abstract ones."[21] An artificial intelligence relieved of the need to move around and cope with the demands of the physical world will inevitably lack human planning and comprehension capabilities, say the authors.

Unexplored Possibilities

More subtle neurological effects of computer use have only been hinted at. For example, the electronic stimulus of video games causes a few children to experience epileptic seizures. Video-game-related seizures (called VGRS by neurologists) are rare, but a recent study indicated they can occur in youngsters without previous seizure difficulties. A 1997 bulletin from Japan aroused concern by reporting that a TV cartoon show modeled after Nintendo games had triggered convulsions among "hundreds of children."[22] The seizures began twenty minutes into the program, when there was a five-second episode of flashing red lights from a character's eyes, and Japanese physicians issued a warning that parents should be aware of possible hazards of flashing lights in TV and video games.

While the games do not cause the condition, which may also show itself in response to other types of flashing or highly patterned visual stimuli, computer games are bringing out enough new cases to also receive attention from pediatricians in the United States and elsewhere. Dr. William Graf, of Children's Hospital in Seattle, studied ten patients over three years and concluded that the disorder may be "more common than generally recognized."[23]

Most common in adolescent boys, who compose the majority of video game players, sufferers may stiffen, shake, or even lose consciousness for a few seconds. In some seizure disorders, the child does not exhibit dramatic symptoms but merely stares for a few seconds and then "comes back" with a start. Of course, most computer aficionados become very engrossed, but the difference is that a child experiencing one of these "absence" seizures is actually "out" for a brief period of time. Robert W. Kubey from Rutgers University points out that less obvious symptoms may also occur as a result of such overstimulation. "I have many parents report to me that, short of seizures, their children have become nauseated, tired or listless, or experience headaches during and after playing a video game," he reports. Kubey blames the "hyperkinetic" nature of these stimuli for upsetting the child's equilibrium.[24] If your child demonstrates worrisome symptoms, get a prompt medical consultation. Fatigue can worsen the condition. The best treatment for sufferers is going cold turkey off video games, says Dr. Graf.

In Chapter 6 we will see how some uses of computers can trigger hormonal changes that raise blood pressure or affect the immune system. The brain is very responsive to small alterations in the hormonal system; even seasonal and daily changes in light intensity cause cyclical patterns of hormone secretion that, in turn, alter brain functions and chemistry. These changes exist to help the individual cope with changing environments, but we do not understand the effects of artificially altered environments (such as too much time on a computer in a dimly lit room) over the long run. Certainly, habitual stress takes a long-term toll, including damage to neurons in the emotional centers of the brain.[25] Exactly how much and what kind of pressures can cause such damage has not been agreed upon, but children differ in their sensitivity to various stressors.

Until We Know More

Science has only begun to give us the answers on how to make new electronic environments safe for our children. My guess is that in the next few years we will see more, rather than fewer, concerns raised—perhaps about issues we haven't even anticipated. In the absence of concrete guidelines, the best advice is to watch the child and use a firm hand in determining how much and what kind of artificial stimuli you allow into your home or classroom.

Growing up Safely with Computers

I must admit that in researching this chapter I have altered my own rather haphazard computer habits. I have moved my chair back from the screen, turned the machine, and used a file folder to shield light reflected from a nearby window. I am also trying to remember to rest my eyes and body with frequent breaks.

We owe our children the concern to monitor screen time and observe current safety guidelines. Given our usual lukewarm attitudes about problems that are not hitting us squarely in the face, I don't hold out a lot of hope for substantive research in the near future. Yet, as someone with responsibility for decisions that may affect your child's long-term health, you will want to practice prudence. After all, we are usually careful about the children we let our kids play with; why would we be any less diligent when offering them an electronic playmate?

Chapter Five

The Growing Brain Meets
Artificial Intelligence

"Yes, computers can think. Because they pick up tons of information. I would think a computer is smarter [than a human]. Because it tells always the right answers."
Aubrey, age eight

"Some people worry that artificial intelligence will make us feel inferior, but then, anybody in his right mind ought to have an inferiority complex every time he looks at a flower."
Alan Kay, "visionary" and innovator in modern computer science

"Things that make us smart can also make us dumb."
Donald A. Norman

As computers edge their way further and further into children's lives, we may begin to see subtle differences in both human brain functioning and our notions of what constitutes intelligence. In this chapter we will consider a number of cognitive outcomes that may arise from working, playing, and learning with artificial intelligence.* We will work from a set of basic facts about brain development to examine

*In this chapter I use the term "artificial intelligence" or "AI" to cover a wide spectrum of computer functions as they interact with the human brain; in Chapter 9, I will view it in its more customary context as a "thinking" or "reasoning" substitute for human intelligence.

how new technologies interact with important aspects of human thinking and learning:

- Changing definitions of intelligence for an "information society"
- Cognitive effects of visual symbol systems and hypermedia
- Learning styles and new technologies
- Video games and changing intelligence
- How boys' and girls' brains respond to technology use
- Computer use and creativity.

Above all, we will be looking for insights into how to use computers to sharpen rather than dull kids' minds. To begin, consider the following observation from a school where innovative technology attempts to expand not only traditional forms of school, but also the sophistication of elementary students' thinking:

Systems Thinking Is Elementary

"It's not working!" wails Maja, straddling her chair in frustration as she watches several small objects gyrate about the screen. As one vaguely resembling a fish bumps into another globular-looking one—Poof! Object number two vanishes. "The zooplankton are eating all the phytoplankton and their food source is going to be gone—then they'll all die."

"Maybe you need to put in a rule for creating more phytoplankton." Attracted by the unfolding drama, a teacher has materialized behind Maja's chair. "Is there some way you could have them reproduce more frequently? Or could they move away when zooplankton come close?"

"Well . . . if I tried . . ." Maja returns to a pull-down window in the top left corner of the screen and studies a group of small icons arranged in patterns. "OK! I'll try this. Every time this one moves down one space, he turns into two thingies—he's reproducing. Now maybe the zooplankton will have more than they can eat!" Quickly she arranges icons in boxes to add this rule to her growing program. This program contains no letters, numerals, or words, but rather boxes and pictures which are laid out to form a series of nonverbal rules. For example, one set of boxes shows this particular type of zooplankton moving into a square next to the phytoplankton; the next set of boxes demonstrate that the phytoplankton has vanished, or been "eaten." Maya herself has created the objects using a computerized drawing program, modeling them after diagrams of the actual biological organisms the class is studying. Now she is simulating on the computer how their behavior translates into "real" life in a virtual underwater world.

"See," she explains, suddenly remembering that I, a bewildered novice, am gaping over her shoulder. "These little guys are all phytoplankton. They move like this: down one and then two over—that's their rule. Now, I'm adding a new rule: Every time they move down, they need to turn into two, sorta like having a baby. See, now all of the phytoplankton follow that rule. The zooplankton have different rules; they go diagonally, and when they bump into phytoplankton, they eat them." Having arranged the small icons to show her new rule (by now I have realized she is really creating if/then statements with pictures), Maja returns to the main screen to discover how the scenario plays itself out, and I reluctantly draw myself away to continue my tour. Meanwhile, Maja and her classmates, aged nine and ten, pursue their excited exploration of systems theory. They seem happily unaware that they are really doing "Artificial Intelligence Programming Using a Rule-Based Expert Systems Language."

David Smith, senior scientist of Apple computer's advanced technology group and developer of this program, is in the classroom with four software engineers troubleshooting, answering questions, and making extensive notes about the children's learning process. Smith's group is trying to develop educational connections between artificial and real-life intelligence.

"Nonverbal rules get beyond the language barrier," Smith explains. "Conceptually it's very abstract, but making it visual enables them to get it. At age eight or nine or ten, if you want them to think symbolically, they have to do it visually. It takes the kids a lot of work to program in the rules and then debug the program, but they don't mind." Although the active presence of six adults for twenty-some children makes me question the practicality of this system, I have to agree that the potential here is fascinating—not only for teaching children new ways to think, but also for observing how they go about it.

This scene took place at the Open Charter School in Los Angeles, California, a collection of drab, low-slung buildings surrounding an asphalt play yard. Its diverse population of enthusiastic students, some of whom ride buses for as long as an hour and a half each way to get there, finds it anything but drab. Open Charter was chosen as a well-funded demonstration project for innovative computer use because of its sound, learner-centered philosophy and curriculum. The school prides itself on using its elaborate technology only as a carefully planned adjunct to a lively, project-based learning environment.

"Technology certainly isn't a cure-all," insists principal Grace Sipper Arnold. "If anything, it's your belief system that's the cure-all." Nevertheless, I see here some of the most interesting applications I have found—seamlessly embedded in real-life activities.

Indeed, as I make my way through classrooms alive with a joyous clutter of learning, I find that, for all the wealth of computer equipment present, the majority of the learning is still low-tech. Eight-year-olds building a scale model of a city of the future investigate structural integrity by piling books on a classmate who lies balanced between two chairs; and students studying "transformations" have modeled an object on the computer and then constructed three-dimensional wearable objects to the scale of their own bodies (e.g., a box decorated as a book, a scotch tape dispenser). Walls are alive with "old-fashioned" student writing and drawing, and language is everywhere. I am not surprised to learn that test scores in this school are high. The entire atmosphere is about teaching young brains to be effective, creative, flexible learners and problem-solvers in many different media.

Computer innovator Alan Kay, who masterminded this project, believes new technology—when combined with active, personal learning experiences—can expand human intelligence far beyond the strictures of traditional education. Most educational computer use, however, misses the real point—getting children to take initiative and think deeply. Kay likens the computer to a piano; the music is not in the instrument itself, but in the feeling and understanding of the artist. If teachers do not nourish the romance of learning, demands for technological literacy become merely a burden, like being forced to perform Beethoven's sonatas with no sense of their beauty. "Instant access to the world's information will probably have an effect opposite to what is hoped: students will become numb instead of enlightened," Kay warns.[1]

Business managers as well as educators realize that an "information society" will place demands on human brains for a wider range of intellectual skills than schools have generally taught. The big question, of course, is how we should be teaching them. Maja and her classmates are learning to think in a screen-based environment where they learn both content and thinking skills by open-ended exploration. Stanley Pogrow, of the University of Arizona, also believes in emphasizing flexible thinking and effective problem-solving, but with much more direct guidance: "specific methodology, structure, dosages, and materials." Pogrow's innovations revolve around software—some specialized, but some standard commercial games—with a cognitive lesson attached, such as analyzing steps in a process, learning mathematical skills like measurement or graphing, or thinking up new strategies. In his programs, called "Learning Dramas" because of the student's level of personal involvement, the software provides only a platform for problem-solving; the skilled questioning of the teacher is what counts. Particularly with educationally disadvantaged students, *producing sophisticated learning is a function of the sophistication of conversation that surrounds the use of the technology—not the sophistication of the technology.* Pogrow claims impressive results in improving logical problem-solving and academic achievement for learning disabled as well as gifted students.[2]

Whatever their methods, it is clear that educators have zeroed in on the fact that the way children use computers may have powerful long-term effects on their minds. The main reason, of course, is that using any medium affects the underlying neural circuitry that is being established during childhood and adolescence. To understand this important issue more fully, let us now digress for a quick explanation of some brain "basics." How do children's brains actually develop, and how will new technologies impinge on this process?

Brain Basics

[In terms of the brain] "timing is everything."

Jason W. Brown, Department of Neurology, NYU Medical Center[3]

Although no studies have been done on direct links between computer use and children's brain activity, enough is known about how the brain develops during childhood and adolescence to draw some general conclusions and guidelines. I will now summarize six of the most relevant principles of brain growth and practical implications that follow from them.*

1. The brain grows as it responds actively to its environment, and it becomes "custom-tailored" to that environment.

Traditional belief had it that you came into the world with most of your intellectual attributes, such as IQ, motivation, special skills, abilities—and inabilities—pretty much predetermined. "I was born poor at math—just like my Mom." Now we know that while genes set parameters and place certain limits on development, your environment—and your response to it—determine how well this potential is realized. Individuals who actively use their mental apparatus throughout life develop strong and diverse connections among nerve cells (*neurons*) in the brain, increasing intelligence and skills. The person who has resigned herself to poor grades in math and science will never be a candidate for a Nobel Prize in physics, but if she had been encouraged to play different types of games and had experienced a different type of teaching, she might have done much better and even enjoyed these subjects.

Technology can subtly nudge the brain to expand certain types of mental skills or neglect others, depending on how it is used. It can produce either flexible problem-solvers or minds intent only on finding

---

*For those interested in a much broader exposition of the points covered here, I refer you to my books, *Your Child's Growing Mind*, which is a practical guide to brain development and learning from birth to adolescence, and *Endangered Minds*, which explains how current media and lifestyles literally change the brains—and thus the learning abilities—of today's youngsters.

one right answer. It can engender either a curious, reflective mind set, or one dulled by spacing out on inconsequential games. *The more actively the child uses her mind as she interacts with the technology, the more active the learning habits she will develop.* With today's software, unfortunately, this is not always the case.

These influences are most important during childhood and adolescence because the younger the child, the more "plastic" the brain. Human brains arrive in the world with excess potential to make connections (*synapses*) between different types of neurons. As a youngster carries out certain types of activities, those connections are strengthened, whereas habits that don't get much stimulation or practice may lack a strong neural base. Repetition of an experience tends to "set" connections to make that particular form of learning more automatic. Many children with school problems lack strong automatic connections for particular academic skills, such as reading or math computation, or for learning habits such as attention, strategic problem-solving, or self-control. The difficulty may be exacerbated because somewhere along the line their brain didn't get the proper experience to set up a strong basis for those particular abilities. *Age-appropriate computer use may help establish some forms of connections, but inappropriate use may also build resistant habits that interfere with academic learning.* Once set into the brain's connectivity, such patterns are hard to break.

Brains tend to become custom-tailored for skills that the environment promotes. For most of us who spent lots of childhood years practicing language and reading, for example, many brain connections have become specialized for these media. If we had grown up in a totally screen-based culture with icons instead of written text, the reading connections might have withered away in favor of stronger visual systems. In fact, we are already seeing a new emphais on "visual intelligence" supplementing verbal forms.

What kind of connections will our children need most? I advocate trying to give them the widest repertoire possible so they will be equipped to deal with multiple eventualities. A child with lopsided experiences is likely to end up with a lopsided brain.

When parents and teachers reflect on this information, they begin to think seriously about what mental aptitudes are really most important to promote. I have asked a lot of folks in workshop groups to come up with a list of their choices of "skills for the future." The things they tend to focus on are not technical skills; rather they nominate mental habits like analytic thinking and problem-solving, communication abilities, imagination, values, persistence, creativity, kindness, and tolerance.

2. "Critical" or "sensitive" periods open the brain to new windows of development at certain ages

At special times during childhood and adolescence, certain brain systems are at vulnerable points and require stimulation. For example, when language networks are maturing, most children acquire first words and then sentences with a minimum of prompting. Before long, the brain seems driven to make connections, as the child begins to place objects, words, and then ideas into mental categories ("Why, Mommy?"). Much later, the young teenager experiences a spurt in brain areas connected to painful, but necessary, growth in self-awareness, reflection, abstract thought, moral reasoning, and planning. He seems impelled to challenge things he has always accepted, argue with his parents, and take issue even with his own previous self. ("No, I'm wearing my hair *this* way now!" "Why *do* you believe that?") *Computer use should be planned to capitalize on these developmental stages.*

The downside in this panorama of possibility is that open windows can also close. For example, if interactive language experiences are slighted during the critical years, erosion of potential soon begins. Introducing too much external programming or too many electronic escape routes—in the form of any seductive medium, such as TV, video, and many forms of computer "education"—can interfere with the brain's own wisdom. No evidence exists that there is a critical period for learning to use a computer; in fact, many who mastered it quite readily in midlife attest to the contrary. If computer time subtracts from talking, socializing, playing, imagining, or learning to focus the mind internally, the lost ground may be hard or impossible to regain.

Consonant with the views of such theorists as Jean Piaget, Rudolf Steiner, and Maria Montessori, scientists now use a "spiral staircase" metaphor for different periods of development. *Children need time and plenty of practice to "play around" (often literally) with different types of learning;* while we can enrich, expand, and possibly pull a child up a step or two, there is little to be gained (except, possibly, an unpleasant fall) by trying to propel someone to the top steps before the lower ones have strong foundations. However, the spiral nature of the process makes it possible to learn a weak skill (such as spelling) when new brain systems mature, enabling different strategies and approaches (e.g., mastering spelling rules rather than trying to remember what the words look like). *Trying to use computers simply to accelerate mental development may backfire, because nature's program is carefully constructed to expand a much broader spectrum of abilities.*

In general, the stages of development move from *concrete* learning (touching, feeling, tasting, manipulating, physically exploring, building) through *symbolic* representations (letters, pictures, words, stories, math problems, mental images) to more *abstract* modes of thought (hypothesis-testing, understanding and applying formal rules of grammar or calculus, metaphor). Computer use, being primarily a two-dimensional symbolic activity, may simply not be developmentally appropriate before the age of seven or eight—a question to be explored in a later chapter. On the other hand, later developmental stages, when the brain is moving into more abstract representation, may be substantially enhanced by carefully chosen computer experiences.

3. *The brain uses multiple systems which interconnect with practice*

One important aspect of development is to integrate the workings of different brain systems—for example, to look at a sheet of music, transform notes on the page to keys on the piano, and add a motor program for the fingers to play the notes—all the while listening to the melody. The drive for this brain integration comes from within but is accomplished by time-consuming practice, as the learner (at any age) actively organizes some sort of raw materials into a new form—clay into figures, boxes into birdhouses, movements into dance, ideas into sentences, commands into a computer program, impressions into philosophies.

Will newer technologies enhance or diminish this process? I have puzzled over this question, and I am still unconvinced that much of what I have seen is an adequate substitute for real experience. Specialized software can improve brain connectivity in children with some forms of sensory disabilities, but whether technology can likewise improve integration for the normally developing brain is unknown. *Having a computer do too much integrating (e.g., combining picture, sound, movement), so the child simply experiences rather than coordinates it all himself, eliminates an active process that may prove to be irreplaceable.*

Moreover, subtle processes exist which we barely understand. One case in point concerns the interconnected systems of *right and left hemispheres,* which must develop multiple connections to function efficiently together for maximum intelligence. Some types of fast-moving and primarily visual software (as in computer games) arouse the right hemisphere at the expense of the left,[4] and we have long suspected that too much use may shortchange left-hemisphere skills such as language proficiency. New research suggests that it could affect emotional development as well. Scientists are now aware that activation of the right hemisphere accompanies negative mood (feelings of sadness, lethargy, depression); and in situations where one feels happy or pleasantly excited, activation is strong on the left side of the brain. Studies also show that prolonged television viewing often results in negative affect and sometimes even mild depression; in the words of one psychologist, "The more one watches TV in one sitting the worse one's moods progressively get."[5] Scientists have also proposed that people whose right hemisphere is chronically activated may be predisposed to depressive or anxiety disorders and have an increased vulnerability to other types of illness because excessive activation of the right hemisphere tends to depress the immune system.[6]

No one knows if too many computer games will make children more subject to depression or affect their immune systems, because no research has considered such questions. Yet it is just one of many that should make us approach any new medium judiciously.

The gradual integration of other systems (e.g., back to front) also holds secrets, barely unlocked, that may account for attention and behavior problems. We will investigate these in the next chapter. *Mean-*

while, we must remember that when children use computers, it is a form of brain-training that we don't yet understand.

4. Emotional brain centers exert powerful controls over learning

Not so very long ago, emotion, motivation, and social development were somehow regarded as being "outside" the brain, but now we know that thinking and feeling are irrevocably linked. Structures far down in the brainstem act together with emotional circuitry to "prime" the thinking cortex for learning. *Unless we get the emotional brain involved, higher-level thinking and problem-solving will be short-circuited.* In the next chapter we will delve further into the potential interaction of cyberculture and emotional stimulation.

5. Language helps develop higher cognitive functions

Language plays a major role in brain development. Unfortunately, solitary computer use limits a child's verbalization. Children need plenty of interactive "talk" for maximum mental development. More on this subject later.

6. The brain makes sense of its world by seeking patterns

Children learn and remember best when adults help them make meaningful connections. Even by age three, children have extracted many patterns from their environmental experience. ("The picture and the teddy bear are both Pooh.") Later, patterns become more complex. ("Oh, that's a lot like the problems I solved yesterday—now I get it!") *Much of today's technology fragments children's experience instead of integrating it and distracts their mind from the job of sense-making.* In later chapters we will find out how to harness its potential for more brain-appropriate uses.

In short, while it is certainly possible for AI and HI (human intelligence) to interact constructively, caution is advised. In planning for computer use, we must remember that building human intelligence is a long, slow process that requires both active involvement by the child and strong guidance by adults prepared to provide appropriate kinds of mental stimulation at each step up the staircase.

Now we must confront the question of what we mean by "intelligence" when we are talking about a world flooded with information and the continual challenges presented by new media.

Intelligence in an Information Society

If our children are to stay afloat in the information sea, they must become accomplished users of high-level cognitive strategies. They must learn to take in massive amounts of data and information and convert them into something meaningful and useful. Getting kids to use information effectively cannot be accomplished simply by sitting them down with computers. Roy D. Pea of the Bank Street College of Education argued in 1985 that the skills most needed for such "new intelligence" would actually be ones good schools have always stressed:

- Cognitive skills of information management
- Strategies for problem-solving that cut across domains of knowledge
- Metacognitive skills: planning, monitoring, and learning how to learn
- Communication skills
- Critical inquiry skills[7]

Robert J. Sternberg, author of *Successful Intelligence*, believes practical and creative abilities must also be included when we define either "intelligence" or "achievement."[8] Especially important are "creative flexibility," the practical application of information, the ability to see things in new ways, and the skill to "sell" one's ideas to others.

We can help students increase their intelligence by teaching them how to go beyond simply accessing information. An effective thinker can work at multiple levels.

Getting Beyond Information

A Scaffold for Effective Thinking

data: isolated bits
   • What is the population of China?

information: collections of bits
   • Chart the population figures for six countries in Asia in the twentieth century.

knowledge: an organized body of information
   • Give the names, dates, and describe the characteristics of the periods of Chinese history.

understanding: ability to generalize and apply knowledge in new contexts
   • Analyze the causes of the Boxer Rebellion and compare with the American Revolution.

wisdom: soundness of judgment, self-regulation, ethics, reflection on consequences
   • Develop, articulate, and implement an effective foreign policy toward China in the twenty-first century.

Assembling information is a foundation but not a goal. The main reason to gain *knowledge* of the multiplication tables is to learn how and when to use them to solve a real problem (*understanding*). *Understanding* and *wisdom* are the qualities (along with imagination) that set human intelligence apart from AI and deserve top priority. Yet much of our schooling seems data- and information-driven.

Developing Knowledge

We hope our children will be able to slog through the swamp of data and information to locate knowledge, understanding, and perhaps even wisdom. To do so, they must develop flexible uses of knowledge.

procedural knowledge: how to do something
   • turn on the computer and insert a CD-ROM
   • follow memorized rules to solve a math problem

- behave appropriately in a restaurant

conceptual knowledge: combining meaningful ideas
- interpret a text and write a report or essay
- explain why to use certain operations in solving a math story problem
- appreciate and interpret a work of art

strategic knowledge: developing techniques for problem-solving
- troubleshoot a computer glitch for a friend
- figure out a more efficient way to study for a test
- know how to get on a teacher's "good side"

Good thinkers use all these interchangeably, and today's youngsters need particular help with the latter two. In fact, strategic knowledge is what differentiates high-achieving students and successful adults in the technical, professional, and creative worlds. Youngsters who have had too much of their thinking and practical problem-solving done for them, either by humans or by machines, tend to have weaknesses in strategic knowledge. On the other hand, technology might also help teach children to develop strategies for difficult tasks.

Today's computer use tends to emphasize procedural rather than strategic routines (e.g., discovering a "trick" instead of developing an original plan). Yet effective problem-solving requires far more than simply romping through information, skipping out when puzzled, or letting the programmer do the thinking. Many standard board and card games, as well as hobbies and personal projects, are much better ways to exercise strategic skills.

Surface or Depth?

A related flaw in today's computer teaching concerns another important distinction: superficial vs. deeper knowledge.

superficial or surface knowledge: neglects the brain's need to create meaningful patterns
- rote level memorization
- software that imparts facts without requiring thought
- games that encourage solutions by trial and error

deeper knowledge: builds strong conections within and between systems
  • comprehension, analysis, reflection, evaluation

Knowledge of one's own thinking process, called *metacognition,* is particularly important for deeper knowledge. For example, poor readers may "read" a page or a screen and think they understand it when they have only read the words, whereas good readers constantly monitor their own comprehension (e.g., "I don't get that," "Why did she say that?" "Oh, that's the same point as . . ."). Likewise, an inferior work of art, music, dance, or drama simply copies something that has been done before without adding new insights.

We must make sure that computer use includes the important step of requiring children to "elaborate" their knowledge—thinking aloud, questioning, communicating ideas, or creating some kind of original representation about what they are learning. These demands cause the brain to process more deeply and will contribute powerfully to our definitions of "intelligence" in the future. One of the best ways to deepen processing is to formulate a message about what is being learned, most frequently by either writing or carrying on a thoughtful conversation. Nonverbal formulation also works. Drawing, dramatizing, or developing a creative musical interpretation of a concept may also enhance processing demands—that is, if the arts budget hasn't been cut to pay for technology!

Now we will begin to consider how human intelligence responds to the symbols found in media that extend far beyond books, paper, and pencils. Will multimedia environments benefit or detract from brain work? Will they subtly push the evolution of the human brain into new directions? While we don't yet have the answers, you can be sure that these radically new forms for representing information are bound to reorganize the lineup on some of academia's playing fields.

Different Media = Different Symbols, Different Intelligences

"Media's symbolic forms of representation are clearly not neutral or indifferent packages . . . they influence the meanings one arrives

at, the mental capacities that are called for, and the ways one comes to view the world. Perhaps most important, the culture that creates the media and develops their symbolic forms of representation also opens the door for those forms to act on the minds of the young in more and less desirable ways." [9]

Gavriel Salomon

"Two-dimensional pages will become the graffiti of three-dimensional space."

Tim Berners-Lee in *Wired* [10]

Any new medium brings with it new symbol systems which, in turn, influence the way the brain learns to take in and process information. Newer technologies emphasize rapid processing of visual symbols (e.g., icons, film clips) and deemphasize traditional verbal learning (e.g., expository writing, text reading) and the linear, analytic thought process that accompanies it. Sequential argument, reflection, and "making pictures in your mind" are diminished in favor of immediate experience. It is easier to convey emotional tone with visual images than with text but more difficult to deal with abstract verbal reasoning, such as analyzing the differences between a democracy and a republic. It is also difficult to convey abstract mathematical concepts, such "evenness" or "primeness" in visual formats.

Nonetheless, looking is easier and more seductive than listening. Visual areas in the human cortex take up far more space and have more potential connectivity than auditory and language areas. For example, if a child is watching TV, he is much more likely to pay attention to and remember the visual effects than the dialogue. A major bone of contention today is how much to allow visual learning to override the verbal, and teachers are often baffled about how to evaluate intellectual integrity in new media forms.

Undisciplined Minds?

"The notion of 'great books' is being supplemented with 'great flicks' as the boob tube and silver screen are now considered coequal

with literature as an intellectually taxing and rewarding learning medium."

J. Martin Rochester, author and political science professor [11]

One of the few researchers who have seriously examined how different symbol systems develop different forms of intelligence is Gavriel Salomon at the Hebrew University of Jerusalem. Salomon showed that children listening to a story or seeing it on video learn and remember different sorts of information and develop different thinking skills. In one interesting study, he exposed Israeli children to a jazzed-up "educational" television program that is a staple for American preschoolers. The result? "Observable decreases in their perseverence."[12]

Salomon has mixed feelings about newer technologies, as they change the meaning of knowledge from something we possess to something we have to access. He worries that these new technologies may cultivate a preference for free association and a quick-paced, undisciplined, chaotic way of handling information (e.g., "web surfing"): "Students may start exploring the life cycles of elephants in Central Africa but very quickly find themselves following a lead that takes them to the biography of Napoleon or to the political situation in Turkey."[13]

Successful use of any symbol system depends on whether the brain is sufficiently mature to cope with it (e.g., few three-year-old brains are neurologically equipped to read with understanding, but children this age can listen to a story and enjoy the pictures in a storybook). Moreover, young or naive learners, without experience in processing different forms of media, are strongly influenced by early exposure to specific symbolic forms. A youngster who spends a lot of early learning time on a computer is being programmed to prefer that type of presentation to reading a book, engaging in a discussion, or hearing a lecture about the same topic.

Salomon points out that visual media are less abstract than written text because things are depicted rather than described. They also require less mental effort ("elaboration") than does reading text, and therefore lend themselves to shallow processing. Any medium can build cognitive abilities if the child is investing serious effort in "knowledge extraction"—expending mental effort to learn something. Such effortful cognitive work can be triggered by adult expectations. When Salomon told schoolchildren they should learn something from a TV presentation, they dramatically increased their expenditure of mental effort. Thus, it is important that parents and teachers choose activities that require children to make some effort to extract and understand information. They should also remind children of the importance of what is to be learned. "*The difference between what* can be *affected and what is* typically *affected is particularly great for media that allow shallow processing,*" warns Salomon.[14]

■ ■ ■

In one computer lab (with one teacher trying to supervise eighteen children and troubleshoot almost continual technical glitches), I observed a seven-year-old girl who provided an unfortunate example of how easily unguided computer use can lead to "shallow processing." She spent the entire period locating, downloading, and staring at a map of Africa. She had obviously done this routine before, and as she gazed intently at the screen, I assumed she must be examining the geographical features of the continent. Finally I inquired, "What do you find so interesting there?"

"Oh, I just like to look at maps," she replied.

"What is the name of that map you're looking at?"

"I don't know. I just like to look at maps."

"What's this line here?" I indicated a large river. "Or this?" for the ocean.

"I don't know," she shrugged. "I just like to look at maps."

Surely there are much deeper and brain-building ways for her to enter the world of visual symbols.

Avoid "Boredom" at All Costs

Skeptical teachers point out that they already see negative effects from television and video games. In fact, students who have spent a great deal of time with video games tend to find even educational computers uninteresting.

"The worst sin today is to be 'boring,' " commented one math teacher recently. "I am so tired of these kids expecting to be entertained—they don't have the patience of a flea!" A social studies teacher agreed, after trying futilely to get her students to consider thoughtfully the issues in a political campaign.

"This generation wants things in an instant," she observed. "They hate to wait. If they can't see results right away, they have no interest in what's being discussed. They don't understand that a democracy isn't efficient."

Employers are beginning to complain that many new workers can't solve problems that require initiative, persistence, and independent thinking. "It's really different from even ten years ago," one director of a company told me. "If the solution isn't obvious, they haven't a clue. What do you suppose this means for the future?"

Gertrude Himmelfarb, professor emeritus of history at City University of New York, suggests that our acceptance of bombardment by disconnected texts, sounds, and images is a by-product of postmodernism, which eschews logical argument in favor of "indeterminacy" and "fluidity." In this view, a comic strip or advertising slogan has just as much validity as the Bible or Shakespeare, since no symbol system or authority is "privileged" over another.[15]

A cognitive scientist who consults for a large computer company also worries that the new media may erode our ability to think systematically or critically. In his book *Things That Make Us Smart,* Donald A. Norman states, "I am concerned that the new tools have moved us in unexpected ways to accept experience as a substitute for thought. . . . Alas, our educational system is more and more trapped in an experiential mode . . . we strive to keep our students engaged in our schools by entertaining them."[16]

Clifford Stoll, vocal apostate from Silicon Valley, also remarks on this issue: "Lacking critical thinking, kids are on-screen innocents who confuse form with content, sense with sensibility, ponderous words with weighty thoughts." In addition, much of the educational software, claims Stoll, "turns science and math into a spectator sport."[17]

SURFING FOR SWIMMING POOLS

As I join the melee of young adolescents bumping into the classroom, I am on my way to a virtual mini-vacation. An experienced teacher who is proud of her computer expertise has invited me on a "virtual field trip." The kids quickly arrange themselves at machines, with little of the reluctance that so often accompanies the start of class with young teens. Working in pairs, the boys set immediately to work—mainly on smash-and-blast games or checking current stock market quotations, while pairs of girls chat together. One boy, a leftover from the previous class, is trying to complete an electronic "scavenger hunt" designed to teach students to use search engines (on-line tools for finding data about a specific topic). He reads the question on the screen: "In what year was St. Augustine, Florida, founded?" Four choices are given (multiple choice being the only way the machine can understand his answers). He does a quick version of "eeny meeny miney mo" and clicks on one alternative.

"Is that what you're supposed to do?" I inquire innocently.

"Who cares?" he shrugs and offers a conspiratorial smile. "It gets it over with."

This is an expensive private school, and the elaborate machines in this classroom represent only the tip of a $300,000 infrastructure that, according to the principal, "is like a big, black hole that you just keep throwing money into." I have been told some interesting Internet projects are being carried out here, and I am eager to see them firsthand.

Class begins. The instructor explains to the students that they will be journeying to Central or South America, which I later learn is a random choice on her part. She explains how to access a commercial travel program to obtain information. I am surprised when, confronted by the machines, many of these students (all of whom have computers at home) respond with the same sort of stimulus-bound behavior expected of preschoolers. They can't wait to start pushing buttons, so they are launched before she stops talking. It doesn't matter much because no outcomes are specified, and they are simply free to roam.

A pair of boys enters a web site for travel to Costa Rica. They click on the name of a well-known hotel chain, and up comes not only a glorious swimming pool but a pulsating full-color king-sized bed.

"Hey, cool! Look at this!"

Within a few minutes, most of the class is enthusiastically comparing swimming pools and beds in various locations. Their comments are about as colorful as the screens. Two students, bored by the activity, surreptitiously boot up an action game. Several girls return to chatting quietly. Mercifully, the period ends.

I wonder if this random "surfing" will satisfy the adolescent desire for quick excitement—or will it inspire more impulsive and alarming thrill-seeking? The parents at this school are particularly proud of the fact that it is the most technologically "wired" in the community—a guarantee they are spending their money on "the latest" in education. I would advise them—and any parent who takes this notion on faith—to observe critically just what their kids are learning. They might discover that the latest is not necessarily the greatest.

Understanding "Hyper" Learning

One way in which newer symbol systems may eventually enhance rather than replace traditional learning is by effective use of "hypertext" and "hypermedia." These methods of presenting information are revolutionary because they don't follow the sequential order of traditional text. If you have used the World Wide Web, you are aware that it consists of branching "nodes" of information consisting of both words and pictures, which you can peruse in any order and at your own pace. Scientists believe that our minds store information in a similar way, using "semantic memory structures" which resemble organized spiderwebs of words and meanings.

Hypertext consists of written material, while hypermedia is a more general term for a mixture of sound, graphics, text, and, eventually, virtual physical sensation. Hypermedia, in particular, taps more right-hemisphere and visual function than does written text. Since the brain's wiring tends to make looking easier than listening, a major issue with hypermedia is whether the pictures distract students too much from reading the words. Another question is whether the random nature of these bits of information will accurately convey what needs to be learned. Will students be better informed—or will they be distracted?

Hypertext and hypermedia are used in basically two ways in schools: either to teach certain types of subject matter or to have students create something, such as an alternative to the customary report. Thus far, research on effectiveness is unconvincing, although when students develop multimedia projects and presentations—*within carefully structured academic parameters*—we see some of the more engaging uses of the technology.

STUDENTS AS CONSTRUCTORS: CREATING PATTERNS IN INFORMATION

Twelve-year-old Kim has always been fascinated by ancient Egypt, but when he moved into this district last year and found a fully equipped media lab, he discovered a new way to explore his fascination. On the day I visited his suburban school, Kim was putting final touches on his presentation about King Tut, and he proudly arranged the setup to run on a large liquid crystal display screen mounted on the wall. As introductory music faded, a map of Egypt appeared and Kim's recorded voice could be heard reading an introduction to his topic. The next screen displayed "buttons" (e.g., "history," "geography," "tomb artifacts"), the selection of which would determine our path through the material. I first chose history, and we were treated to a slide show augmented with video clips, oral commentary, text screens, and appropriate sound effects. The entire production revealed an impressive depth of understanding of the technology and the subject matter. Kim is also a good example of a student using the different types of knowledge mentioned earlier: procedural knowledge of how to use the equipment and how to organize a report; conceptual knowledge of the topic, deepened by the need to summarize information from a variety of sources; strategic knowledge to decide how best to get his point across or to deal with technical challenges that demand new solutions.

When I asked this bright-eyed young man how he organized the presentation, he displayed his computer program layout, which looked something like an outline of rectangular boxes—the "cards" that described each individual effect to be rearranged in any format. (As I struggle to describe in words what I experienced, I realize how difficult it is to translate this event into verbal form. My difficulty illustrates the differences I am attempting to demonstrate!)

To achieve all this, Kim had used an array of gadgets such as camera, scanner, video connection, and tape recorder, not always available in a school setting. I was, frankly, somewhat dazzled by his expertise. Had he been working with computers since infancy? On the contrary.

"Two years ago, when I was in fifth grade, I didn't even know anything about computers, and I never even used one until last year," he confided from the newly sophisticated perspective of age twelve. "It's not really that hard. You just fuss around until you get it."

Such intuitive "fussing around"—sometimes termed "bricolage," from the French root that gave us bric-a-brac, a miscellany—is one of the new hallmarks of the multimedia generation. Kids learn to use computers by trial-and-error, not by following a direction manual of sequential steps. (This accounts for many of the tech services required; kids aren't afraid to push buttons—even the wrong ones.) This approach comes naturally to individuals with a "kinesthetic" learning style, which masters material more effectively through manipulation than through verbal or mathematical abstractions.

Experimentation comes more easily to those who are willing to make a mistake or two. One of the reasons given for exposing youngsters to computers is to make them comfortable with the technology before they develop a fear of "fussing around." My own guess is that, while younger children are certainly able to work with hypermedia, the late elementary years are an ideal time to capitalize on the brash curiosity of childhood, while still tapping the nascent judgment of preadolescence.

In another class of twelve-year-olds, who lacked the fancy gadgetry of Kim's school, students were divided into teams of two to prepare reports on countries in Africa. Like Kim, they used a preplanned "hyperstack" of "cards" to develop their nodes incorporating assigned categories of information (e.g., demographics, geography, government, social customs) gathered both from text and on-line sources. When the viewer/reader ("experiencer?") clicked on a link, a certain category of information unrolled. Following clear steps laid out by their teacher, the students had read the sources, written up information for each card, created a bibliography, determined the setup, added visuals and sound effects, and arranged the branching of the program. Was it better—or worse—than a similar class who developed reports in booklet form with straightforward expository text, handmade drawings, and a typed bibliography? At this point, such a question requires a judgment call which I am both unable and unwilling to make. Doubtless traditional scholars would suggest the straight textual form is more intellectually taxing, more central to the exposition of the issues involved, and more demanding of abstract cognitive resources. Yet as I left the computer room and heard two students engaged in an intellectual debate about what icon to use to represent government (a balance scale for justice? a law book? a picture of the president of the country? a soldier?) I realized that if hypermedia—and a good teacher—can push kids toward spontaneously debating abstract ideas, these new symbol systems may soon be solidly afloat in the intellectual mainstream.

"Postliteracy," Brain Rot, and the Erosion of Self

Two recent books illustrate the views of scholars who deplore this switch from traditional forms. In *The Gutenberg Elegies: The Fate of Reading in an Electronic Age*, Sven Birkerts warns that increasing multimedia experiences at the expense of written text risks "language erosion," decline of analytic and logical thought, "flattening of historical perspectives," and "the waning of the private self."[18] Texts viewed as "difficult," predicts Birkerts, will increasingly be glossed over (which is, in fact, happening as students are both unwilling and unable to grasp the more subtle meanings or attend long enough to read them). As we forget or ignore the complexities of history's lessons, a bland "electronic collectivization" will render us ripe for political totalitarianism. Is it possible for language still to flourish "among the beep and the click and the monitor . . .? I hope so, for language is the soul's ozone layer and we thin it at our peril," comments Birkerts.[19]

In *A Is for Ox*, Barry Sanders, professor of English and the History of Ideas at Pitzer College, argues that "the idea of a critical, self-directed human being we take for granted . . . develops only in the crucible of reading and writing."[20] He describes a world of "young folk who have bypassed reading and writing and who thus have been forced to fabricate a life without the benefit of that innermost, intimate guide, the self. . . . It is a world in which young people seek revenge and retaliation rather than self-reflection."[21] These "postliterates" drift through life as through a mall, unable to connect even to their own selfhood.

In my travels I have frequently delighted in observing hypermedia use, but I always find myself wondering afterward if I am so taken by the kids' enthusiasm that I lose my objectivity about what they may or may not be learning. Entranced by the pictures, cut-and-paste text, amusing noises, and animation, students (and even adult authors!) are tempted to flit over the harder work of reading, writing, and reasoning. Moreover, with much hypermedia experience occurring as group work, those who choose not to read or write can often avoid these skills entirely by relying on the good readers and writers to do this part of the job.

HYPERMEDIA AS TEACHER

Nonetheless, more and more teachers are going hyper. One argument is that hyperlearning can tap whatever representational tool is best fitted for the ideas being expressed and deepen student involvement. Enthusiast David Thornburg emphasizes that while pictures and words are not interchangeable, the quality of student engagement is the main issue in either symbol system. He joins other critics, however, in observing that what is currently sold as "interactive" is often limited, as in merely allowing the user to punch icons to choose the pace at which a story unfolds ("high-tech page turning" as opposed to "crafting a personal pathway through the material"). "True interactivity provides, at the minimum, the capacity to branch to different scenarios, to gather additional information, to take new twists and turns and, when very well done, to explore avenues never anticipated by the creator of the program," states Thornburg.[22]

Screens vs. Books: The Research

> *"It is not even the case that new technologies have just produced new problems; they have, but they have often failed to solve the old ones too."*
> Andrew Dillon [23]

To conclude this section on hyperlearning, here is what the research tells us about the effectiveness of these new forms.

HYPERTEXT

In most studies, hypertext has come in as a poor second to traditional text.[24] Reading from a screen is slower, more fatiguing, less accurate, and more subject to information overload than standard reading. In several studies, students tested for comprehension after reading from a screen demonstrated less understanding and poorer memory than those getting the same information from a book. They tended to get lost or flip too quickly through the screens without reading.

Youngsters who grow up reading and writing on screens may or may not become more comfortable with them than with traditional print sources. Curiously, one of the main things lacking in screen-based text is smell, a sense powerfully linked to the emotional brain and thus to learning, comprehension, and memory. My guess is we will soon have simulated olfactory features added to hypertext (eau de library?) to make us want to curl up more cozily with our coolly reflective screens.

HYPERMEDIA

Research thus far has mainly looked at students trying to learn from—as opposed to creating—hypermedia presentations. Adding digitized pictures, sound, and animation to learning has not yet proven any more effective than studying illustrated books. Novice users of hypermedia tend to become easily distracted and confused by the lack of organizational structure. Some researchers feel students should be given a structured overview before they are turned loose to explore at random. Others claim that providing less structure, at least for older students in certain types of material, forces them to develop a mental organization for the topic, thus processing the information more deeply.

With or without computers, "showing" and "telling" complement each other, at least in a narrow range of scientific topics. Richard E. Mayer of the University of California at Santa Barbara tried out various types of presentations with college students who were learning about a scientific subject that lent itself to illustration. Presenting both pictures and text was most helpful, especially for students who started the lesson knowing little about the topic and who had relatively high spatial ability. Two very interesting findings: (1) It did not matter whether the presentation was on a computer or in textbooks. (2) Visual material alone, either illustrations or animations, was comparatively ineffective.

As we will hear again and again, Mayer found the essential variable not to be the medium of delivery (e.g., computers or textbooks) but *whether the presentation engages the students in active "knowledge construction."* He also criticizes most current applications. "Technological advances in computer-based graphics . . . have not been matched by corresponding scientific advances in understanding how people learn from pictures and words," he explains.[25]

There is no question that hypermedia is highly motivating to most of today's kids. Nonetheless, I find myself doubting whether students, after having studied endless CD-ROM encyclopedias or produced their fifteenth hypermedia term paper, will retain the initial level of excitement. An even more important reason for exploring hypermedia is its ability to broaden traditional academic discourse, reach into different learning modalities, and thus offer success to a wider swath of students, particularly those with divergent learning styles or learning disabilities.

Different Learning Styles in the Digital World

"Learning was easier because we were able to invest ourselves in it, to do our own set of things. Not everyone had to do the same thing, and everybody became good at something."

Middle school student, Evanston, Illinois

Although the environment does shape the growing brain, genes have already established the parameters within which this force works. Thus, family members often share similar preferences for learning (e.g., being an early reader or having talent in visual arts). Such differences are now termed "learning styles" or "multiple intelligences."[26]

Verbal-analytic intelligence has been the traditional passport to academic success, yet not all talented people have the same learning style. Today's "difficult" students (many of whom are labeled "learning disabled" or "attention deficit disordered") may actually be showing us the way into hypermedia's new world of parallel processing. Three-dimensional visual-spatial understanding will assume new importance, and the ability to "see" meaning may become as valued as the ability to "hear" or "read" it. In fact, when I'm told about "hyperactive" kids, I remind myself that some of the most successful minds in the emerging technology industries are, likewise, "multi-taskers" who can think and work in multiple modes at any given time. For example, one of Hollywood's most successful screenwriter-directors includes a small screen in the upper right-hand corner of his computer which plays reruns of "Star Wars" to keep his peripatetic mind engaged. "I just can't deal with him any more," confided one software designer. "The guy is so wired!" The fact that the intellectual journal of the cyberculture is also named *Wired* should probably tell us something about the future of thought.

In a multimedia world, even definitions of literacy may fall into question. One thoughtful tech director asked me, "If a dyslexic student dictates a text which the computer then writes, prints, and reads back to him, can we say that the student is literate?" Clearly, new possibilities— and new questions—are on the horizon.

"Seeing" New Potential

A burgeoning field called "image processing" (IP) involves collecting, manipulating, and analyzing visual data. It allows students to edit, filter, enhance, alter, and even animate pictures—from CAT scans to space probes—to reveal relationships and information not visible to the human eye.

Image processing often enables so-called learning disabled youngsters to release their creativity by working, as many talented scientific and mathematical thinkers do, through visual and kinesthetic rather than verbal intelligence. When these highly original minds can learn by graphing algebraic equations, geometric proofs, or the molecular structure of matter through dynamic three-dimensional models, who knows what new discoveries and theories may emerge?

"Here [in the computer lab] I'm a creative genius. In other classes I'm a goof-off. I don't think I'd be interested in school at all if I didn't have this class," stated high-school student Zack Alvey when he was interviewed by a reporter for the *Wall Street Journal*.[27]

Mary Mitchell, a tenth-grade biology teacher in Orlando, Florida, describes a lesson on measuring microscopic bugs in which she used IP to teach the use of small metric units—an abstract concept difficult for many students. One student, Brian, who had been uninterested in school, displayed an intuitive grasp of image processing and was suddenly energized.

"I never understood millimeters or micrometers until today," he told her at the end of class.

"Since that day," claims Mitchell, "Brian comes to class and does his work." He has not only gained respect from his peers, but he also has become an IP assistant to other students.[28]

Maria, another student previously "at risk," was introduced to IP in ninth grade as she was seriously considering dropping out of school. She "fell in love" with the computers and was soon coming in early in the morning to work on IP activities so she could be an "expert" helper in science class.[29]

Any student who has learned to work through visual or kinesthetic channels may have a better chance to shine in newly developing fields than students overly limited to linguistic and linear forms of reasoning. Both sets of skills are important—and will doubtless continue to be. Fortunately, computers can also help develop verbal abilities in youngsters whose brains don't take to them so readily.

Rewiring "Different" Brains

Six-year-old Susan concentrates intently on the sounds coming through her large earphones. On the computer screen in front of her, an animated clown presents a game in which Susan must distinguish between simple sounds (in this case, "pah" and "bah"). For all her hard work, Susan is enjoying her success; as she graduates to the next level of difficulty (figuring out whether the syllable "bah" comes first or second in a word), a large smile brightens her face. Her parents are especially delighted, because Susan hasn't been smiling a lot since she started first grade. She is one of the 5 to 8 percent of children who suffer from a brain-based disability in processing what she hears which makes it difficult for her to sort out the sounds of ordinary talk. According to neurolinguist Paula Tallal, who developed Susan's computerized remediation program, such children are often of normal or above-average intelligence, but their brains have difficulties with "temporal processing"; that is, the normal tempo of human speech is too fast for them to discriminate and sequence the sounds in words—the foundations for language comprehension and reading.

The gamelike programs Susan will use for fifteen to twenty-five hours a week for four weeks are designed to retrain her brain by slowing the rate at which phonemes (the individual sounds in words) are heard, emphasizing rapidly changing speech components such as short vowel sounds, and giving Susan exercises in careful listening. Program developers claim the computer's ability to control the quality of the sound and the rate of presentation, gradually increasing levels of difficulty, is superior to that of human tutors. Initial trials showed an impressive degree of success for twenty-two language-impaired children between the ages of five and ten,[30] and corresponding gains may follow in reading. Dr. Tallal and her colleagues believe their invention has succeeded in reshaping the brain's language areas, making the computer a powerful ally in treating learning and even behavioral difficulties.

Unfortunately, I do not have room in this book to do justice to the wonders being accomplished by "assistive" or remedial technology as it harnesses the power of computers to help children with various sorts of learning differences or handicaps. For example, children with cerebral palsy can now move a cursor on a computer screen by moving their eyes; the computer measures movements with small electrodes placed near the eyes.[31] Legions of poor spellers and nonfluent writers have already benefitted from spell-checkers. Language training similar to Susan's is helping adult foreign-language speakers master the accent.[32] Computer "readers" with synchronized visual and auditory text are useful aids for poor readers motivated to teach themselves.[33] Autistic individuals report that communicating electronically is much more comfortable for them, since they do not have to process the confusing stimuli of face-to-face communication.

These are only a few of the remedial and assistive computer technologies now in development, but this set of applications is very promising. And with scientists suggesting that eventually computers may be able to read our thoughts, stay tuned!

Video Games and Changing Intelligence

Parents often ask what video games will do to their children's intelligence. Could they be building useful skills that we don't yet understand? It depends, of course, on how they are used. Games may have some redeeming qualities, depending on their content and whether they are allowed to steal time from developing traditional academic, social, or personal skills.

Playing them may develop certain forms of visual-spatial reasoning, although we do not know yet how these abilities will relate to school learning. Patricia Greenfield, cultural psychologist at UCLA, became interested when she was trying to grope her way through one of her son's favorite games. She had to navigate spatially between different rooms in a visual maze, but it was not until her son explained it to her that she realized she had been moving from one floor to another of a virtual structure.

"But, Mom, it's so *obvious*," she was told. "*Anyone* can see you're going up to the next level!"

"Well, *I* didn't see it," this highly intelligent woman told me. "And at that point, I began to wonder what his brain could do that mine couldn't—probably as a result of playing these games."

Greenfield and her colleague Rodney Cocking recently edited a book, *Interacting with Video*, in which they report on her research.[34] She learned, first, that because video games strongly engage the player, they have more profound effects (good or bad) than viewing TV. Second, some games increase certain visual-spatial skills, such as those needed to navigate a plane instrumentally or accurately locate a target. However, "visual-spatial skills" covers a wide array of abilities, which have yet to be specified and understood. The exploratory mental stance of game players may be valuable in open-ended problem-solving, but it is equally possible that single-solution games will constrain thinking. Unfortunately, Greenfield and Cocking's work predated the development of even more entrancing multimedia CD-ROMs.

"Different forms of tools, with different technical requirements develop different forms of intelligence," Greenfield adds. In the case of video games, visual perspective-taking and iconic (pictorial) and spatial representation may lead to new discoveries or new thought forms, even using pictures to represent sound.[35]

One important theme in Greenfield's book is the "decreasing psychological distance" between child and medium as we connect children to ever more realistic representations. Particularly if content is ill-chosen, as in games where one must kill first to survive, such experiences can negatively influence behavior and worldview (this is a violent place where I can't trust anyone), as well as cognitive skills.

So, do the positive findings in this research mean we should all start urging our children to settle down to play video games? Caution! Like most experiences for the developing mind, video games should be taken only in reasonable doses and at the proper ages—in a setting where adults carefully monitor usage. Because programmers know how to make games so psychologically compelling (some say addictive), they have a power far beyond most childhood games. It is impossible to prescribe how much is appropriate for each child, but whatever you do, please make sure your children are developing minds of their own, not just virtual replicas of a programmer's distorted fantasies.

If you also encourage your child to develop a wide variety of interests—including literature and the fine arts—he may even have a chance to join a highly select group of video connoisseurs. At Vancouver's DigiPen (short for digital pencil) college, students spend four years—often after four years at another university—learning to create video games. Applications for admission at last count were running at 12,000 for 77 places. Clearly not an intellectual cop-out for Nintendo-heads (although the project has been heavily funded by the video-game manufacturer), the program selects talented youth with academic backgrounds in fields such as cognitive science or English literature.

Have these young minds been rotted away by their screen fascination? Evidently not, as students' book-reading tastes ranged from authors Martin Amis to Umberto Eco. Nor have they abandoned academic rigor. DigiPen director Claude Comair expects his students to study hard. "If these kids are indeed more graphic-minded today, and less print-oriented, it's up to them to make something of that," he says.

Guidelines for Video Game Use

   ❦ Screen and supervise content carefully for violence, antisocial messages, gender stereotyping, and other issues that may be important to you.

• Discuss content with your child; lend him your adult perspective on issues raised. You can challenge his thinking without being an autocrat (e.g., "Would you really do *anything* to win?" "Is anything more important in life than winning?").

• Homework and household chores should come first.

• Develop your family's own guidelines for reasonable time limits.

• Don't allow cyberworlds to substitute for social encounters or physical exercise.

• Be alert for abnormally "spaced-out" behavior that can signal rare video-game-related seizures (see Chapter 4).

• Seek games that encourage reading and original problem-solving instead of memorizing procedural routines.

• If you believe your child might be addicted, check out the suggestions for Internet addiction in the next chapter.

Gender Differences in Computer Use

One of the most interesting findings to come out of current brain research is that male and female brains appear to be constructed in somewhat different ways. When we add in the powerful effects of a culture that tends to treat boys and girls differently from birth, we find notable dichotomies in attitudes toward technology by the time students enter high school. We must take these preferences into account when planning for technology use.

■ ■ ■

I am in Delta, Colorado, visiting a high-school technology center straight out of *Star Wars*. At roomy workstations around a domed space, students gather to pursue assignments in word processing, spreadsheets, statistics, image processing, multimedia production, and computer-aided-design. All students in the high school take a required course in basic technology, and many spend extra time on specialized projects.

I am immediately attracted to one corner of the room where a group of youngsters, obviously "regulars" in the lab, are deftly manipulating animation software to supplement personal biographies they have written for English class. Only one of them is a girl. Elise, long blonde hair swinging with energy, intently puts the final touches on her project. She is a good writer and all-round student as well as a technological whiz-kid, which makes her something of a gender exception.

"The minute I saw these computers, I was hooked," she explains. "Of course, I've had one at home since I was about ten. But there's so much here to work with."

Across the room, three girls form a disheartened cluster around another machine. As I approach them, they turn quickly from their conversation back to the screen where a statistics problem blinks a challenge.

"Sorry, I just don't get it," says one. "Why do we have to do this stupid stuff—we'll never use it!"

"Sounds as if this isn't exactly your favorite class." I am trying to be tactful.

"That's putting it mildly. They make us go through all these stations, and we hate it," she confides. "We wish we were in Spanish class or something that's at least interesting."

"Well, you probably know that everyone has different learning styles. I bet you're all good at something," I venture.

"Yeah, but not this stuff!!"

This scenario is a typical one. On average, females tend to be more verbally fluent and adept at fine-motor sequential movements (e.g., finger dexterity), whereas males, in general, are better at certain visual-spatial skills, such as the ability to rotate a three-dimensional object in one's mind. Of course, there are enormous variations among individual girls and boys in these "typical" skills, but research on computer use has tended to support sex-linked differences. Some may be related to innate differences, some to social assumptions about appropriate interests for young boys and girls, and some to the contents of available software.

In examining patterns of cognitive skill, Pat Greenfield and colleagues found that boys playing video games made fewer errors than girls in mental rotation of objects on the screen and in judging speeds and distances. Playing certain types of games could improve girls' performance; the worse they were at the beginning, the more improvement was seen. These authors again point out that this type of training is useful primarily for learning things like mechanical tasks, machinery operation, or tracking with radar.[36]

Significantly fewer girls than boys play commercial video games, partially because content has tended toward violent or sex-stereotyped themes which girls tend to avoid. Manufacturers are now developing strong female heroines and trying to make games friendlier and less violent. Girls prefer more constructive themes: fantasy and cooperation, open-ended challenges, or nonviolent spatial-relations games (e.g., moving marbles through mazes, navigating an unfamiliar "building").

Similar gender differences emerged in an interesting study conducted by Yasmin B. Kafai in an inner-city magnet school in Boston. Sixteen ten-year-old children in a six-month project each designed an imaginary world, characters and story, in a video-game format. Almost all the boys created adventure hunts and explorations, whereas the girls' games were equally divided among adventure, skill/sport, and teaching games. Girls' games were more personal, gave gentler feedback to the player, and featured few evil or malevolent characters; most boys' games included violence and had a moral contest with a hero on the side of good fighting off the villains. Girls attempted more complex programming maneuvers, whereas boys focused more on animations.[37]

In many schools, boys are the ones using the lab during free time. Girls' avoidance may result from perceptions that computers are linked to traditional male-dominated fields (science, technology). In one major study of a "typical" high school, boys used the machines more—even for class assignments—and everyone tended to refer to the computer as "he."[38] Parents have been more likely to buy home computers for boys than for girls, and much educational software also has themes of more interest to males. Yet in single-sex schools or settings where software is carefully chosen and girls are encouraged to take equal time, their computer prowess and interest are equal to boys'.

In New York, the Center for Children and Technology has piloted a project in which successful women in science, engineering, and computing "telementor" female students who display talent and interest in these fields. By communicating with their mentors through e-mail, these young women receive practical advice as well as the inspiration to pursue technological study that is lacking in some educational settings.[39]

Different types of software and teaching methods appeal differently to boys and girls. Richard H. Hall, a University of Missouri researcher, showed web pages with different types of formatting on a scientific topic to twenty-seven undergraduates. Males and females both preferred a combination of pictures and text but disagreed dramatically in other preferences. For example, young women were put off by "cluttered" backgrounds; young men thought they were "the coolest thing around."[40]

Even if girls don't choose technology-oriented careers, they should probably have a chance to develop these abilities by the end of high school.

Girls in the Technical World

&- Choose software with nonviolent, nonsexist themes.

&- Look for themes featuring cooperation, teaching, open-ended problem-solving.

&- Support emphasis on positive female characters and role models.

&- Give girls access to successful women in technical fields.

&- Schedule equal time for girls and boys at home or in computer lab and classroom.

&- Encourage girls (and their mothers!) to play nonviolent games that may build visual-spatial skills.

&- Understand that girls prefer to use the computer as a medium for creativity and communication rather than as a toy.

&- Solicit girls' opinions to make sure a format is not an automatic "turnoff."

&- Start a computer club for middle- or high-school girls.

Creativity in Cyberworlds

"Much serious thought must be given to the appropriate educational use of the computer with its powerful but highly specific, and exceedingly limited, form of imagery."

Douglas Sloan, Teachers College, Columbia University[41]

"You are absolutely right about [a popular multimedia drawing program]. Not only do the kids in my grade two class devalue their crayon drawings, but worse—they devalue their computer drawings in favor of [the program's] 'stamps' [the canned artwork that kids can select]! I'm ready to get rid of [this program] in my class because the stuff they create on it and save, including their slide shows, they rarely if ever revisit. On the other hand, the little books they write and illustrate they revisit again and again: reading, rereading, trading, and carrying around the classroom."

Carol Buell, teacher, grade two, Oregon

The fullest development of human intelligence includes the ability to use one's mind in creative ways. In fact, this particular facet of mind is doubtless the one that will enable our children to stay in charge of their ever-"smarter" digital servants. Whether and how early computer experiences expand or contract creativity is one of the most important issues in today's research agenda.

No one is sure how "creativity" arises in the brain, but it appears to come about as an interaction of innate tendencies and environmental stimuli. Its full expression awaits the final stages of brain maturation, but foundations are laid throughout life. Proponents laud the opportunities for creativity that new technology offers children through programs that facilitate drawing, music composition, multimedia design, and the like. Detractors insist that computers will stifle children's creativity. The only study thus far to look at the issue (reviewed in Chapter 2) supported the latter view, as one of the most popular software packages to teach reading reduced creativity scores in preschool children.[42]

"Creativity" is often thought of as a property of the arts, and researchers in artificial intelligence hotly debate whether computer-generated art, music, or literature shows creativity or just superficial originality. I prefer a broader view of creativity that incorporates the ability to come up with new and useful ways of looking at the world, solving problems, expressing thoughts and emotions, and having the wisdom to evaluate one's own work. Critical is the ability to imagine, moving beyond the here and now to a mental landscape enriched by *personal* and *original* visual, physical, or auditory images ("mind-movies" in the words of one child).

Much creative invention depends on *mental imagery*, yet teachers find that today's video-immersed children can't form original pictures in their mind or develop an imaginative representation. Teachers of young children lament the fact that *many now have to be taught to play symbolically or pretend*—previously a symptom only of mentally or emotionally disordered youngsters. (More specifics for the preschool brain in Chapter 7.)

Creative thinking and problem-solving will be necessary as individuals in many walks of life adapt to rapid change and uneasy certainties—struggling to find solutions to questions that have never been asked, much less answered, before. Creativity, coupled with the wisdom to apply it, will be critical in burgeoning scientific fields, among many others. But Ron Haybron, physics professor at Cleveland State University, is among those who doubt that computers will do much to enhance—and may seriously detract from—scientific creativity. The computer's memory contains only things we already know, he points out, arranged according to how some programmer thinks they fit together. Creative scientific thinking, on the other hand, is personal; every scientist develops her own style of "seeing."

As a physical scientist, Haybron believes in learning about scientific thinking in real-world rather than virtual contexts. "My concern is that we are tending to expose students to too many contrived, controlled versions of reality rather than nature as its raw, untidy self. If our schools' curricula included an hour of birdwatching or rock collecting, or fossil hunting or astronomical observing for every hour spent in virtual reality, I could be content, but increasingly that seems not to be the case," he laments. If parents want their children to develop this type of creativity, they must provide the training in field observing, which is at the heart of all science—make sure kids rub shoulders with the real world in the wild, not just the illusionary world of computer reality.[43]

In the world of the arts, computers can make available to children the wonders of the world's finest museums, facilitate creative writing, and enable students to compose music. Many experts are skeptical, but June L. Wright, one of the foremost authorities on early childhood computer use, believes computers can enrich children's aesthetic experience. She cautions, however, not to let convenience (e.g., lower-resolution video disc images of great art, or musical composition programs with poor timbre and pitch) triumph over quality, yielding nothing but "junk learning."[44] And children are certainly better off when they can also visit real museums, music, drama, and dance.

Even high-tech corporations seeking creative employees rarely hire people who are primarily computer experts, reports Todd Oppenheimer in a revealing article for the *Atlantic Monthly*.[45] Rather they look for innovation, teamwork skills, flexibility, and innovative thinking—qualities they find lacking in many "technology nerds." In fact, to boost creative skills of the future employee pool, a major hardware manufacturer spends a substantial amount of money each year donating materials such as dirt, seeds, water, and magnets to school districts. Recruiters in high-tech film and computer-game industries look for artists who have had traditional art training and are sensitive to body movement, feeling, and expressiveness. Artists who have spent a long time on computers, they find, tend to have "a stiffness or a flatness, a lack of richness and depth" in their work. A prominent architectural firm looks for graduates with "knowledge of the hands" gained from building three-dimensional models. The requisite skills with computerized drawing tools can be acquired in a two-week training course.

Two researchers prominent for their work in creativity are Mihaly Csikszentmihalyi and Howard Gardner. Csikszentmihalyi originated the concept of "flow," when people involved in a difficult challenge enter a state of consciousness that focuses both energy and creative ability.[46] According to this expert, creativity and high achievement in the arts and sciences are closely connected to a sense of play—the "spontaneous joy of a child's natural learning experience," as opposed to externally imposed demands for learning. The goal in truly creative work is *the activity itself, not the reward that will follow.* Equally important is an *inner sense of one's goal and some internally guided ability to judge one's progress toward it.*[47]

I asked this noted scholar whether he thought computers enhanced or impeded creativity and "flow" in youngsters. While there is no doubt that computers are useful devices and can induce a state of pleasure, he replied, he is unconvinced that this relatively shallow form of pleasure contributes positively to creative development. In his opinion, anything that "soaks up psychic energy" without delivering true satisfaction may be more dangerous than helpful.[48]

Harvard's Howard Gardner was also judicious in his comments when I asked him how he saw new technologies in relationship to creativity. On the one hand, he suggested, some skills can be learned from computers, and some applications, such as drawing programs, may help clumsy children create more enjoyably. Yet, he pointed out, there is a great deal we don't yet understand about why—or even how much—"the natural way" of physical and manual experience is necesary in learning about a domain; computer use may activate different neural pathways. In short, "It's always a bad thing to put all your eggs in one basket and to spend too much time on one thing." Gardner cautions not to confuse the present state of technology and the "dismal level of software" with what will eventually be possible.

If we really want our children to learn to be creative, he says, we should focus on how much imagination is being shown by parents and teachers in their personal dealings with children. If a child is spending too much time with the computer, that is a parental decision. Says this scientist, who is also a father, "Any parent who thinks the computer can substitute for a parent is just stupid."

Is there an age at which children should be introduced to computers? When will they do the most good?

"Children would not suffer the slightest disadvantage if they didn't see one till age nine or ten," Gardner answered unhesitatingly. "But these nervous and uptight parents—they're afraid their kids will lose out."[49]

Artificial and Human Experience: Uneasy Companions

Technology can assist the human brain in compensating for weaknesses and even in expanding traditional forms of intelligence. Yet our relationship with our machines is still an uncertain one. As we increasingly expose our children to the seductions and potential benefits of artificial worlds, we should keep in mind the brain's fundamental need to grow and integrate itself through active, meaningful involvement. We must beware the dangers of information unclothed in understanding, of "hypermedia" devoid of intellectual integrity, of mind separated from body, or of "creating" without imagining.

The human brain has survived and flourished because its plasticity enables it to adapt in wondrous ways to changing environments. Electronic worlds will inevitably influence its functioning, whether for better or for worse depends on decisions we make now. Mental habits, once formed, stick with the individual and also with the general society. Likewise, skills such as literacy or the ability to reflect deeply, if lost to a generation, may not be regained. Using computers to enhance abilities is one thing; allowing them to replace our intellectual value systems is quite another.

Earlier in this chapter we looked in on a school where children were exploring a "microworld" designed to guide them into sophisticated reasoning about systems and rules. If such applications can improve on human thinking abilities, they will open new panoramas of possibility. First, however, we must consider another aspect of human development which is even more important in the long run—the social and emotional ramifications of interacting with minds that think but do not feel.

Chapter Six

Emotional, Social, and Personal Aspects of Children's Computer Use

"When we guide our lives by our own pondered thoughts, it then is our life that we are living, not someone else's."
Robert Nozick in *The Examined Life* [1]

People aren't living; they are gathering information.
High-school history teacher, Brattleboro, Vermont

Connecting or Disconnecting?

It is hot in the computer room this May morning in central Pennsylvania, but no one seems to notice. At each machine three heads bend earnestly over the keyboard, and today gray and white heads mingle with those of the children. Several "students" occupy wheelchairs. I am observing the eagerly anticipated "Elder-Kids Connection," when nine- and ten-year-olds entertain their new friends from a nearby retirement home. Each elder faces a computer, with student teachers flanking each side.

"I'll never get it," sighs a crinkly-eyed grandmother. "These old hands and this old brain just can't . . ."

"Here, I'll help you." A young hand guides hers. "It's OK, you'll get it, you're doing great! Everyone has trouble the first time."

A robust lady across the room is telling an enthralled audience about her early life in this part of Pennsylvania. "Well, when I was in school, if

169

you were bad the teacher put a pointed hat on you and made you sit in the corner!" She chuckles to the delighted horror of her young partners. "These days that teacher'd probably get sued."

Farther down the line, a small boy strokes the hand of an elderly man, who smiles broadly as he puts his other arm around the child's shoulder.

"Wow!" whispers the associate from the retirement home. "That fellow hasn't smiled for months, and look at him. He's grinning from ear to ear."

The children's teacher has tears in her eyes as she watches a lady in a wheelchair exchanging a gentle hug with two youngsters. They have been doing mental math problems; the kids have discovered their guest is faster than they are at this form of "computing." The teacher draws me aside. "I can't believe it. Some of these kids act barely human most of the time, but they're the best ones."

Judy Ulrich, technology coordinator for the district, agrees. "By the end of the day last year we were all in tears. The kids are studying Pennsylvania history, and these elders have so much to contribute. First they meet and the kids interview them about the history of the area. Then they help the elders compose a short personal history on the computers. But the best thing is just seeing the responses. Even with troubled kids, their compassionate human side just comes out in buckets and barrels."

Ever the practical observer, I ask, "Of course, you wouldn't have to use computers to get this kind of interaction, would you?"

"Certainly not. But the elders love it, and the kids are so proud of being teachers. Now, if they get the home up on e-mail, we're going to start writing to each other."

∎ ∎ ∎

By age sixteen, Dania knows she wants to be a veterinarian. In her small southern town, however, girls don't often go to college, and no one at the high school can advise her. She is about to give up her dream when her science teacher learns about a program sponsored by the Educational Development Center for Children and Technology in New York City. Young women interested in technical and scientific careers meet on-line with women who work in these fields. Dania and her new mentor, Laura, communicate regularly; Laura is an engineer, but she takes a personal interest in Dania's courses, helps her find a summer internship in veterinary medicine, and encourages her to go to college.

"I learned something else from Laura," Dania told Dorothy Bennett, senior project director. "You can be passionate about your work. I never realized that before."

"We're excited about some of the stories coming out of this project," Ms. Bennett told me. A lot of work and "a huge human infrastructure" are necessary to develop guidelines, train mentors, and build the appropriate safety nets. The result? New communities linking people together.

∎ ∎ ∎

I am at a reception in a university town on the West Coast, talking to a professor who has discovered I am writing a book about kids and technology. He wants to tell me about his six-year-old son.

"You should see Justin on the computer! Right now he has this thing about geology, and he's memorized all the different kinds of rocks from a program I got him. He's learning the names of the geologic periods, too. He's used the computer ever since he was two—he'd see my wife and me on ours and he wanted to do it too. Now he'd rather work the computer than play with his toys."

"How much time does Justin spend on his computer?"

My new acquaintance looks uncomfortable. I have the feeling he has been asked this question before. "Oh, well . . . um, well . . . we try to limit him to maybe three hours a day. We have trouble keeping him away from it—but we think it's great how much he's learning."

"Does he play with other kids?"

"Well, um . . . his brother some, but he's so eager to learn, we don't want to discourage him."

"How about reading? He's in first grade—is he starting to read?"

"Well, um . . . that's not coming along quite as fast as some of the other things."

I decide, during my consultation at Justin's school the next day, to take a look at this mini-prodigy. I locate his first-grade classroom and slide quietly in the door. All the children are working in pairs, reading to each other from beginning-reading books. All, that is, except one pale little fellow who crouches under a table, nervously leafing through a stack of pictures of rock formations. As the teacher calls the class to line up for gym, this youngster is the only one who resists.

"Now, Justin," she says, gently prodding him out from under the table. "Remember, you agreed you would try your best today."

Reluctantly, Justin unwinds himself from the table leg and joins the group. Two classmates move to make a place for him in line, but Justin pushes them aside and goes to the end where he stands slightly apart.

After the class has left for gym, I chat with the teacher and learn the following: Justin has severe social problems, is totally "uninterested" in reading or in most other school activities, and reacts to emotional stress like a much younger child. Even when the class goes to the computer lab he is unable to work cooperatively.

"I really can't figure him out," comments his teacher. "It's like he missed a few steps somewhere in his development. The psychologist came in to observe him last week and told me she thought his social skills were about on the level of a three-year-old."

"But isn't he quite bright?" I inquire.

"You'd never know it in here," she sighs. "He can spout a lot of facts—he's into rocks now, earlier this year it was dinosaurs—but he can't seem to make connections. We're very concerned about him."

I follow Justin, curious about what I will see. He appears to have the symptoms of a disorder called social-emotional learning disability (SELD). Often, these youngsters are also clumsy, poorly coordinated. I watch Justin dribbling a ball—by himself. He is apathetic, but certainly not clumsy. Nothing seems quite to fit here. Eventually, I track down the psychologist.

"What's the deal with Justin? Are we looking at SELD?"

"He doesn't really fit the profile. He's a mystery to us," she replies.

"Do you suppose all the time he's spent on a computer instead of playing and socializing could have anything to do with it?" I ask gingerly.

She rolls her eyes. "Of course it does, and we're starting to see more kids like this. But Dad thinks it's a sign of genius. They've got a very unhappy little boy, and I'm afraid they're in for big trouble. We've got a conference scheduled next week."

■ ■ ■

At a reception on the White House lawn following a conference on early childhood brain development and learning, I am talking with two noted pediatric neurologists who are interested in the book I am writing.

"Well, tell those parents not to let those kids spend so much time on the computer!" exclaims one doctor. "I'm seeing these kids who've spent hours and hours, and some of them actually look autistic."

The other nods her head. "It's true. We're seeing more and more. The computer is substituting for personal contact and for other activities in so many households. Language, social skills, the ability to play imaginatively—they're all suffering."

"Are you serious? Surely, computer use couldn't *make* a child autistic." I am incredulous. I have read the research and I know that true autism is a brain-based disorder that develops irrespective of home environment, although extreme variations in experience can either mimic some of its symptoms or bring them out in a vulnerable child.

The doctors exchange a knowing look. "These days we're not exactly sure how we're defining autism," one finally says. "Well, let's just say 'autistic-like,' " they agree.

Temple Grandin, successful autistic professor and author of several books in which she describes the painful social isolation of autism, believes she finds in the computer an analogue of her own "wiring." "I use Internet talk because there is nothing closer to how I think," she stated in a recent interview.[2]

■ ■ ■

Computer technology can be used either to help connect children to the world of humanity or to separate them from it. In extreme cases, like Justin's, too much virtual life can bypass critical experiences and result in lasting handicaps. Yet some adults are so focused on their children's mental abilities they neglect human qualities that extend beyond IQ.

Success Lies Beyond IQ

In his book *Emotional Intelligence: Why It Can Matter More Than IQ*, Daniel Goleman collated decades of research on intelligence and concluded that as a culture we underestimate the importance of social and emotional skills.[3] In the long run, they are much better predictors of success than so-called mental ability. The fact that this book catapulted to the best-seller list and stayed there for a long time suggests that Goleman hit a resonant chord in today's information-saturated culture.

Goleman warns of a dramatic drop in "emotional competence" over the past two decades, what other psychologists have called an "emotional deficiency disease." Between the mid-1970s and late 1980s, American children on average had gone down on forty indicators of emotional and social well-being. These findings are worrisome since Goleman finds that IQ, or tested intelligence, contributes only about 20 percent to financial and personal success; the rest is highly dependent on social-emotional abilities.

Social-emotional factors are also astonishing predictors of mental ability. For example, in one study preschoolers' self-control was assessed by determining whether they could delay the instant gratification of eating one marshmallow in favor of waiting fifteen to twenty minutes for the promise of two marshmallows. Fourteen years later, the same children were evaluated; those who had been able to control their behavior were more emotionally stable, better liked by teachers and peers, and scored an average of 210 points higher on the SAT. While such correlational studies do not prove this one ability caused the differences, factors far beyond IQ are increasingly associated with effective mental habits.

Dorothy Rich, popular author of *Megaskills*, has shown that teaching children lifelong habits such as motivation, initiative, caring, teamwork, and common sense causes significant differences in both academic and personal outcomes. Youngsters who lack important personal and social habits will be at the mercy of computers, rather than in control of them, she suggests.[4]

So why are these skills in such a state of decline? Goleman doesn't mince words when it comes to attributing much of the slippage to newer media—including computers.

"Kids are spending more time glued to a TV or in front of a computer, away from other children or adults. And most of the emotional skills I've discussed aren't learned on your own, they're learned through your interaction with other children and adults. That's why the emphasis on computers concerns me, helpful as they can be. More time with computers and TV means less time with other people,"[5] he stated in a recent interview.

Many prospective employers worldwide express more interest in social and emotional intelligence than in technical skills. A recent survey in Switzerland revealed that large firms (e.g., engineering companies, banks) wanted employees with the following characteristics: self-discipline, initiative, ability to concentrate, communication skills, creativity, team effort, flexibility, honesty, enjoyment of people—the very skills that are in decline. Good grades in secondary school were mentioned far down on the list, and computer expertise did not make it at all.[6]

Psychologist Robert Coles agrees that today's culture is neglecting important personal values, but he places his emphasis on the development of "moral intelligence." Many of our children today are in great need of adult guidance—"moral companionship" in Coles' words—but no one seems to have time to give it to them. One casualty is the ability to be morally introspective and to reflect on one's own values.[7] Many of today's youngsters reflect more on the video display terminal than muse about themselves and their values.

So how much does computer use affect social, emotional, and personal development, including important life habits such as motivation, attention, and memory? How do we help youngsters develop all the characteristics that make up "selfhood"—self-knowledge, values, reflection, caring, spontaneous play, and personal joy? If we develop children who are empty of all but what is beamed into them from outside, we will have begotten nothing but the sad shells of our own ambitions.

Emotion and the Brain

"A central theme in the study of critical periods in brain development is that the effects of disturbances are likely to be more profound and longer lasting for a growing brain than for a mature brain."

Ottfried Spreen in *Developmental Neuropsychology*[8]

In our increasingly electronic world we witness escalating attention-deficit disorder, antisocial behavior, poor motivation, depression, and ineffectual work habits. All these originate in the brain's emotional centers. As in the thinking brain, the habits and connections in this "feeling" brain are sculpted during childhood. Its most important needs can't be met electronically: frequent and affectionate human interaction, models of thoughtful behavior, and physical exercise are far more important. As part of this system, for example, circuits regulating aggression are malleable through childhood,[9] and many scientists are convinced that too many violent computer games—coupled with too little human affection—may negatively affect susceptible individuals. In fact, conduct disorder—in which the rights of others and the rules of society are violated—has increased dramatically in the United States and is now one of the most frequently diagnosed problems of childhood and adolescence.[10] While computer use alone is certainly not going to bring on such serious consequences, it may subtly contribute to problems that result from neglect of the "feeling" brain's development.

Thought, Emotion, and Physical Development: Partnership in Learning

For many years, neuroscientists focused most of their work on cognitive abilities. That is changing.[11] Because the emotional brain has close links to bodily states as well as setting the tone for the thinking brain, it is impossible to separate mind, body, and emotions. This entire complex is like a two-way circuit from lower to higher centers, headed by the "executive system" in the *prefrontal cortex*, located just behind the forehead. The prefrontal cortex is responsible for self-control, among many other things, and is closely linked to motor planning areas and to the emotional *limbic system*, which lies closer to the center of the brain.

These circuits are relatively late-maturing and need a lot of refinement as they become responsible for "higher-order" functions, such as paying attention, becoming "motivated," sequencing and organizing information and actions, planning ahead, resisting impulses, interacting socially, and reflecting on ethical questions. This system is also linked to immune function, and to the neurotransmitter *serotonin* that influences mood and aggression. Serotonin levels are at least partially habituated or learned by the brain as a result of positive or negative childhood emotional experiences. Personally responsive human faces are a large factor in this process.

"The most important message our research can make is that experience is as strong or stronger than anything that's inherited," states psychologist Stephen Suomi of the National Institute of Child Health after researching this aspect of development.[12] Lasting patterns of impulsivity, aggression, or depression can be set up by "poor rearing environments" in which adults have emotionally distant or damaging relationships with children. Even infants show different neural activation depending on the emotional responses of caregivers, and positive social feedback increases secretion of positive brain chemicals such as serotonin.[13]

Physical experience helps integrate the emotional and executive circuitry. "There's a reason we're wrapped in skin, with all systems waiting to be awakened," stated Marian Diamond, noted neuroanatomist from the University of California at Berkeley, when I asked for her opinion about children's computer use. "Do not neglect the fact that the cortex does not work alone. Children need a multisensory, enriched environment; computers can be a part of that, but they may only develop one area of the brain. Children need to run, and hop, and jump and do all the other things that kids do to develop the whole [cortical] mantle."[14]

Who knows how much of the escalating degree of social and personal malaise present in today's young people is a function of too much electronic stimulation replacing physical activity and interpersonal experience? The frontal-limbic systems develop in stages from infancy through adolescence, so there is never a time they can be neglected.

STAGES OF DEVELOPMENT

The first stage is tied to *infant/toddler* body experiences, as the child begins to get the hang of planning, coordinating, and sequencing movements. Loving contact with adults is especially important now. A computer can't supply this.

Between ages four and seven, when technology pushers are accelerating marketing appeals, prefrontal development should be pushing youngsters to develop an internal mental life, to imagine, wonder, and practice managing behavior. These young children begin to

- use language to guide motor actions and attention
- plan and sequence their own behavior (as in tying one's shoes or planning ahead)
- learn to switch activities ("I guess I'd better put those toys away and get ready.")
- keep concentrating even if something is distracting or "boring"
- complete tasks without having to be constantly reminded or entertained
- learn to stop and think before acting impulsively or hurtfully
- understand other people's feelings

As I watch children with computers, I am troubled by how often the machine is supplanting this valuable mental work. Prestructured programming dictates that the child only follows—rather than initiating with mind and body—a sequence of actions. Attention is guided by noise, motion, and color, not by the child's brain. Feedback is ready-made and prepackaged ("Good job, Arthur!"), and the child doesn't have to evaluate his own performance and how to improve on it. Necessary input from human facial expression is ignored, as are other people's points of view or even basic courtesy.

Between the ages of nine and twelve another prefrontal growth spurt occurs, refining the skills just mentioned and preparing for adult behavior.[15] Contrary to popular belief, says Robert Sylwester from the University of Oregon, "adolescence occurs mainly within our brain."[16] Substantial time spent with trivial, violent, or socially isolating technology can distort the process. On the other hand, exemplary uses of technology at these ages (see Chapter 8) can "scaffold" development. Young teens should make major emotional/rational leaps in the development of moral reasoning; they particularly need feelings of social connectedness, integrative experiences in the arts and humanities, good models of value systems, and ethical concern. While young teens' behavior sometimes suggests otherwise, they still require close and caring relationships with responsible and responsive adults. Don't let computer experiences substitute for this critical—and sometimes painful—learning. According to Sylwester, experiences of isolation may predispose a young teen to lasting tendencies for depression, lowered self-esteem, and antisocial attitudes.[17]

Older teens still need lots of real-life learning, but new waves of neural maturation make them better equipped to handle new technologies. Although frontal-lobe maturation is not complete until at least age twenty (perhaps even thirty or later for some), this is the age when socially grounded uses of computer learning (e.g., collaborating with peers on a hypermedia project or programming language; teaching others) have a great deal to offer teens.

The Human "Executive" vs. the Computer

The emotional and executive aspects of brain development may well be the ones most threatened by kids' computer use. Let's look more closely at two aspects of emotional intelligence as we evaluate how technology can help or harm development.

DEVELOPING MEMORY

The prefrontal and limbic brain are integral to memory skills. One form, "working memory," acts as a desktop to retain things in need of direct attention. Like a desktop, working memory has limitations; one of the reasons older people (I prefer the term "chronologically gifted") have difficulty remembering to take the car keys if they are thinking about their grocery list (or forget the list if they go to get the car keys) is that working memory starts to shrink in the aging brain.

During development, working memory gradually increases in size and efficiency, and youngsters learn to hold enough alternatives in mind to make comparisons, understand a math story problem, or take notes from a lecture. Children with learning disabilities often have difficulties with age-appropriate working memory.

What will be the effects on human working memory when children spend a great deal of time staring at a video display terminal (VDT) instead of using their memories and imaginations? We don't know, but if the computer gets most of the practice, there may be very little space left for exercising the growing human mind.

LEARNED EMOTIONS

Even adult brains are sometimes at the mercy of emotions or impulse. For all of us, massive doses of neurochemicals and hormones quite literally "change one's mind" in the face of fear, anxiety, or excitement. The *amygdala,* a mass of gray matter at the base of the brain, can register the emotion of fear without conscious awareness;[18] the brain and body respond to threat, but the person is unaware of his own physical response. Children are even more susceptible, not always knowing what is best for them, so many computer "games" may have more profound effects than the player realizes. Repeated experiences set lasting patterns that may prove detrimental in the long term.

For example, the brain is hard-wired to produce a fear response to sudden loud noises, as well as to competition or violence, as the adrenal glands pour "fight-or-flight" chemicals into the system (e.g., adrenaline), increasing heart rate and preparing the muscles. This hyperactivation of the adrenaline response that may accompany even "educational" computer games, will, with repeated experience, become an ingrained physical habit. Measurements of blood pressure, heart rate, and even brain waves during virtual interactions mirror those that would be present in a real-life situation—all without conscious control. The brain will also respond to subliminal images, which are flashed so quickly as to be outside conscious awareness. These have been federally regulated in television and film, but computer applications are thus far unregulated.[19]

The full effects of such continual "downshifting" to primitive fight-or-flight responses are unknown, but they could habituate the brain to a need for "extreme" experience or chronically affect blood pressure. Some individuals are more constitutionally at risk than others. If, as some research has hinted, such computer uses also "idle" the prefrontal cortex,[20] we should be especially vigilant, as a child with a lazy or undeveloped executive system is at risk for many kinds of problems.

Computer Influences on Habits of Mind for Lifelong Success

"These days it seems as if most of my referrals show up with 'executive function' disorder."

School psychologist, Illinois

"He Just Can't Get It Together . . ."

Boyd was an eleven-year-old student referred to me because his teachers had reached the end of their collective rope. "Would you please find out what's the matter with this child?" pleaded his adviser. "He's falling farther and farther behind, and he doesn't even seem to care. He's totally stopped doing his homework, and if anything looks the slightest bit 'hard,' he won't even try it. He's hopelessly disorganized, can't ever find his books and stuff, but he's always blaming someone or something else. The other kids avoid him because he seems so silly and immature. He's a really nice kid at heart, though, and he means well. He just can't get it together."

Boyd's parents were equally concerned. They acknowledged that he had always been somewhat disorganized and irresponsible, but now these habits were highlighted because his classmates were acting more mature. Neuropsychological testing showed that his basic language abilities and routine academic skills, such as reading and math calculation, were on an appropriate level. He had real difficulty, however, with any task that required judgment, strategic planning, persistence, describing thoughts and plans, or juggling abstract ideas. He was impulsive, tending to jump on the first available answer and sometimes making the same mistake over and over, but he seemed unperturbed by failure. He had surprisingly little personal insight compared with other youngsters of his age; he seemed unable to explain to me his feelings about how he was doing or why he was failing. As I listened to him trying to describe his mental and personal life, the word that came to my mind was "shallow." In short, Boyd had a problem with "executive function." Still, like his teachers, I found this boy extremely engaging, and I was eager to try to help.

Such cases are not the easiest to deal with, and family support is very helpful. Boyd's parents were devoted to him, but they were busy—they always had been, according to his account—and had little time to spend talking to, playing with, or doing projects with him. Boyd had spent his early childhood and elementary years mainly with caregivers, and he had turned to watching a great deal of television and, more recently, to playing computer games alone by the hour. His parents were delighted with this development because they thought the computer was more educational than TV, and they readily provided him with whatever software he requested.

To make a long story short, I gently read them the riot act. Among other suggestions, we decided it was time for Boyd to have direct help in planning his homework, to take on some household responsibilities with specific consequences if he "forgot," and to have more opportunities to interact socially with classmates. Sometimes the only way a child will develop skills of planning and organization is to have them directly modeled and supervised. Moreover, we agreed that he must cut down his screen time and get some parental input on appropriate software choices. (Incidentally, when his parents found out what was inside some of those glossy packages they had bought for him, they were both horrified and angry.)

We replaced some computer game time with regular family dinnertime, including conversation about current events and issues as well as about daily happenings. I encouraged his parents to both model and "push" him toward deeper consideration of issues that interested him, along with reflecting on his present and future plans. Moreover, they agreed to play card games with him and to purchase some nonelectronic board games involving strategy and planning ahead. They promised to help him plan and execute some family projects, such as redecorating Boyd's room in a more "grown-up" style. I really admired these busy people for making such an effort, and their attention soon began to pay off. Boyd and his family are still working on making up a lot of lost ground, but we are all hopeful.

Boyd couldn't manage his own brain; my guess is that one reason lay in the fact that he had never been required to. He didn't know how to go about it. There are three crucial higher-level skills that Boyd lacked—attention, motivation, and metacognition. All of them can be influenced by electronic technology.

Attention

Children come with differing ability to "pay attention," screening out extraneous stimuli and focusing on what is appropriate. Some youngsters have constitutional problems with attention, but experiences during critical periods also affect the system. Software programmers know exactly how to keep kids' attention riveted with exciting and visually distracting input. To understand just how damaging this can be, let's consider how the attention system develops.

First comes *selective attention,* the ability to control the brain's focus, which has its critical period during the years *before age seven.*[21] Children whose minds seem "jumpy," who respond indiscriminately to irrelevant noises, sights, or thoughts are still immature in selective attention. Others may seem "tuned out" or distracted much of the time. Too much sensory bombardment may reset normal levels. I have worked with children from homes where there is a lot of shouting or constant noisy media who have quite effectively tuned out human voices. In fact, teachers believe that increased "tuning out" by media-blunted brains is one factor in the growing "epidemic" of attention problems.

A second aspect of attention, called *response organization,* develops most rapidly in late childhood, with a particularly sensitive period *between ages seven and nine.* As the brain learns to control where it focuses, it must then learn to do something about it—form a plan and act on it in an organized, efficient manner. Many children's software programs—even nominally "educational" ones—take responsibility for selective attention and response organization away from the child by running the show themselves. In the real world, when doing a project, a hobby, a chore, or tackling a long-term homework assignment, the youngster must independently focus on relevant materials and goals while organizing some sort of response. She must figure out the sequence of the steps to be taken and monitor the ongoing project. When a child is "exploring" a preorganized computer environment or following a simulation with "guess and test" strategies, there is little demand for response organization. On the other hand, some computer use may demand self-organization: e.g., gathering data and then organizing a spreadsheet or data base, or planning and implementing a hypermedia presentation.

Sustained attention, the ability to stay involved, is the final step. This occurs mainly *from age eleven on.* Now the brain can persist on a problem even when the material is not terribly interesting. Sustained attention, or "vigilance," is probably the aspect of attention most in jeopardy in a media culture. We should make sure the child is the one initiating and sustaining the concentration, not being "hooked" by the program's high stimulus value. In Chapter 8 we will investigate positive examples.

One final note is in order here regarding "*multi-taskers,*" whose attention systems allow—or even require—them to be doing more than one thing at a time. In a hypermedia world, this type of intelligence may become increasingly adaptive—so long as it allows sufficient attention for some sort of accomplishment. Since many children with attention problems in other settings can remain glued to a screen for extended time periods, their computer use requires special care, and some researchers are already pursuing this challenge. I expect computers will eventually lay new routes to good mental habits. Above all, we want our young people to be in charge of their own minds, not so mentally scattered that they are at the mercy of each passing impulse or sensation.

Practical Tips for Improving Attention

1. Especially for young children, be wary of software or multimedia that is excessively stimulating to the senses: loud, surprising noises or movement, garish color effects.

2. Make sure your child gets sufficient exercise. In school, insist on exercise breaks during long stretches of computer (or academic) time.

3. Don't let screen time interfere with bedtime. Lack of sleep can cause symptoms that mimic attention-deficit disorder.

4. Anxiety or depression also interfere with attention. Insist on age-appropriate content.

5. Watch the child. Ask yourself, Who is controlling his attention?

Who is organizing his responses? Who is really in charge? If it is not the child, dump the program.

6. Show your child how to talk through her plans and discuss strategies before jumping in.

Motivation

> *"Some people enjoy sitting and doing a Web search. I would rather look it up [in a book]. It's more work so I think it is more rewarding when you have finished doing the work."*
>
> Christopher, age ten

> *"The lack of internal locus of control translates into a missed connection between effort and outcome; underachievers haven't learned about hard work."*
>
> Sylvia B. Rimm, psychologist [22]

"Motivation" is arguably the most critical ingredient for long-range success, and researchers Geoffrey and Renata Caine are authorities on how to develop activities that promote it.[23] They say that appropriate levels of challenge and complexity can stimulate curiosity. Other researchers point out that a motivated child feels confident enough to be willing to take on new challenges ("self-efficacy"). Computers may improve motivation if they can individualize a lesson's degree of challenge and offer useful feedback for improvement. They should not use challenge and complexity to engage the brain around trivial content (as in numerous games supposedly designed to teach). When they take human interactivity, emotional tone, or the sense of "self-efficacy" out of learning, they ultimately reduce motivation.

Children come into the world strongly motivated to learn, but "motivation" feeds on reinforcement. If the child learns that it feels good to try hard and succeed, he will strive to do more. If, on the other hand, he develops feelings that his own efforts are not effective or even necessary, he may lose that important drive to succeed.

When our children eventually join the work force, they will need sufficient motivation to work independently and to retool frequently. To meet these demands, psychologists have identified two attributes of motivation that should be emerging by age eight or nine: (1) a strong sense of oneself, sometimes called "autonomy" or "internal locus of control"; (2) Embracing learning goals instead of performance goals. How do computers affect these motivational attributes?

Autonomy: Autonomous people are motivated because they feel capable and have "intrinsic" motivation—they want to feel personal satisfaction at success. Those lacking autonomy work mainly in order to attain a reward or avoid a punishment; they doubt their own ability and attribute both success and failure to luck or to powerful others. ("I was just lucky," or "It wasn't my fault I failed the test. The teacher isn't fair!") Parents and teachers can foster autonomy by acknowledging the child's perspective, providing age-appropriate choices, and helping the child take responsibility for his own successes and failures. In a machine age, it is often all too easy to blame "powerful others." ("It's not my fault. The computer ruined my homework." "Yeah, it looks great, but all I did was cut and paste—the computer did the work.")

Children accustomed to being passive or even helpless because they feel someone (thing) else is running the show are at risk for external locus of control and poor motivation.[24] For example, if their decisions are only trivial ones (which button to push), they may feel someone else (the computer) is doing all the work, and they really can't take much credit. Young children, in particular, have a great deal of difficulty understanding what makes the machine do its "magic," so it is important to check on whether the child believes he is personally accomplishing something or whether he thinks the machine is doing it for him.

Even bright children aren't guaranteed success in school or life unless they develop autonomy, take personal responsibility and try new challenges. Can computers help? Certainly not with software that dishes out false praise for little effort or encourages the child to "cop out" when the going gets tough. And certainly not by replacing valuable time spent mastering the physical environment where children learn firsthand about autonomy from natural challenges.[25] Youngsters weaned on a media culture tend to have trouble taking responsibility and exercising persistence. "If they can't push something and make it happen, they don't want any part of it" is a litany I hear with alarming regularity.

To succeed and feel good, people must experience "feeling bad" about minor defeats, insists Martin Seligman, an authority on self-esteem. For example, if a parent continually completes a child's homework so the youngster is never forced to face the unpleasant consequences of minor failures, big-time difficulties are down the road. Likewise, if computer use gives a child an exaggerated idea of his own importance or unrealistically cushions failure, he may crumble when tough real-life challenges appear.

Seligman objects to any medium that falsely makes kids feel good. He believes that retreat into media worlds may blunt warranted sadness and anxiety, thus putting them at risk for depression. "By encouraging cheap success," he says, "we have produced a generation of expensive failures."[26]

Learning Goals vs. Performance Goals: Learning-oriented students are motivated because the material is interesting or they want to improve themselves; the performance-oriented care more about beating someone else. Children with learning goals show more interest and motivation, develop better strategies, and do better schoolwork. Adults with learning goals are motivated to be lifelong learners, to adopt or invent new methods and new technologies, to create something because it is pleasurable, and to keep their brains alive and growing with curiosity.

"People who have only performance goals often show a range of maladaptive responses, such as avoiding challenges, giving up when a task becomes difficult, and experiencing anxiety and lowered self-esteem," concludes a report from the National Mental Health Advisory Council.[27] Yet software manufacturers, parents, and teachers seem to have bought into the dangerous notion that children will not work unless they can win something.

Individuals with learning goals are more likely to come up with original (divergent) answers. Those with performance goals just want to win, so they try to find the "right" answer. Watch out for computer use that emphsizes too much *convergent* thinking. While there is clearly a place for some "right" answers, the successful minds of the future will contain a hefty mix of divergent abilities as well. We need to be constantly on guard that new technologies do not rule out innovative ideas or original problem-solving.

In a Nutshell: Using Computers to Boost Motivation

1. *Let the child be an active agent rather than a button-pusher.* Offering the child reasonable choice within limits builds internal controls. Good software offers real choices ("What kind of ending will you write for this story?"), not just trivial ones ("Choose the weapon you want to use to smash the alien.").

2. *Avoid programs that give "rewards" for completing tasks,* particularly easy ones. Emphasize that the pleasure should be found in using one's mind to solve problems and feeling good about success. One of the surest ways to turn off motivation is to dispense external rewards for something that the child finds innately pleasurable (e.g., creating a drawing, solving a puzzle, or solving a challenging math problem). Good educational software can "plug in to" the student's ability level for success with an appropriate amount of effort.

3. *"Corrective feedback"* develops thinking skills and confidence by helping a student understand a mistake and how to correct it. For example, instead of simply saying "right" or "wrong," electronic (or human) tutors should guide the learner toward understanding the "why" and the "how" of solving a problem. If a program can also help a student reflect on his own thinking or evaluate strategies in advance, all the better. Otherwise, he may need a human helper.

4. *Cultivate the notion that learning is inherently interesting, rather than something so boring that one must be externally rewarded to do it.* "Skill development" rewards, such as giving more advanced problems or assignments once the student has mastered easier ones, tend to increase motivation. They are likely to increase confidence and help a student learn to take constructive intellectual risks.

5. *Well-designed hypermedia programs can enhance motivation,* especially for youngsters with more visual or kinesthetic learning styles.

6. *Check whether the program requires only convergent answers* or whether it allows the child to do some original thinking. Is it possible to come up with a solution that even the programmer didn't anticipate? Programs that encourage creative thinking are always to be preferred.

7. *The depersonalized computer may help uncertain students* take more risks in the service of learning because no one is there to make fun or criticize. It can motivate older students who already feel embarrassed or "turned off" by past failure.

8. *Insist that the child take reasonable responsibility.* Don't let him believe the computer does the work or blame it for making the mistakes. Early and middle childhood years lay important groundwork for autonomy, and too much computer use may interfere before parents realize what is happening.

DESIGNING SOFTWARE FOR MOTIVATION

A few researchers are studying how computer software can motivate and teach without having the "game" aspects take over. In one study, they designed variations on a computer game to teach math concepts (order of operations and proper use of parentheses) to nine- and ten-year-olds.[28] When they questioned the students afterward, they found three simple changes had improved both motivation and learning. The addition of personalized elements (incorporating the student's name, names of friends, or favorite foods), giving choices to enhance the student's sense of control, and embedding the concepts to be learned in an interesting and understandable context (in this case a fantasy adventure) were all effective. Despite these encouraging results, however, the authors add several cautions: First, for highly motivated students, such "embellishments" may be an irritating distraction; second, questions about novelty (how soon will this sort of format lose its novel appeal) are unanswered; and third, the amount of time the "motivation" takes away from actual learning time should be considered.

Particularly important, these authors emphasize, is to examine the relationship between the goals of winning the game and learning the material. The two should reinforce each other, rather than winning becoming more important. They also comment that observing these principles—making learning personal, meaningful, and incorporating student choice and learning goals—does not require a computer.

Metacognition: No Downtime?

Metacognition is a technical term for self-evaluation. It enables us to monitor intelligently what we are doing, evaluate what we have done, figure out why we did or didn't succeed, and develop strategies to use on similar problems. Since metacognition appears to be controlled by the prefrontal cortex, it is not surprising to learn that highly gifted children seem to have enhanced prefrontal functioning, just as learning disabled children show less.[29]

Since metacognitive skills develop rapidly *between ages six and eight* and again at *adolescence,* these are special times to watch out for mindless stimuli. Instead, does the child have (1) models in older children and adults to show him how to reflect on his thinking and insist that he do it ("I wonder why that didn't work? Oh, I guess I should have . . ."), (2) enough quiet time to stop and think things through, and (3) sufficient language ability to plan strategies and "think aloud" about how they are working?

My own feeling is that few of our children have sufficient "downtime" these days, and we risk raising shallow minds that never learn about self-reflection. Language is one commodity that suffers in such circumstances, yet it is a foundation for metacognition as well as many other aspects of self-expression.

LANGUAGE AND METACOGNITION

Even toddlers solve problems better if they are taught to talk about what they are doing. Elementary-age children talking in pairs reason more effectively—on or off a computer-based scientific reasoning task, for example—than either children alone or children in pairs not instructed to talk.[30] Adolescents prone to antisocial behavior show dramatic improvement when they are helped by peers trained in "verbal mediation" to discuss their disputes rather than act them out.

What is the magic of language that helps the brain control itself, think more effectively, and deal with stresses of all types? Language actually serves as "brain food" for the prefrontal cortex, enabling it to make effective connections and organize the confusing assault of information from sensory and emotional systems. Children without the ability to receive and use language effectively are at risk not only for academic failure but also for personal and social difficulties.

Technology should never be allowed to separate a child from his own self as expressed in talk. Most software or "surfing" precludes discussion, reading, or even talk beyond single words ("There," "Oops," "Yes!!"). This is a poor recipe for a well-developed brain. More extended reading and conversation, on the other hand, will encourage youngsters to articulate and mediate problems with words. If this important groundwork is neglected or subordinated to electronic babble, it will never be regained.

Computers, Relationships, and the Development of the Self

"When Max is at home on a Saturday, or on vacation, he may hit the computer as soon as he gets up, ignoring repeated entreaties to eat breakfast, and finally ignoring bowls of cereal placed under his nose as he plays one of the war-strategy games he currently loves. . . . What's lost is the old dream that parents and teachers will nurture the organic development of the child's own interests, the child's own nature. In this country, people possessed solely by the desire to sell have become far more powerful than parents tortuously working out the contradictions of authority, freedom, education, and soul-making."

David Denby in *The New Yorker* [31]

We turn now, finally, to "soul-making." Instead of merely asking what our children will *learn* with computers, we also need to ask what they will *become*. Will the mediated self be merged with—or even subordinated to—the "values" of efficient data processing or the elaboration of special effects? Will our children's minds become so saturated there is no room left for moral reasoning? Or will they emerge with higher personal resolve and a deeper sense of identity?

One way to answer these questions is by considering the relationships people have with computers. Children tend to personalize computers and accord them intelligence, wisdom, and authority. The need for relatedness is so ingrained in the human brain that even adults treat computers a lot like human beings—one more bit of evidence that they possess far more power than "just tools."

Having an Emotional Relationship With Your Computer

"OF COURSE IT'S NOT HUMAN, BUT . . ."

"People don't have social relationships with tools," assert Stanford University professors Byron Reeves and Clifford Nass, authors of *The Media Equation*.[32] In experiments looking at human-computer interactions, they found that even sophisticated technology users respond to computers more as humans than as machines. In one typical study, adults who had worked on a computerized tutoring program answered a set of questions evaluating the computer's performance. Half completed the evaluation on the same computer with which they had worked, while the other half moved to an unfamiliar computer. Those questioned by the familiar computer were much more complimentary, seeming reluctant to "hurt the computer's feelings" with low ratings. This study used only text; voice or graphics would make the electronic personality even more compelling.

Reeves and Nass believe that because the human brain has not evolved to deal with technology, we tend to treat anything that communicates with us as "human"—no matter how irrational we know this to be. We are particularly susceptible to flattery by a computer, and when computers use voices, we respond differently to male and female; male-voiced computers are seen as more authoritative.

If the emotionally impaired personalities in current software can engender social responses, just wait until computers can read your expressions and body language and tailor their responses accordingly! A few can already recognize simple facial expressions (happiness, surprise), and they will soon have more realistic voices. As this "affective computing" advances, wearable computers might warn individuals when they are becoming overwrought or encourage students when they start to look frustrated.

How will our children relate to machines that behave so much like humans? Will they come to prefer the easy friendship of an undemanding pal who reflects and serves only the ego of the user? Neil Postman believes that such a computer culture may raise egocentrism to the status of a virtue.

Some scientists are concerned that computers that can read and express emotions—without the corresponding human value systems—would potentially be capable of impersonating human intelligence and even harming real people. "Do we really want to build an intelligent, friendly machine? I'm not sure people are ready for computers with emotions," commented one expert in the field of artificial intelligence.[33]

Our children, in their lifetimes, will confront challenges to traditional value systems that extend far beyond new electronic companionship. According to Gregory Rawlings in his provocative book *Moths to the Flame* (which, by the way, is dedicated to "the next generation, both human and machine"), image-processing already makes it difficult to distinguish between what we see and what is real (e.g., models with blemishes removed and legs elongated). Before long, as new techniques "sample" appearance and mannerisms, virtual copies of real people (e.g., Humphrey Bogart starring in a new movie), artificial "news" (or propaganda), and visually synthesized humans are only a few of the near-term possibilities. Basically, says Rawlings, the next generation will be living in a world where they may not be able to believe anything they see or hear. Moreover, "when body images and movements become copyable information, what happens to personhood?" he inquires.[34]

Our children will be confronted by never-imagined problems of what it means to be human. Already advertisers are on deck, capitalizing on youngsters' belief in computer-as-authority-figure. How should we prepare them for such challenges? Let me respectfully suggest that a thorough grounding in values, empathy, and a core sense of self should be our primary goals. If we consign our children to surrogate minds instead of human companionship, we should not be surprised if they neither understand nor value the difference.

Helping Children Deal with the Computer Personality

"I think that some computers are too smart for you!"
Rebeca, age nine

"Some people choose computers over their own family!"
Christopher, age ten

1. Make sure your child has plenty of opportunity to develop close human relationships, and do not let computer time steal from informal play time. If you believe your child is showing signs of tuning out the real world in favor of cyber-companions, pull the plug.

2. Make it clear to children that the computer is not real; they do not need to believe what it tells them, and what they read or see on the Internet is not necessarily true.

3. Make sure your child understands that computers only "know" what human beings have programmed into them.

4. Be specific in teaching children that computers do not have feelings as people do, no matter how it may seem. Talk about what "feelings" are, and why they are important.

5. If your child acquires an electronic "pet" or "playmate," discuss the difference between organisms that have feelings and devices that don't—and how we need to treat each.

6. It's OK to laugh about how "dumb" the computer is when it makes a mistake and how we have to help it understand things because we are smarter.

7. Children who have learned to use a simple programming language (e.g., LOGO) are more aware of digital limitations and gain a sense of power in machine interactions.

8. Pretending to be "in charge" behind the scenes demystifies the machine. Imagine that you and your child are computer programmers. Discuss ways in which programmers have made computers easier to use (e.g., icons such as a desktop or a trash can to represent real-life objects; can you think of some new icons or ways to improve the help screens?).

9. Collaborate with your child in designing a robot. If someone

wanted to make a computer seem more like a human, what would have to be done?

10. Talk about ways in which human beings are different from computers (make sensible judgments, appreciate beauty, have a family, etc.).

Emotionally Lost in Cyberspace

> *"Maybe for a lost soul, badly hurt by the world and its unreliable occupants, computers are a haven we should not begrudge. But what happens when people start going straight to computers for their companionship, bypassing the danger of hurt but also the hope of transport?"*
>
> Gregg Easterbrook in *Questioning Technology* [35]

> *"We hear constantly about cyberspace as a place of connections made between all kinds of people who would not have come together before. Perhaps. But every one of them has connected by being alone, in front of a computer screen, and this is a poor excuse for what community has meant for most of history."*
>
> Paul Goldberger, in the *New York Times*

Human emotional vulnerability in cyberspace is nowhere better illustrated than in the bizarre phenomenon of computer as psychotherapist. Who would possibly confide their deepest feelings to a machine? Who, indeed! Anyone who has the chance.

John: "I feel rotten today."

Therapist: "You are not feeling at all well. Do you know why?"

John: "I'm really p—ed off at Ruth. She's ruined my day!"

Therapist: "Ruth must have done something you disapprove of. What made you so angry?"

John: "Well, let me tell you . . ."

This "therapist" is a software program which elicits powerful emotional responses merely by reflecting back the user's thoughts. Joseph Weizenbaum, who moved from designing artificial intelligence to criticizing it, calls this practice "immoral," raising "somber questions about the authority our society invests in machines."[36]

MIT psychologist Sherry Turkle is one of the wisest researchers into the interplay between human and machine. In her engrossing book *Life on the Screen: Identity in the Age of the Internet,* she sees this interaction as one of many ways in which our "nascent culture of simulation" breaks down boundaries between people and machines.[37] Turkle is not anti-technology, but she believes we risk losing respect for emotion and genuine relationships as we blur the line between simulation and reality.

Turkle has analyzed the Internet relationships teenagers and college students have with anonymous social worlds, namely MUDs (Multi-User Domains) and MOOs (MUDs of the Object-Oriented variety). In these simulated environments, users type in descriptions of "rooms" which others may visit; the ensuing conversations may be joined by anyone on-line, entering as any character (e.g., a young man could assume the role of a female, a dog, or his real self). Some participants begin to confuse what happens in their simulated life with their real one.

Turkle gives mixed reviews to the psychological properties of this immersion. Teens and young adults often need to experiment and "try on" different personalities in a relatively unthreatening forum. Nevertheless, for some young people this can be a route to arrested emotional development. "MUDs can be places where people blossom or places where they get stuck, caught in self-contained worlds where things are simpler and where, if all else fails, you can retire your character and simply start a new life as another."[38]

As computer simulations add ever more "real" physical sensation, we will increasingly question the very notion of selfhood: Who am I? What is the nature of my relationships? What is the connection between my real and my virtual body? Turkle compares an adolescent girl taking a rafting trip down the Colorado River to using an interactive CD-ROM to explore the same territory. In the trip, there may be physical danger, real consequences, a real need to "strain one's resources to survive." In the virtual version, she would be flooded with graphics, maps, and information, but unchallenged in any sort of transition to adulthood. Clearly, the real and the virtual offer very different experiences; Turkle suggests we should make them complementary, yet it's tempting to go for the "easy fix," believing that simulations can effectively substitute for the real thing.

I am reminded of educators' growing tendency to cut funds for "hands-on" field trips in favor of virtual ones. Experiences that make the fake seem more compelling than the real (e.g., exciting nature programming has made slow-paced, real-life nature seem "boring" to many children) devalue direct, unmediated contact with the real world .

Turkle concludes, "The new practice of entering virtual worlds raises fundamental questions about our communities and ourselves. . . . For every step forward in the instrumental use of a technology (what the technology can do for us) there are subjective effects. *The technology changes us as people, changes our relationships and sense of ourselves . . . there is no simple good news or bad news.*"[39] (Emphasis added.)

Addiction

It's 4:00 A.M. and Steve is engulfed in the green glare of his computer screen, one minute pretending he's a ruthless mafia lord, the next minute imagining he's an evil sorcerer or an alien life-form. According to a recent report by the American Psychological Association, Steve is far from unique. More and more college-age students are addicted to their computers. Social lives and studies suffer as a result of forty to sixty hours a week in MUDs, often from midnight until the sun comes up. Many recognize they go on-line to escape life's pressures, but they can't quit as they increasingly feel "fidgety and nervous" during off-line time. Some forget to eat.

Psychologists liken this to any other form of addiction. "Substitute the word 'computer' for 'substance' or 'alcohol' and you find that Internet obsession fits the classic definition of addiction," says Kimberly Young of the University of Pittsburgh.[40] It offers escapist, pleasurable feelings and an alternative reality that masks depression or anxiety. It may also produce changes in the normal functioning of the brain by stimulating deep "pleasure centers" in ways similar to addictive drugs.

Internet social interactions are more addictive than television because they offer contact with other people. Assuming new identities, individuals may begin to believe they are loved and cared for in their new "selves." We humans have a need for companionship, a need to belong. Individuals without close relationships are at serious risk for major personal and social problems.[41] Yet the capacity to get along well with people outside one's own family must be learned. Inasmuch as artificial cyberworlds offer an easier alternative, they are a tempting replacement, especially for young teens, whose self-conscious concerns make social relationships a special challenge.

Psychiatrist Ivan Goldberg, originator of an on-line Internet Addiction Support Group, recommends five steps to overcoming this affliction.

Overcoming On-Line Addiction

1. Recognize overuse patterns. "Pathological computer use" can be identified by obsessive need, missed classes and appointments, forgotten homework, loss of contact with friends and family members.

2. Pinpoint underlying troubles. Depending on the age of the individual, issues such as uncertainty about the future, pressure to perform academically, or problems in social relationships can all cause a youngster to flee to ever-welcoming virtual worlds.

3. Tackle the real problems. Avoiding stressors only makes them worse. You might find a tutor to help with schoolwork, start to confront social difficulties, write about what is "bugging" you, or even seek professional therapy (human, that is).

4. Control computer use. While it is not necessary to go "cold turkey," on-line time must be limited. Depending on age, parents or the student himself may have this responsibility. Activities should be prioritized and no on-line chatting should take place before homework and other obligations. Avoid the most addictive activities, such as chat rooms, and settle for e-mailing friends.

5. Distinguish between on-line fantasy and helpful uses of the Internet, such as doing research.[42]

Values and the "Saturated Self"

"Human lives seem most meaningful and satisfying when they are devoted to projects and guided by values that transcend the self.

Lives organized around self-actualization and the pursuit of gratification are particularly vulnerable."
M. Brewster Smith[43]

"If I fear anything, really, it is that soul—that unitary, charged, and purposeful core of the self—will not be able to find sustenance in a mediated environment, banished from things and relations in presence, and suspended in an information system where all is proxy."
Sven Birkerts[44]

"Basically, if you're me, you do whatever you can to win—because I'm invincible!"
Shawn, age thirteen

Overall, it is far more important to raise our children to be good people than to be founts of information. After all, Hitler had plenty of information. The term "saturated self" was coined by psychologist Kenneth Gergen to describe an empty individual at the mercy of a constant bombardment of information and input. "What I call the technologies of social saturation are central to the contemporary erasure of the individual self," he warns.[45]

Recently, educators and legislators have mandated programs in U.S. public schools to teach values such as trustworthiness, civility, fairness, caring, and citizenship. Yet it is hard to teach "values" in a culture that fails to respect them. What has gone wrong?

I would suggest that our passion for the fruits of technology has caused us to separate intellectual and moral values, mind and soul. We seem to care more about how fast our children can learn than how deeply they can feel. We are increasingly dependent on abstract expert systems rather than on other human beings, and it is tempting to abdicate to technology the job of society's elders to initiate the next generation. Instead of offering children our own thoughtful companionship, we saturate them with the noisy and temporarily self-gratifying objects of an electronic world, hooking them on artificial stimulation and self-gratification. As we thus drown out their inner voices and their inner selves, should we be surprised if they lack a stable core?

As we replace our concern about human progress with excitement over technological progress, we increasingly confuse humans and machines. Yet "values" spring in great part from the ability to live fully within our humanness, with space left over for the quiet and painstaking process of constructing a self. Self-knowledge helps us understand other people's emotional responses and view things from various perspectives. For children, these qualities are strong predictors of "moral" behavior: Those with higher levels of moral reasoning relate much better to others, even in early years. Researchers know that the foundations for moral behavior are set by a long progression of human interactions that teach children to interact appropriately and to respect and care for themselves and others.[46]

The Carnegie Council on Adolescent Development in 1995 released a ten-year study confirming that youngsters are not getting enough interaction with either parents or other mentors. To some adults' surprise, kids want more. The message here: Slow down, turn off the media, and spend some time just being together for a while. And, while you're at it, urge the school to allocate the technology budget toward better teachers and smaller classes!

Parents and teachers today must prepare children for an unfamiliar technological frontier, far from traditional choices and boundaries. Our children will confront the challenge of pushing on humanity's borders, and they will travel in the company of rapidly evolving species of virtual companions. Not only will their computers be assistants; they may eventually become rivals. How should we equip our children for this journey? In the long run, the best preparation may be simply to help them become as human as possible.

PART THREE

Doing It Right When the Time Is Right

Chapter Seven

Cybertots: Technology and
the Preschool Child

"After you've developed your own brain, then you can have an artificial one to play with."
Mother of a six-year-old, Vancouver, Canada

"We bought our three-year-old this great computer, but all he wanted to play with was the box it came in."
Father, Florida

"People are horrified when I tell them my own [six-year-old] child's not on the computer. I think my child is extremely generous and empathetic; she can entertain herself and is very imaginative. I don't have computers in my classroom because I think they interfere with social interaction and imagination—no matter how creative it's supposed to be, it's still dictated by the computer. Actually, I think it's our job as adults to protect them, not expose them to all this stuff."
Marie Randazzo, preschool teacher, Illinois

What's Wrong With This Picture?

Caroline is having separation problems. When her parents decided to include her on their ski vacation in Colorado, they understandably refused to pack up Caroline's personal computer, her mouse, and her collection of thirty CD-ROMs. But Caroline misses her accustomed jolts of electronic pleasure so I arrange a "play date" with one of our school computers.

Caroline is four and a half years old. Growing up with technologically inclined parents, she has used the computer since she was very small—sometimes up to four hours a day. Her parents encourage her interest, although they allow her only one-half hour of daily television. They purchase mainly software that sounds educational and accelerative, with titles featuring words like "knowledge" and "jump start."

"She could spend the whole day on the computer if we let her," her mother confides with a certain degree of pride. "On weekends we have our family breakfasts together in front of the computer. Wait till you see how she handles these programs!"

Perched anxiously on the edge of a school library chair, Caroline attacks some game-format software with almost frantic intensity. Her entire body tenses and quivers as she is instantaneously lost in maneuvering her way through mazes and puzzles. I wonder, as I watch, whether Caroline's spatial skills with the mouse might possibly transfer to math and science (unproven by research) or if she will enjoy a career as a fighter pilot. Or would she develop better spatial-relations skills by creating something with a set of wooden unit blocks?

I am also struck by the level of stress in this child's tense body. She knows her parents are proud of her ability, and she doesn't want to disappoint them. I think of the studies showing that the young of any species, if exposed to continued stress during early years, are likely to undergo subtle alterations of neurohormones which will leave them more prone to stress and depression throughout a lifetime.[1]

"Yes! Level five!" she exclaims through clenched teeth as her parents smile approvingly. Quickly, she switches to another familiar program, in which she "drives" a car through an animated landscape, picking up items as she goes to solve a problem (this type of software is sold as "interactive problem-solving"). Caroline races her vehicle around the screen, following the "tricks" she has already learned (e.g., pick up the rope here) and repeatedly bumping into blind alleys. Her hand on the mouse is lightning-quick, and she maneuvers with the expertise of an Indy 500 driver.

"Why did you pick up the rope?" I inquire.

Caroline shrugs. Her eyes never leave the screen.

"What will you use the rope for?" I gently insist.

"'Cause you're s'posed to," she mumbles, navigating another corner.

In fact, it turns out that Caroline doesn't understand either the "mental map" of the space she is speeding through or the cause-effect nature of the problem; rather than "problem-solving" in the cognitive sense, she is simply jumping through alternative hoops as fast as possible.

We race through several more programs. Everyone but Caroline is getting tired, so we adjourn.

I am curious. These bright, concerned folks are adoring parents who have a lovely, intelligent child. Does the amount of time she spends on the computer worry them? How are her social skills developing?

"Well, sometimes we worry a little," her mother admits. "But then we look at all she's learning and how much she loves it. She sees us spending a lot of time on our computers. Yes, she does have some difficulty sharing with other children. You should ask her teacher."

Caroline attends a noted and innovative private school with a top-notch early childhood program. "How does her teacher feel about computers for four-year-olds?" I ask.

"She won't allow them in her classroom!" laughs Caroline's mother. "She doesn't approve of them for preschoolers."

∎   ∎   ∎

Debate rages among parents and educators as to whether and how computers should be used with young children. Thus far, however, public discussion of technology has skirted important questions of age-appropriate use, with marketers cheering when someone opines: "The earlier the better. Let's prepare these kids for the *future!*" Yet, as we have seen, preparation for the future involves a far different set of abilities. Time spent with computers in the early years not only subtracts from important developmental tasks but may also entrench bad learning habits, leading to poor motivation and even symptoms of learning disability.

Children in different stages of brain development have different needs. Just as in shoes, mathematics, or sports, there is no one-size-fits-all in electronic learning. I have recently come to believe that computers—at least as they are currently being used—are not necessary or even desirable in the lives of most children under age seven (with the exception, of course, of children suffering from certain handicaps). I realize this opinion is not a popular one, especially with parents like Caroline's who have invested money, time, pride, and faith in an electronic tutor. It will be even more vocally scorned by those who stand to make substantial profits from those parents' good—if misplaced—intentions.

Research supporting preschool computer use is almost nonexistent; what is available has mainly been promulgated by those who stand to gain in some way from their advocacy. And there's plenty to gain. Software for toddlers is a rapidly growing market niche, and computer "classes" have parents enrolling their children as young as two and a half—and many arrive already familiar with the machine.[2] A favorite cartoon in my file shows a young boy entering his mother's kitchen with a downcast expression. "I got sent home from computer camp because I couldn't button my shirt," he announces.

I believe we need a reality check, which this chapter attempts to provide. Because some parents and teachers will rush to new technology anyway, I will also mention a few applications for tots that may prove useful or at least benign, along with realistic guidelines for those who insist on believing that digital technology can improve on nature's program for childhood.

A Busy Time for the Brain

"Buy my four-year-old a computer? What nonsense! She needs first to build up her own mind, to learn writing, math. You must realize the computer can do only what the human mind tells it to. Our children need good minds so they'll be able to run the computers!"
Industrial software engineer, Frankfurt, Germany

To review some points covered earlier: During the early years, the brain has a staggering number of developmental tasks to accomplish, and environments influence its formation. If the environment is a poor one, final sculpting of neuronal connections will bypass or distort important aspects of development. During these critical periods when the brain is changing rapidly, we may see relatively sudden growth (interspersed with needed regressions, or "rest periods") in a child's ability to perform certain types of mental operations.[3] Since virtually all parts of the brain are active during these years, anything that limits appropriate experiences or sets up undesirable emotional/motivational patterns will have profound and lasting effects.

Birth to Two Years

Networks of connections are forming for social, emotional, and cognitive capabilities—with *emotional and language interaction from human caregivers* the main impetus.[4] Eighteen months is an extremely important juncture when a mental growth spurt opens new windows for conceptual understanding of natural laws governing both human behavior and the physical world. This age is also a turning point in sociability and for organizing the child's senses around movement. Putting normally developing babies on computers for any length of time is so ridiculous that it hardly bears further comment. In fact, animal studies looking at "augmented sensory experience," or abnormal overstimulation of more than one sense too early in life, have shown it has lasting negative effects on attention and learning.[5] Scientists can't ethically do this type of research on humans, but some parents seem to be trying!

Ages Two to Seven

Profound developmental tasks to be mastered include the following seven types of learning which may be distorted by too much electronic stimulation:

1. Learning in a Social Context

> *"Can a computer cheat at tic-tac-toe?"*
> *"Yes, it's alive, it cheats, but it doesn't know it's cheating."*
> Robert, age seven, quoted by Sherry Turkle in *The Second Self* [6]

Since even older children and adults have trouble sorting out the "humanness" of electronic brains, young children may be profoundly affected by the social and emotional relationship they develop with their machines. Computers must never supplant supportive human environments. In a large study of day care, researchers at fourteen universities found that children's intelligence, academic success, and emotional stability were determined primarily by the personal and language interaction they had with adults.[7] Optimally, the brain does its important work in a context of relaxed exploration guided primarily by the child and supported by helpful and emotionally responsive but not overly intrusive adults.

Digi-tykes may be especially at risk if certain types of software induce overactivation of the right hemisphere and concurrent underactivation of the left (see Chapter 5). In one provocative study, four-year-old children with greater amounts of left frontal activation displayed more social competence, while children who showed more right activation displayed social withdrawal.[8] Whether computer use will prove to be related to similar electrophysiological changes is an interesting question.

2. *Learning to Use All the Senses*

From birth, sensory areas in the back of the brain refine their ability to perform basic functions effortlessly: listening, looking, touching, and moving. These systems should become automatic so that around age seven children can integrate them smoothly (e.g., watch a guitarist and move to the beat; think about story content while writing words; look at the chalkboard and listen to a teacher). This "intersensory integration" is critical for good learning, and it takes lots of practice.

Open-ended computer use—such as a drawing program—offers some combining of sensory abilities but differs qualitatively from nature's programming of whole-body, three-dimensional sensory experience. A time may come when specially designed software can "teach" intersensory integration, but I haven't seen any yet that I would trust to do the job.

3. *Learning to Be a Powerful Learner*

Early years are a time for learning one's "stance" toward the world. Children are wrestling with important personal issues: (1) Should I trust or mistrust others—or myself? (2) How does the world really work? (3) How powerful am I as an independent learner?

Autonomous control of play materials by the child (as with nonelectronic toys or materials) is very important because the child is laying the groundwork to be either an internally motivated or a weak learner. Young children naturally tend to disbelieve their own power as compared with a computer, which is "opaque"—that is, one can't really understand or see what makes it work. Even though youngsters become adept at running programs, they can't ultimately control the computer's behavior (with the possible exception of LOGO programming). On the contrary, good play materials (paints, empty boxes, nonanimated dolls, toy tools, Tinkertoys, playing cards, for example) are fully under the child's control (in accordance with natural scientific laws, such as gravity). They not only empower the young learner/problem-solver, but subtly convey major principles of how the world works. For example, cause and effect—as well as self-control—are easy to learn when you're trying to hammer a nail into a board (if I miss, then I might hurt my finger), but hard to learn when a system crashes for no apparent reason or things jump around the screen without a visible source of propulsion.

As frontal lobe development sets up the basis for executive control systems, the preschooler needs experiences in managing his own mind—not having it distracted or programmed from outside. Among other skills, children of this age should develop:

- ability to regulate one's own emotions
- problem-solving skills, flexibility, originality
- motivation and persistence
- attention
- social skills
- body rhythm and coordination of movement
- imagination

If these foundations are neglected during a critical period, they may be difficult—or even impossible—to regain.

4. Learning to Pay Attention

As we saw in the last chapter, one of the most important learning skills threatened by electronic stimulation is *selective attention*: the ability to direct one's own attention and focus clearly on what is to be learned without succumbing to distraction. Children who can't resist touching anything that comes into sight or whose mental focus shifts every time something happens are said to be "stimulus bound."

Little children's attention naturally jumps from thing to thing, but some forms of electronic media may prolong this immaturity. Distracting graphics and special effects, coupled with the temptation to click impulsively, encourage stimulus-bound behavior which, in turn, contributes to attention problems.[9]

I believe it is possible to develop software to improve attention skills. A few programs are in the works, and we may hope for some good research on this issue.

■ ■ ■

The crowded computer lab in this elementary school has been carved out of a spare room next to the front office. In it, a veteran kindergarten teacher is attempting to demonstrate to a group of eight students at one machine how to make alphabet cards with a hyperstack she has developed. Later they will learn to illustrate them with an electronic drawing program. She is shouting a little to hold their attention, since sixteen five-year-olds and a teaching aide are arrayed around the other machines in the room. Most are playing with edutainment software, including "reading" and "writing" programs, and their choices consist mainly of flashy graphics and noise. The entire room sounds like the video arcade of an amusement park.

The alphabet card group moves to computers to work in pairs. They need to follow a fairly complex sequence of steps to complete the assignment, but they set to work diligently. Gretchen McFarland, my host for the day, agrees with my observation that this activity incorporates some worthy educational goals (as it would, of course, if they were making illustrated alphabet cards by hand). As I circulate around the room, however, I find myself wondering how much mental energy these young brains must expend to keep focused on a complex task in the middle of this electronic cacophony. While most youngsters eventually learn to screen out background noise (an ability called "auditory figure-ground perception"), it takes an unconscious toll on a child's resources and may result in subtle overstimulation and accumulating stress. A young child stressed by such sensory overload usually reacts in one of two ways: either he shuts down or he gets "hyper"—both physically and mentally. A child genetically at risk for learning or attention problems may be particularly affected. Many of today's youngsters have grown up in these taxing environments—television, videos, loud music, and now the beep, beep, beep of computer games—so they almost need stressful background noise to feel "normal."

The period ends, and the children line up to file out. Their teacher looks tired, although it is only 10:00 A.M.

"These kids get more hyper every year!" she comments to me, as she tries to establish order in the line.

No kidding.

5. *Learning Visual Imagery and Memory*

Frontal lobe maturation throughout childhood and adolescence gradually enables better "working memory," the ability to juggle a number of ideas or thoughts at one time. For example, preschoolers naturally have difficulty visualizing a story while paying attention to the plot and the characters' names all at the same time; they are not terribly efficient in their thinking because they can't hold many alternatives in mind. With maturation and practice, the brain learns to visualize and hold alternatives. Children with weak visualization skills may always be plagued by inefficient memory and difficulty with more formal symbol systems (e.g., reading, math).

Research suggests that the way adults help children learn to practice these skills makes a clear difference in their thinking abilities.[10] For example, suggesting such exercises as, "Can you make a 'movie' in your mind of how Cinderella looks in the story?" can aid kids in expanding their abilities. For youngsters on a computer, no such spur is available, as the computer simply makes their pictures for them.

6. *Learning to Think Logically*

If-Then (Causal) Reasoning

Children between the ages of three and four years are beginning to make logical inferences with "if-then"—or causal—reasoning. It is difficult for adults to understand just how elementary their reasoning really is. For example, when three-year-old Paul sees two balls hitting each other and then one rolling off, he is likely to view these as two unrelated incidents. By age five, Paul will be able to infer that the second ball rolled away as a result of being hit by the first. Very young children like to play around with causality (Paul used to drop cookies off his high-chair tray, then look up at his mom with an anticipatory grin: If I drop the cookie, then Mom will . . .), but this form of reasoning takes a significant jump between ages three and four.

How do children learn to reason about these abstract relationships? Psychologists have concluded that, along with requisite brain changes, they need *physical experience of action sequences that they themselves control* (e.g., first I do *x*, then as a result *y* happens—and I can change that if I do *x* differently). Thus, the years between three and four may be a particularly bad time to introduce an opaque and arbitrary electronic "toy" into the child's world. Better quality children's software tries to address this problem, but there is no evidence it can do the job.

If we confuse children of this age about cause and effect by giving them too many things to select and watch, as opposed to doing, will we jeopardize their causal reasoning? Teachers today tell us a surprising number of older children don't seem to "get it" in the realm of "if-then" logic; they struggle with math and science concepts as well as with social relations, strategy use, and ethical choices.

Social Causal Reasoning

Social causal reasoning—the ability to infer how someone else might be feeling ("If I don't come when Dad calls me, he might feel worried")—is also important. Progress requires interaction with human beings and human emotions (e.g., "I took Jimmy's toy and [as a result] he got so mad he hit me!"). Physical and social experiences are intricately tied to the young child's mental development.[11]

Barbara Bowman of the Erikson Institute in Chicago worries that too many children learn to use computers without understanding their "social contexts." Three- and four-year-olds cannot fully understand that real people with particular points of view produced what is on the screen, she points out,[12] and they need human mediators to help them make sense of what they see. "Even in the age of technology, it is through relationships with others—through joint activities, language, and shared feelings with other human beings—that children grasp meaning."[13]

FACT OR FANTASY?

Children under age five have a tendency to confuse appearance with reality. If something moves, for example, they may believe it is really alive. They tend to have difficulty taking another's perspective; they are a bit hazy on "theory of mind," understanding what it means to have a mind containing thoughts or being a discriminating judge of another person's motives and point of view. Thus their gullibility to Internet advertising or implicit messages in children's computer games.

By ages five to seven, children start to move outside their own perspectives. They begin to discriminate fact from fiction in television viewing. By age seven most understand that fictional characters do not retain their roles in real life and that fictional shows are scripted and rehearsed. But this development is *inversely* related to the child's viewing experience—the more TV, the less he tends to understand the difference between fact and fiction.[14] For children unable to discriminate what is real from what is not, electronic playmates may be more confusing than we think. Even older children have trouble deciding whether computers are alive or not, and tend to place too much trust in them.

7. *Learning New Symbol Systems*

"The importance of embedding educational technology in other instructional activities grows out of a disadvantage of technological

media: that they always 'disrupt' reality to some extent and put de-
mands on symbolization capacities that younger learners might
lack."

Heinz Mandl, University of Munich, Germany[15]

Between ages four and seven, children begin mastering formal symbols of adult reasoning (written words, numerals), and it's a tempting time to introduce software for phonics or early math skills. Yet the four-, five-, and even six-year-old brain is not necessarily ready for this disembodied learning. A symbol is not really useful until it has been *internalized*: a young child may be able to count to ten or recognize numerals, but until he really understands what "3" represents in the real world (e.g., he can give you three objects when you show him the numeral, or understand that "3" is less than "4"), he has not connected the real number concept to the symbol.

If you want your child to be good at reading, you should *contextualize* the learning, that is, read with him, talk with him about stories and daily events, expand vocabulary, listen to him, and provide him with open-ended manipulative materials (e.g., aides for pretend play, rocks or button collections, building or sewing materials, puppets, costume box) to encourage concepts and problem-solving skills. If you want him to be good at math, you should talk about number concepts (e.g., "We need *two more* place settings when your aunt and uncle come to dinner") and play board and card games with him. Such games, by the way, constitute the strongest predictor of math ability that researchers have yet found, and thus far even well-constructed computer programs can't achieve the same result.

One experiment cited by psychologist Robbie Case compared young children's math learning from board games played on computers with the same games played by a child with an adult.[16] Although the researchers thought they had developed a software package to duplicate the benefits of real-life experience, the one-on-one contact with an adult still produced far greater gains. What was the difference? It was the spontaneous language interaction when the adult played with the child. Older children, ages ten and eleven, on the other hand, learned some difficult concepts (e.g., inventing a function) more readily from carefully designed math software than from classroom experiences.

Another reason young children don't profit as much from computer simulations as from real activities is something developmental psychologist Irving Siegel calls "representational distance."[17] Children who understand "representational distance" do better in school because they can separate themselves from the "here and now." They understand a thing or name can stand for something else (like a flag representing a country) and that something happening in one place can represent something happening in another (like reading about Alaska when you're sitting in Brussels). Children under age seven are only beginning to learn representational competence; computer simulations may confuse them. Even the physical distance between the mouse and the screen (or the two-dimensional touch screen) makes the simulation less powerful than physically holding and moving a piece on a three-dimensional game board. Siegel also found that a big boost in representational competence comes from close conversations with parents and caregivers ("Let's talk about what we did at the park today.").

A Study in Early Learning

Ralph and Marco are enjoying their scheduled time in the prekindergarten computer corner. Flipping through the menus of a math software program, they settle on a game, giggling and gently fighting over the mouse as colored icons flash onto the screen.

"Be quiet over there, you two." The teacher is helping children paint in the easel corner. With eighteen four-year-olds in the room, she and her assistant have their hands full keeping order and seeing to individual needs.

From a help menu which they can't read, Marco randomly selects a subtraction program. A problem appears on the screen. 8–1=?

Now the boys get down to business. Fingers come into play. Ralph assiduously counts eight fingers, and then another one. Nine! Smiling, he presses the key to enter his answer.

"Sorry, try again!" replies the computer. The same problem reappears. Ralph's face falls. Marco loses interest and moves away.

Ralph tries again. "One, two, three, four, five, six, seven, eight." He is counting very carefully, touching each finger in turn. "Now, one more—nine!" He counts them all again and defiantly punches in the answer.

"Sorry, the right answer is seven." The computer is impassive and nonnegotiable.

Ralph looks puzzled. He regards his fingers once more as if mistrusting them, shrugs, sighs, and walks off.

I mention this incident to the teacher. I believe the boys have learned some important lessons. Marco has learned to flip from thing to thing and give up quickly with no consequences. Ralph has learned to mistrust the evidence of his own mind and his own senses, to feel powerless in a relationship with an implacable and incomprehensible authority, to believe that math is, after all, difficult and confusing.

"Why are they doing a subtraction program when they don't know what the signs mean?" I ask his teacher later.

"Oh, I didn't know that was happening. But you surely understand I just can't stand over them every minute—I've got a whole classroom full of kids. We really need someone in the computer corner, but we don't have the staff. As a matter of fact, it was Ralph's grandfather who donated those machines—he was convinced his grandson needed to learn computer as early as possible. The software came in a package with the machine. Frankly, I think the kids are better off without computers, but there's so much pressure from the families these days . . ."

∎ ∎ ∎

In a classroom next door, almost-five-year-old Sam is preparing to build a sailboat. He got the idea from the shape of a flat piece of wood he found while rummaging in a large box of miscellaneous materials his teacher keeps in the carpentry center.

"This looks like the bottom of a boat," mumbles Sam, eyeing the wood scrap speculatively. He runs his fingers over the smooth surface. "But it needs a stick—here," indicating a mast. He rummages futher and comes up with a small length of dowel. He smiles. Sam holds the dowel in place, pushing down hard, with the superb confidence of almost-five that it may somehow magically stick. It doesn't. Sam looks puzzled.

He casts about the carpentry table and finds a hammer. He pounds on the top of the dowel. It falls off. Sam replaces the hammer and thinks for a minute. Now he spies a drill, seizes it eagerly and applies himself to drilling a hole in the wood. This is hard work, because drill and wood keep slipping apart, but Sam is determined, and it certainly appears that his brain is fully engaged. Finally, he succeeds. Now he tries inserting the dowel. Once more it falls out. Sam looks discouraged.

A teacher passes by. She sizes up the situation and picks up a container of glue.

"Would this help?"

Good teachers are able to achieve what this one just has, deftly reaching Sam's "zone of proximal development"—that exquisitely sensitive gap between actual achievement and potential—where the right question or suggestion from a perceptive adult can help the child solve the problem himself. Although some software marketing has adopted this claim as a gimmick, it is difficult at best to program a computer for this type of sensitivity.

Sam applies some glue, inserts the dowel and now has to wait until the glue dries a bit. He is fidgety, but he manages (attention and self-control areas of his brain hard at work). When the boat is completed, the expression on his face is wonderful to behold.

What lessons has Sam's brain learned? Among others, a feeling of autonomy and power as a learner and problem-solver, systematic planning, creative strategy use, attention, motor coordination, patience, perseverance, visualization. And Sam has something all his own to be proud of.

Two visitors from the central office enter the room. Ignoring other displays of children's work, they stop to examine some computerized printouts in a wall display. These are "drawings" comprising mostly clip art selected from a menu and "pasted" on with a quick click. They admire these fruits of technology.

"Isn't it amazing what today's kids can do?" one comments.

Sam watches them. He clutches his boat.

Why Age Seven?

Most thoughtful professionals I have interviewed agree on one particular philosophy about computer use. It is, simply: If the computer can accomplish the task better than other materials or experiences, we will use it. If it doesn't clearly do the job better, we will save the money and use methods that have already proven their worth. In the case of the child under seven, there are few things that can be done better on a computer and many that fail miserably by comparison.

Because age six to seven represents such an important developmental milestone for the human brain, I believe it is a realistic stepping-stone into constructive computer use. In fact, for children above age seven, combining computer and manipulative activities may result in better learning. Younger children, however, are better off spending this valuable time in a physically and linguistically enriched environment. Even for children who lack this type of privileged experience, there is no evidence that today's computer applications will make up the inevitable gaps. Spend the money on better early childhood programs.

Physical Development and the Importance of Play

Because of the developing nature of preschoolers' eyes, wrists, hands, and backs, and the suspected sensitivity of fast-growing organisms to electromagnetic radiation, we should be very cautious with our youngest pupils.

To fully understand what forms of technology are right—and wrong—for young children, let us now delve into the elaborate process by which young children use their bodies to acquire mental habits and skills.

Body and Mind: Learning Together

Imagine you just bought a new word-processing program. If you're like me, you start by reading the manual, but soon you feel swamped with abstract information and simply start punching buttons.

"Let me get my hands on it and try it myself!" is the plaintive cry of even competent adult learners as they approach new symbol systems. The need to be physically involved is many times as strong in young learners. Moreover, they are the world's greatest experts at exploratory learning—the main reason our young surpass us in mastering newer gadgetry. This is why middle childhood is a good time to introduce computers, as children are sufficiently mature to profit intellectually from the new media, but they haven't yet lost the ability to explore and learn physically through spontaneous play.

Motor Development: Building Intelligent Muscles

> *"Could a lack of motor development contribute to a child becoming learning disabled? You bet it could! We see more and more kids now who have all these fancy gadgets and machines, but they don't know how to coordinate their bodies and they can't have a decent conversation. They spend hours on these computers and mostly they're playing games. Their motor development is retarded, and later on they struggle with reading."*
>
> Bob Sorensen, Executive Director, Special Education Services, Michigan

> *"This hi-tech world has created many passive participants in life."*
>
> Phyllis Weikart, High Scope Foundation

> *"Compared with their American counterparts, Japanese five-year-olds spend four times as much of their school day in free play."*
>
> Catherine C. Lewis, researcher on Japanese educational system, Developmental Studies Center, Oakland, California

For the young child, movement and physical experience provide the foundation for higher-level cognition through integration of the brain's sensory association areas,[18] and educators in many cultures make sure to incorporate physical play with formal instruction. Language, foresight, and other hallmarks of cognitive intelligence are connected in the brain through performing rapid movements in sequence and by developing a bodily sense of "beat." The brain areas responsible for playing the piano, doing needlework or carpentry, forming words into a meaningful sentence, understanding language, or planning a party in advance all require specially ordered sequences of movements and thoughts. These find their roots in early object and social play.[19]

Certain visual-spatial skills that contribute to mathematical and scientific thinking are also learned from using the whole body to navigate through space while running, jumping, climbing, etc. The child's muscles are "smart instruments" that register the spatial properties of objects in the environment and build a foundation for higher conceptual understandings (e.g., proportion, velocity, engineering, design).[20]

Many adult experts in fields such as math, science, technology, and the arts still do much of their reasoning with bodily intelligence. Frank Lloyd Wright remembered all his life the blocks that got him started on his career. At the age of eighty-eight, Wright commented, "The maple wood blocks are in my fingers to this day." Kindergarten experiences where children manipulated sticks, modeling clay, and paper to make geometric forms are also given credit for inspiring the works of painters Braque, Klee, and Mondrian.[21]

Yet today's potential creators may never have the chance. Phyllis Weikart, consultant for High Scope early childhood programs, is concerned that "because of today's fast-changing lifestyle, we may have overlooked development of the kinesthetic intelligence, which is essential from birth to approximately age seven."[22] For example, every year she finds more children who can't keep a beat, signifying that their brain has been shortchanged on experiences that will help it work efficiently.

The "Concrete" Learner: Messing Around with Real-World Materials

> *"Some recently released programs let them cut out snowflakes, design jigsaw puzzles, make origami art, and create and print out fashionable clothing for dolls. And there are no messes to clean up!"*
> Software review, *Early Childhood Today*[23]

At a small conference on computers and young children, I was having breakfast with several scientists and educators, including Douglas Sloan of Teachers College. We were, I must admit, making fun of the current tendency to put tried-and-true childhood activities into computer software. We were particularly taken by the ludicrous quality of an ad for a digital "fingerpainting" program.

"Why would anyone want to buy such a thing?" questioned Doug, who understands as well as anyone the value of real fingerpaints in a young child's life (which require planning to get out materials, arranging the space in an organized way, enjoying the sensory experience, integrating brain and body, helping clean up and put things away, etc.).

"Well, you avoid the messes," responded a couple of veteran moms at the table.

Doug considered this for a moment.

"Why don't they just throw out the child?" he inquired.

■　■　■

"I cannot think of any case in which computers could be considered developmentally appropriate for children in nursery school. . . . Since we agree that 3's and 4's need to have plenty of time to explore mud, sand, water, and blocks, etc., where do you fit in a computer and what would it replace?"

Preschool teacher[24]

It is no accident that formal schooling in most countries begins at the time when the brain is sufficiently organized to grasp abstract symbols. Prior to that time, young children are "concrete learners": they need to "mess around," experiment, and create meaning with their own symbol systems. Preschoolers don't learn language and concepts from two-dimensional flash cards but from multidimensional experience.

Some early childhood researchers contend that such experiences as a computerized drawing program, which the child controls and understands, may be "concrete" if it is meaningful and personal to the child. One might also argue, however, that computers minimize three-dimensional motor and sensory experiences (including smell, a powerful brain stimulus). Even for older children, a computer simulation of a chemistry experiment is decontextualized: no smells, no broken test tubes, nothing goes wrong, except in a preprogrammed way.

Real-life context, usually developed by the child herself in the course of play, allows her (at her own pace) to derive important cognitive principles, or rules, for the way things work—e.g., smaller goes inside bigger (math); liquids are runny and solids are firm (science); "you" means one thing if *I* say it and another if *you* do (reading, writing); if I do this, then that happens (behavioral control, problem-solving)—to pave the way for an understanding of more abstract symbolic forms and concepts.

The greater danger, of course, is not that children will occasionally enjoy an interesting software program, but that in spending too much time on two-dimensional computers, the child will adopt an iconic mode of reasoning that bypasses real-world foundations. While the "learning" gained there (e.g., knowing letters, geometric shapes, reciting the names and characteristics of all the dinosaurs) looks impressive to adults, it may be only superficial mastery. Children playing with unit blocks may not know the name of a "rectangle," but they have a gut-level understanding of its properties and how it works. At a later point in childhood, such terms become important, and computerized concept-building and even "drill" on symbols such as spelling rules or math facts will be useful—but only after the child has understood concepts at a personal and physical level.

Real-World Play: Brain Food for Tots

> *"I shudder when I think of teachers spending $2,000 on anything if they don't have blocks and paint. We must keep our priorities straight! One screensaver I previewed was so engaging that children tended to simply sit and watch it."*
> Warren Buckleitner, software reviewer

> *"These plug-in kids don't know how to play!"*
> Kindergarten teacher, Iowa

> *"A good toy is 90 percent child and 10 percent toy."*
> Joan Almon, President, Waldorf Early Childhood Association

> *"Most children's software is 90 percent computer and 10 percent child."*
> Response from first-grade teacher

Another major criticism of media technology—no matter how "interactive"—is that it subtracts from a child's unprogrammed playtime. Although many adults regard play as "only fun," it is the young brain's primary means of intellectual development and creative expression. Adults who have retained their ability to play (with ideas, inventions, materials) are the most productive and innovative people.

The prevalence of spontaneous play across cultures suggests it has important adaptive value. Even the young of animal species spend a great deal of time and energy on play. Studies show a striking correlation between the period of greatest playfulness and the time when brain connections are most actively made.[25]

Not long ago I accompanied Rene, almost three, and her mother to a children's museum and a special hands-on exhibit she had previously loved. On the way to the exhibit, we passed by some fish swimming in a tank. Rene was enchanted. She displayed absolutely no interest in what we had planned for her but played for as long as we could let her by the fish, mimicking their movements, dipping her fingers into the water (forbidden, but irresistible), and presumably puzzling deeply about questions which our adult minds were too thick to grasp. We thought the exhibit looked much more interesting; Rene needed to interact with fish that day. I'm glad we gave her the chance to follow the dictates of her brain. "Hooking" youngsters to electronic stimulation prevents such serendipity.

Play and spontaneous physical activity have other important functions in early life, including stimulation of the cerebellum, which coordinates motor activity, balance, and higher cognitive functions. In early childhood the child is naturally impelled to jump, hop, spin, and interact with playmates. (Organized sports do not qualify as "play" in the same sense because they are structured by adults and lack spontaneity.) Because the cerebellum is integral to many mental skills, restricting physical play may have serious long-term consequences.

Informal play helps children gain social skills and learn to handle aggression appropriately. The more an animal—or a child—plays, the better its chance of becoming a well-adjusted member of the society. "Through play bouts, an animal's aggressive tendencies are socialized and brought under control," states Dr. Stephen J. Suomi of the National

Institute of Child Health and Human Development. "Play seems to make the difference in quality of life, between merely surviving and really thriving."[26]

The level of a child's play correlates with intelligence, language development, general well-being, and the ability to understand others. Play reduces stress. It also enhances latent creativity and original thinking. As children use symbolic objects to "pretend," they are broadening mental landscapes and building abstract abilities. It is very troubling to hear from preschool teachers that stimulus-saturated young children are losing the ability to play spontaneously. "It takes me until after Christmas to get them to pretend that a block is a loaf of bread," worried one teacher of four-year-olds. "If they lose their imagination and their spontaneity, what's left of childhood?"

ELECTRONIC "PLAY" AND THE OVERPROGRAMMED CHILD

Parents tell me their child loves "playing" with the computer. Naturally, such an engaging object may be a source of excited exploration, but not everything that looks like play is necessarily beneficial. Hundreds of volumes have been published on the value of natural, unprogrammed play,[27] but children oversaturated with other people's scenarios may lose the ability to create their own. In natural situations, children tend to model or copy what they see and repeat it (sometimes endlessly, it seems) in play, so pretend play prepares children for adult roles as they observe and practice many of the adult functions of their society. Meanwhile they also master language in spontaneous interactions with peers or adults. They invent stories, fantasies, and adventures. They learn to give and take, to regulate their emotions (e.g., pretend fighting vs. real fighting).

Parents should know that the greatest stimulation to a child's natural play is seeing adults engaged in constructive real-world work they enjoy. It is doubtless beneficial for today's children to incorporate "pretend" technology into their play (imaginary phones, cars, computers), yet many of today's children spend playtime at school only mimicking electronic program plots. Is this because screen life is replacing real life for all of us?

"Dramatic (pretend) play is the most important thing a child can do at this age, but my students have already had so much television and computer at home that it takes them a while to learn to play imaginatively," sighs preschool teacher Marie Randazzo. She compares children creating a pretend play scene with clay to children working on a computer. The children working with the clay are deciding what figures to construct and how to do it, and they are using their bodies to mold them, place them, move them about. Then they make up and dramatize the action and the dialogue. In contrast, those using the computer are selecting and "placing" icons in a similar, but vastly impoverished, scene as far as sensory experience, intelligence, or imagination are concerned.

Comments this veteran teacher, "The clay is so open-ended, and it generates much more interaction and dialogue as the children negotiate decisions and enter into fantasy play. With the computer, it really dictates and limits everything. Besides, I like to see children's bodies move in my class; when they're pounding clay or molding it, there's so much imagination and creativity wrapped up in that physical movement."

After viewing a popular software program in which children "play" at creating a story by placing clip-art on a landscape, physicist Fritjof Capra deemed it "a teaching tool for reductionist thinking par excellence. A landscape is composed of items. There are no relationships between the components; you can change them around and replace them. Things aren't connected; it doesn't matter what you do with them; there are no natural consequences."[28]

Electronic landscapes reduce reality in many ways. Fewer than ten percent of children in the United States now learn about nature from the outdoors, about one-third from school, and more than half learn about it from some sort of electronic device (e.g, television nature shows, CD-ROMs). Yet, remarks Clifford Stoll, "no computer can teach what a walk through a pine forest feels like. Sensation has no substitute."[29]

Socializing in the Virtual World:
Risky Business

How Much Is Too Much?

Clearly, a small amount of computer use is not likely to seriously alter anyone's brain at any age. But a "little" has a habit of becoming a lot before anyone realizes it.

How much is too much? How do you keep a little from becoming a lot? Here are three possible alternatives:

1. Forget the computer, and limit other "screen time" (TV, videos) to a maximum of one hour a day. This option would be my preferred one for preschoolers.

2. Allow limited and supervised computer time in the company of a mediating adult. Perhaps one-half hour a day maximum, with this time subtracted from television and video viewing. Make sure the school also places limits on trivial technology use.

3. On the other hand, you can let the chips fall as they may, buy whatever software turns you on, and let your child stare at the screen and push the mouse to his heart's content. Just don't be surprised when he starts to have attention, learning, or social problems.

Computer "Addiction": Get Help Fast

Some children are more susceptible than others to computer "addiction" and its negative accompaniments. As it happens, these youngsters are the ones who seem to be most powerfully drawn toward the virtual life. For them, any amount may be too much.

If you have a child with any combination of the following chronic symptoms, please seek a professional evaluation from a children's neurologist or psychologist and consider very seriously the amount of computer use you allow:

Danger Signals

1. Social withdrawal; problems relating to peers or adults
2. Lack of eye contact
3. Language delay

4. "Echolalia": repeating canned messages such as commercials in place of spontaneous and appropriate speech

5. Unnaturally obsessive behavior; fixation on the computer

6. Repetitive body movements (rocking, twiddling, spinning)

7. Attention problems atypical for age

8. "Little professor" behavior: repetitiously reciting facts or repeating other material out of context

9. Exceptional clumsiness or difficulty with motor coordination and age-appropriate physical activities

10. Difficulty playing imaginatively or symbolically (pretend play)

In my clinical experience, I often find that parents of computer-addicted children are so relieved that their child seems to be doing something intellectually advanced that they allow themselves to overlook the fact that he has serious problems in other areas. This denial of a problem is dangerous, since these difficulties are far easier to remedy at younger ages than when the child is older.

Imagination and Creativity

"Young children, ages six and below, really need to do a lot of kinesthetic action in the world around them. To be totally in an image-based world is not a good idea [and things like] painting software can destroy their imagination."

Alan Kay, technology innovator [30]

"If there's not a way for them to enter their own creativity into it, I don't do it."

Teacher, Ft. Myers, Florida

One of the new software barons rhapsodizes as he watches a three-year-old play with an animated book program. "Her ability to influence what she sees on the screen—to answer the question 'What happens if I click here?'—keeps her curiosity high."[31] Sorry, wondering "What happens if I click here?" and watching some flashy canned effects is a pretty low-level definition of curiosity, the cornerstone of creativity. With unconscious irony, this same gentleman goes on to say that his own creativity stems in great part from being lucky enough to be raised in a family that encouraged him to ask questions—real, live, open-ended questions—not programmed ones with programmed answers.

In two other areas, early computer use may block development. The first skill in question is *mental imagery*. A computerized, animated storybook is just one controversial item that might contribute to its decline. Imagery is closely related to imagination and the second skill, the child's level of *creative fantasy play*.

Children's creative play has a clear developmental trajectory. Around two or three, a child who spends a great deal of time pretending is demonstrating maturity and cognitive competence. From ages four to six, children who share their pretend world with peers and play out original scenarios together tend to be more socially and cognitively skilled. From about age six on, pretense diminishes in favor of rule-based games. For good emotional and mental adjustment, children should have their fill of pretend-play in early years.[32]

In their book *The Development of Imagination*, David Cohen and Stephen MacKeith examine the imaginary worlds, or "paracosms," that have been the childhood realms of many creative adults.[33] Many children have imaginary playmates at some point in their lives, but some youngsters create whole fantasy worlds. Vast differences exist, however, between electronic fantasy worlds in which older youngsters sometimes spend a lot of time—often to parents' concern—and the uses of a young child's imagination.

You might be interested to know that much of the software your children are playing with was developed by a company founded by two brothers who, as children, created their own secret world in an alcove under the stairs based on their reading of the Hardy Boys adventure series. Although their software is among the "better" products, I am quite sure its manufactured delights don't hold a candle to that wonderful secret kingdom that occupied so many of their hours—and later enabled them to make a fortune from parents who feared their own children might have too much unscheduled time.

Pretend play is also correlated with intellectual abilities. Dorothy and

Jerome Singer at Yale University have shown that children who are good at imagining (i.e., creating scenarios from their own mind, not from a menu of possibilities) have superior concentration, less aggression, more sensitivity to others, and the ability to take more pleasure in what they do.[34] Researchers now suggest that parents play fantasy games with their children to encourage their imagination and divergent thinking.

Young Children and the Arts

"In spite of the powerful opportunities for symbolic representation, the computer as an artistic medium requires careful monitoring. It does indeed have rich capabilities for appreciating and creating art [but] it is often too easy in the media world to choose convenience over quality . . . then we have junk learning. Saying that a program addresses a certain intelligence is not the same as saying that the program offers an opportunity to enhance that intelligence."

June L. Wright, authority on young children and computers [35]

There is sharp disagreement about whether computers enhance or limit artistic tendencies in such forms as dance, painting, poetry, sculpture, drama, and music. Alan Kay is only one expert who thinks computerized drawing is dreadful because it reduces the dimensions of a child's experience and makes it overly formulaic. One popular software program enables children to design birthday cards and invitations by choosing among 1,000 different card elements—click and paste. Or they can "create" a picture by dragging and dropping characters from a popular TV series. Or they can "create" a banner welcoming Mom home from the hospital with a new baby. Unless a child is physically handicapped, one can hardly come up with a justification for such activities. Surely adults haven't lost so much sense that they would value such products over a smudged, laboriously hand-lettered greeting card or banner, or an original drawing—however "primitive" it might look.

On the other hand, computer enthusiasts like software reviewer Warren Buckleitner believe that the home computer, used correctly, can be a constructive addition to artistic development. He claims good drawing programs that enable the child to reverse an action with an "Oops" button cause youngsters to become less inhibited in their creativity. Still, he hopes, computer software and good color printers—which can be expensive as well as time-consuming—will never take the place of the joy of a fresh box of sixty-four crayons. He suggests combining computer-aided productions with tried-and-true art materials.[36]

Early experiences in the arts are important because they produce intellectual as well as aesthetic gains. In the best-researched example, participation in music seems to do mysterious but wonderful things for the human brain. Music educators have recently become so concerned about parents and educators sending kids off to computer camp instead of music lessons that they have begun funding expert studies on music and intelligence. Although one might wish for a more objective funding source, the results have been provocative. In one example, piano lessons, but not a comparable amount of computer training, had remarkable carryover value to academic skills. Researchers from the University of California, Irvine, compared the two forms of experience in their effects on children's spatial-temporal skills—their ability to form mental images from physical objects or to see patterns in space and time. Such skills are key to understanding proportion, geometry, and other mathematical and scientific concepts. They will also be requisite for the select group who eventually become creators of new technologies. After six months, the piano-taught children had dramatically improved their scores on a spatial-temporal task that involved putting a puzzle together, whereas the computer training had shown little effect. "Obviously, there's more work to be done," commented one of the researchers, "but if I were a parent or an educator, I'd want to take these findings into consideration."[37]

Young children can now presumably "compose" music with a special computer program. We do not know what effects this may have on their eventual abilities, but we should bear in mind that unless preschoolers have significant motoric and rhythmic (kinesthetic) experience connected to the music, they may not derive much benefit from the time spent. One noted music instructor told me, "I have no use for those programs at the elementary level. The experience of what it means to be a composer must come first—with the body, as in getting the feel of playing an instrument or moving to music. The things that are on the software we need to unfold with children, not have the computer do it for them."[38]

Language Development and Literacy

Language Development in a Visual World

Language development is one of the most obvious victims of too much visual experience. Even in the adult brain, visual, spatial, and verbal (semantic) attention are handled by different systems that compete for circuitry.[39] Since there are a limited number of circuits, it is hard to pay attention to both pictures and language at the same time. For children, the pictures usually win, as any parent can attest after trying to get a child to *listen* to her while he was *looking* at the TV or a computer game.

A critical period for language development occurs during preschool years. At about age two, language systems in the left hemisphere start rapid development. During the next few years groundwork for the adult language system is laid—if the child both hears and uses the grammar and vocabulary of the language(s) in his environment. Most children have almost fully developed oral grammar by the time they enter school. Unlike natural languages, computer languages have no critical period and can be learned at any age. It makes sense to concentrate on the natural language while the brain is most open to this important form of stimulation.

Cybertots with too much screen time and too little talk time may have difficulty listening accurately or expressing themselves well. They may have good thoughts and even a decent vocabulary, but they lack practice in formulating ideas into succinct and meaningful sentences. Language problems extend into social relationships, reading, and writing; they also limit the child's inner voice—called "inner speech" or "self-talk"—by which the brain regulates behavior, attention, metacognition, and understanding.

Orality, the cornerstone of language, must be practiced with human companions, both adults and peers. In studies of the way literacy skills are developed, we find that children who talk to each other while play-ing, and particularly those who play together with language (e.g., silly rhymes, riddles, and tongue-twisters as well as discussions, arguments, negotiations), will tend to become earlier and better readers.[40] Talk bridges the gap between a child's concrete, sensorial world and the world of images and abstract concepts; thus, it teaches "representational distance," so important for learning to think about symbols and things that aren't immediately present (as in math concepts, or reading com-prehension). To expect children to become literate before they have a base of language understanding is an exercise in futility. They may learn to sound out words, but that's where the story ends.

Adults reach a child's "zone of proximal development," where learn-ing is primed to happen, by constantly challenging her to understand and express herself in more mature ways.

Father: "What's Peter Rabbit doing?"

Child: "Going in the fence."

Father: "Yes, he's crawling *under* the fence. Why do you think he's doing that?"

Child (pointing): "Lettuce! Him wants lettuce."

Father: "You bet! He's hungry and *he wants* to eat lettuce."

One ideal time for this type of interaction is when you are reading aloud to your child. In fact, training mothers in dialogic reading of pic-ture books—i.e., learning to ask meaningful questions and encourage the child to discuss the material as you go along—had powerful effects on children's language and reading skills in several studies. In one case, the computer was used effectively *to train the mothers* to do a better job when reading to their children. There is no way it could do this job for the children.[41]

Developing an Inner Voice

Nature has also given young children the delightful assignment of telling themselves stories. In fact, their planning abilities develop from personal narratives, which also become a foundation for ethical choices. Talk-ing—either out loud or, by around age seven, in one's own head—helps them pay attention, imagine a course of action, predict its effects on oth-ers, and decide whether or not to do it.

This inner speech originates from talking with adult caregivers—and then having enough time and quiet space to practice it alone. Children vary dramatically both in the amount of and in the timetable for inner speech, which is also related to parenting style and socioeconomic group. Normally, it should become well-developed between four and six years of age in children from middle-class homes, where parents have traditionally had the time to talk and interact closely with their children. For children from less verbal environments, including middle- and upper-income homes where screen time substitutes for family conversations, this development may be delayed.

Inner speech is important to academic as well as personal development.[42] From ages six to nine, gains in math achievement as well as in other subjects are related to the use of self-talk. ("How should I do this problem—oh, I think I'll try . . .") Delays in acquiring and using "self-talk" may interfere with attention and behavior, as well as effective performance in sports.

"When a child tries new tasks, he or she needs communicative support from an adult who is patient and encouraging and who offers the correct amount of assistance. . . . Gradually, adults can withdraw this support as children begin to guide their own initiatives," states language specialist Laura Berk.[43] Can a computer offer similar experiences? Not yet—if ever. Even if software were sufficiently advanced, the emotional importance of human interaction is too important a part of the package.

Early Literacy

One of the most promising uses of computer technology with children aged five to seven is as a supplement to a well-planned literacy program. My classroom visits have included some large urban classes of six-year-olds where one or two computers really helped the teacher in motivating children to practice talking together, writing, and reading, as they collaborated in creating, printing, and rereading their own stories. Moreover, computer word-processing with large, clear fonts is useful to a parent or teacher who wants to write down a child's dictated story and give him an easy-to-read printout to illustrate. (Of course, the same effect can be achieved with pencil and paper if you don't have a computer.) As computers gain more real-sounding voices, "learn" to read back a child's written words, or someday even write down his spoken ones, they may yet find a place as language and reading tutors. (In the next chapter we will discuss why children should still physically practice writing the words themselves.) The jury is still out, however, on other popular "literacy" applications—despite the elaborate claims of enthusiasts and hucksters. Please recall Gavriel Salomon's studies described in Chapter 5 showing that children who learn in one medium (screen vs. page) will always be inclined to prefer the one in which they learned. So if you think books are important, you should probably start there. We all have plenty of screens in our lives; it's books that are in jeopardy.

As I have explained in *Your Child's Growing Mind,* reading consists much more of a person's "habits of mind"—e.g., sustained concentration, language, imagery, questioning strategies—than it does of reciting words or alphabet sounds. Computers most readily lend themselves to drill-and-practice software ("electronic workbooks"), which may do more harm than good if used too soon and too extensively. Generally speaking, the better programs do build certain skills (and thus may be useful at the right ages), and they tend to raise older children's scores if the tests focus more on mechanics of reading than on deeper comprehension skills. But drill-and-practice may have subtle negative outcomes, especially for very young children. In one study children using very popular reading software drill-and-practice (disguised as games with reward screens) demonstrated *a 50 percent drop in their creativity scores.* This decline was not found for either noncomputer-users or children using "open-ended" (e.g., writing, drawing) programs. The researcher who conducted this study is editor of a computer journal and one of the major boosters of "developmentally appropriate" use of computers in preschool. He concludes that if computers are used, they should be integrated with a regular curriculum and complemented with hands-on activities to reinforce the major objectives of the software.[44]

One school I visited used an elementary-level reading package in kindergarten—which necessitated keeping the classroom unnaturally quiet all day because a small group was always working on the computers. ("They have to be able to hear through those earphones," explained the aide.) Although some of the exercises were useful, the dictum of a silent classroom for five- and six-year-olds runs counter to every recommendation by early childhood experts, not the least of which is the limitations it places on oral language and "self-talk." Unfortunately, the school was unable to purchase new materials or upgrade software because of the considerable expense (their grant money was gone), so children in all grades used the same stories and exercises year after year. In short, there are better, less expensive, and more interesting ways to teach most children beginning reading skills. If the aide were trained in teaching reading instead of teaching computer, for example, she could use the same exercises in a much richer educational context and achieve equal or better results with small groups of children.

Symbol Use in Screenland

Among the few who have looked closely at "developmentally appropriate" computer use is Linda Labbo of the University of Georgia, who observed five- and six-year-old children exploring a multimedia program she termed "screenland." Labbo was interested in finding out how youngsters in the early stages of reading would interact with multimedia symbols. This classroom, contrary to the norm, had eighteen children and two experienced teachers (described as "exemplary"), with two computers and a printer. Under Labbo's supervision, the youngsters, most of whom were still nonreaders, used the computers to create pictures that would tell stories, with the occasional addition of alphabet letters (e.g., typing their names or random letter combinations).

Labbo observed that the children enjoyed the experience, and she felt it also enhanced cognitive and social skills as the youngsters explored the computer environment with classmates. Engaging in "dramatic symbolism," they invented characters and dialogue to supplement role-playing. The freedom to erase work quickly and try again, she believes, encouraged them to take risks and be more imaginative. On the other hand, they tended to lean heavily on prepackaged clip art. Even more troubling is her observation of relatively sparse use of language, as the children were deeply engaged in the visual aspects of the experience.

Labbo's aim was to watch how children would "create meaning" from the unstructured use of multiple symbol systems. She believes they did, but no assessment of the children's progress in standard prereading skills is presented. In fact, Labbo's main conclusion is that we broaden our definitions of literacy beyond "verbocentrism." "How can we conceptualize literacy if our notion of print-based literacy is no longer adequate?" she asks.[45]

Did the children gain anything unique from this experience compared with a noncomputerized setting? Would adventures in screenland be either practical or productive in a more standard classroom setting? Clearly, multimedia influences the types of symbols young children generate. The unanswered question is whether these new forms will positively supplement or negatively detract from print literacy. Because of the compelling nature of the visual display, I am skeptical that it will aid literacy. Lacking more definitive research, I would advocate a consciously balanced curriculum, reserving such classroom computer use until at least first or even second grade, when children have the skills to add written stories into the multimedia mix. We must not underestimate the unique qualities of young children's language in shaping and expanding thought.

Making Choices

From his earliest months, Brent was accustomed to seeing his mom at her computer, and by the time he was two, he was clamoring to play with this fascinating adult toy. Of course, Brent also wanted to play with other adult toys such as his dad's carpentry tools and the stove in the kitchen, but his parents wisely diverted his attention in favor of more suitable activities. Should they encourage his interest in the computer? After considerable discussion, they decided it would be OK for Brent to sit with one of them on occasion and help find pictures of cars, tractors, and trucks (his current passion) on-line. They decided against purchasing or downloading children's games or "educational" programs until Brent was older; thus, he spent most of his early years happily playing in a real world of three-dimensional toys, objects, and people.

He gained independence and self-confidence, language and listening skills.

Brent viewed the computer as a useful part of the household, not as an entertainment center for his amusement. He learned about literacy from real books and mastered mathematical principles as he built elaborate constructions with unit blocks, "helped" his dad install kitchen shelves, and accompanied adults on shopping trips. His creativity flourished along with his conceptual development as he made messes with sand, water, fingerpaints, and clay. He learned to play cooperatively with other children and began to display leadership skills.

When Brent was four and in preschool, his parents confronted a financial decision. Should they buy him a new multimedia computer with sound card, color printer, and accompanying CD-ROMs—or should they invest in an after-school program featuring creative rhythm and movement activities to music? After reading an article that cited scientific studies demonstrating the importance of music, beat, and body movement to the development of the brain during the preschool years, they chose the latter. Brent thrived, and they breathed a sigh of relief.

"I'm really glad we didn't have the money to do both," his mother now comments. "We might have broken down and bought a computer, and I really think he was better off without it."

Around the age of five, Brent began to show interest in reading, and he followed his parents around asking, "What word is that?" He began playing with his mom's word-processing program, typing letters at random as he dictated original stories. He loved to have his mother type these stories and print them out for him to illustrate. He still made his drawings with crayons, markers, and paints, and he also displayed quite a talent for creating "inventions" with found objects such as boxes, used envelopes, small toys, buttons, and picture wire. Many of his friends were spending a lot of time with their CD-ROMs, but Brent's parents by now were convinced they had made the right decision and held firm on the limits they had set. They explained to Brent that the computer was useful and interesting, but they cared enough about him to make sure he had plenty of time for things that were better for children his age. The computer would come later. Fortunately, the parents of another child in the neighborhood shared their views, and the two children spent hours roughhousing, playing with toys, making up games, and enacting fantasy dramas.

After he began first grade, the stories Brent typed became longer and better spelled, but he still practiced writing and illustrating by hand. He began to read. Because his language was so well developed, he not only understood what he read but began to enjoy independent reading. His teacher commented he was one of the few children in the class who knew how to listen and follow directions, and because of his good social skills and self-control, he was a popular friend and playmate.

Not long after he began to read, Brent's parents finally upgraded their household technology and bought him a CD-ROM encyclopedia, which the family enjoyed together. Within one week, Brent had become more adept than his parents at manipulating the program. A multimedia authoring program followed. At first he was "glued" to the screen whenever possible, but because he already had so many interests, the computer soon became simply one of his many activities. Brent's software preferences were typical of a high-ability child, since he liked open-ended problem-solving programs best. (Lower-ability children, on the other hand, are drawn more by lots of animation and graphics. They are bothered by the lack of structure in problem-solving software, and need the close assistance of an adult to use it successfully.)[46]

Brent's parents were pleased that his development was so well rounded, and they secretly congratulated themselves for resisting all the pressures to turn Brent into a cybertot.

If You Must . . .

The reality, of course, is that many parents, teachers, and day-care providers will continue to believe they must propel their young charges into the electronic future. The powerful National Association for the Education of Young Children has reversed its previous stance and squeezed out a limited endorsement of "developmentally appropriate" computer use for children in preschools. Many parents and teachers firmly disagree, and it should be noted that the caveats in this report are so stringent as to make "appropriate" use difficult or even unlikely in most schools. NAEYC recommends that teachers take much more training, spend more time observing children for computer-related problems, make an effort to avoid the flood of bad software, take responsibility to guarantee that computers serve the curriculum in appropriate ways, and participate more in technology decision-making. Appropriate use also guarantees that the cost of new technologies will not subtract from other learning materials. In other words, if you already have an exemplary program, it's OK to add a little computer experience if you have time to plan and supervise extra activities that will dovetail with your regular instruction.

With young children it is even more important than with older ones to determine what we want them to learn before choosing the technology to do the job. Purchase equipment because it fits a specific need, not because it's "cute" or novel. In fact, if we define "technology" more broadly as "any tool that extends the senses," such as hand lenses, magnifying bug boxes, string telephones, compasses, thermometers, creative art materials, rulers, and audiotapes, computers become only one of many options for early learning. Moreover, because young children require thirty to fifty minutes of free play or independent exploration to become fully engaged in learning materials,[47] occasional large blocks of time with adult supervision—not superficial jabs at software—should be scheduled.

As technology and software progress, we will doubtless see increasing numbers of worthwhile applications. In the meanwhile, if you must plunge your preschooler into an artificial world, you might review the following suggestions for computer use and software selection:

Guidelines for Young Children Using Computers

    ➤ Starting children on computers too early is far worse than starting them too late.

    ➤ A child should be able to understand the cause-effect relationship of moving a mouse or touching the screen to get a reaction before she starts to use a computer.

    ➤ Look for software that makes the child feel independent, e.g., being able to navigate in and out of activities, hear spoken directions, or access understandable help screens.

&❧ Downplay skill-and-drill math and phonics activities in favor of interactive problem-solving or more open-ended uses where the child is free to explore and discover ways to use the materials.

&❧ Discourage impulsive clicking. Stop the program occasionally to encourage the child to talk about what is happening, what he is doing, and why. You may need to turn off the visual distractors at this time. Describe what he has done and ask questions about how he accomplished something. If there is an icon or image on the screen, make sure the child understands its relationship to real-life objects and events.

&❧ Supplement "eyes-on" with "hands-on." Find real-life experiences that extend and complement the virtual ones.

&❧ Help the child understand how the computer works and what is going on as he manipulates a program. Let him see how you physically connect computer, printer, and other components. Keep emphasizing that people control the computer, not the other way around.

&❧ Don't let screen time substitute for lap time and don't expect books on CD-ROM to substitute for interactive reading with loving adults. Be sure to take the time for questions about and personal discussion of the story you are reading. Encourage children to dictate stories. Young children tell more complex stories, using more mature language, when they dictate rather than type them.

&❧ Consider eliminating the use of clip art if you decide to let your child use digital drawing tools.

&❧ Evaluate the aesthetic qualities of software, including, of course, CD-ROMs.

&❧ If your child goes on the Internet, closely supervise him.

&❧ Whenever possible, make computer use a social experience by putting two chairs at the machine and encouraging conversation and collaboration with peers, siblings, or adults.

&❧ If your young child begins to show signs of computer addiction, cut down on or eliminate screen time and make sure plenty of alternative activities are available.

&❧ Don't ever forget that the best multimedia, interactive environment is the real world.

Guidelines for Choosing Early Childhood Software

A useful checklist for early childhood software is presented by Susan Haugland and June Wright, authors of *Young Children and Technology*.[48] I have adapted some of their suggestions below, many of which are similar to the guidelines for children of all ages given in Chapter 2.

- Is the child in control, an "actor not a reactor?"
- Does the child set the pace of the activity?
- Are instructions clear?
- Does it teach powerful ideas, not just trivia?
- Can the child operate it independently?
- Does it feature discovery learning, not skill drilling?
- Does it capitalize on the child's intrinsic motivation rather than using external rewards?
- Is process more important than product?
- Does it reflect the child's experience in the real world?
- Are technical features well designed (e.g., runs quickly, saves child's work, has uncluttered graphics)?
- Does it display gender and role equity?

Conclusion

"Children do not have to be amused, cajoled, or tricked into learning. This is only an American problem and it's disrespectful of children."

Lillian Katz

"There seems to be this frenzy to get them to push the right buttons early."

Gretchen McFarland, teacher training specialist, Lancaster County, Pennsylvania

The immature human brain neither needs nor profits from attempts to "jump start" it. The fact that this phrase is being successfully used to sell technology for toddlers illustrates our ignorance of early childhood development. Our wish to rush young children willy-nilly into the electronic grip of an unproven medium also reflects a belief that learning is something the young must be enticed into, whereas it is, in fact, the driving force of their existence. Unfortunately, many adults don't recognize real learning when they see it—as with Sam and his toy boat.

The brain tends to seek what it needs at each stage of development, and it doesn't need the blandishments of software programmers to distract it. Why, after all, are we so unwilling to trust the wisdom of the young child's brain to seek out the stimulation it needs from a naturally enriched environment? The minute we introduce an artificially engaging stimulus with fast-paced visuals, startling noises, silly scenarios, and easy excitement, the brain is diverted away from its natural developmental tasks. Kids will be enthusiastic about any novelty, but their enthusiasm is uncritical. It's up to the mature minds in the situation to discriminate and select what is truly valuable.

"Yes, we get a lot of pressure from parents, but we believe the gains from working with computers do not outweigh the losses for four- and five-year-olds," states Mary Ucci of the Wellesley Child Study Center. "At this age they need to be pushing Play-doh, not buttons."[49]

David Elkind, child development authority, laments our failure to respect the unique qualities of childhood learning. It has become fashionable to try to bring children into many aspects of the adult world too soon, he points out, "collapsing" the stages of childhood and thus depriving youngsters—and their brains—of the opportunity to complete necessary developmental tasks. To enter school successfully, Elkind suggests, children don't need technological expertise. Instead they should be able to

- express themselves, listen, and follow directions
- start a task and bring it to completion themselves before jumping off to another project
- cooperate with other children[50]

As we have seen, all of these qualities may be eroded by the wrong kind of computer exposure.

MIT's Joseph Weizenbaum was once a booster for everything digital but now offers articulate warnings about its use. Do we want, he asks, to expose our young children to artificial minds that possess no human values or even common sense? The physical world, not the two-dimensional screen, is where they will learn the real skills for the future and become complex "systems thinkers"—able to relate things to each other, to see real-life connections, patterns, and context.[51]

One preschool teacher says it eloquently: "Let us not let our adult excitement with what computers can do in the adult workplace deter us from offering to children the squishiness of making mud pies, the scent of peppermint extract when making cookies, and the feel of balancing a block at the top of a tower. . . . The adult world of the plastic workplace comes all too soon."[52]

Chapter Eight

Learning With Computers in Elementary, Middle, and High School

*">During our experiment we discovered that our hypothesis was
>unfortunately
>incorrect."*
Internet posting by middle-school students, Mott Hall School, Harlem, New York

">Ah ha! You have done science!"
Response from scientist at Global Atmosphere Program, Environmental Defense Fund

Can technology contribute to learning? I think it can . . .

If a child has sufficient cognitive skills and social development

If technology is not substituting for important developmental experience

If we are not expecting it to do what it cannot do

If parenting and teaching retain priority

If the technology complements a well-planned curriculum

If it does not steal funds from more important needs (e.g., early childhood education, arts programs)

If we are judicious in planning and selection of software and activities

If we don't become seduced by flashy graphics and digital legerdemain

If parents and teachers are willing to provide a human "scaffold" for technology-assisted learning . . .

. . . then young people may profit from wise choices in this emerging field.

In this chapter I will try to show what it means to "scaffold" electronic learning for children of different ages. We will look at good examples of innovative computer use and at thorny but practical issues, such as whether, when, and how to teach students to write on a keyboard, how to use technology to teach basic skills, and how to assess student work in a new era of glossy cut-and-paste scholarship. Because telecommunications are such dramatic features in the electronic landscape, we will also take a serious look at some of their uses and misuses.

Anyone who is the least bit savvy about young people sees the enormous individual variations among kids at any age. For the purposes of discussion we will adopt some normative terms, but with the understanding that such generalizations have very fuzzy boundaries. For our purposes, "primary" will denote children of approximately five to seven years, "elementary" eight to ten, "middle school" eleven to thirteen, and "high school and beyond" fourteen and up.

My notes for this chapter include so much material that this topic should itself comprise a book. Therefore I apologize in advance for presenting only the barest outline of how digital teaching may prove to be a useful and appropriate assistant to mental development.

General Principles for Meaningful
Technology Use

First, some general principles for educators and parents. If your child's school neglects these "basics," it may be wasting students' time and your money.

1. Fit the activity to the students' level of maturation and cognitive development.

2. Make the activity meaningful by linking it with students' interests and experiences.

3. Start with hands-on and interpersonal activities (e.g., practicing face-to-face interviewing skills before questioning "experts" on-line;

building a classroom replica of the rain forest while participating in a simulated adventure in Central America).

4. Set clear outcomes and standards for learning. Help students evaluate when and how well these goals have been reached.

5. Ask for student self-reflection—preferably in writing—on work habits and process as well as on the outcome.

6. Plan for a meaningful and useful way for students to "show off" what they have learned (e.g., a multimedia demonstration about planets in the solar system; an explanatory guide to local historic spots; a virtual tour of Shakespeare's England; a musical performance incorporating original digital composition; an essay or letter to the editor expressing the student's point of view on a topic studied).

7. Don't be seduced by technical effects. Be sure technology use is always cloaked in understanding (e.g., require the child to explain the meaning of the data and to justify the formats chosen to present the project).

8. "Support" the organization and quality of long-term projects with clear written directions and expectations, checklists, and checkpoints for each step. Elementary-age children especially need adult supervision in planning and completing each step.

9. If students work in groups, make sure all share in total workload and various types of tasks (e.g., all have experience with designing graphics, and all must do some reading and writing). Acknowledge that some students are better at some types of tasks, and encourage all to enjoy exercising their talents as they also improve less-favored skills.

10. Encourage integration of understanding across modalities (e.g., prepare an original—written—script about something viewed; represent historical information in dance; draw illustrations for mathematical data in a spreadsheet; compare and contrast emotional response and learning from reading a book vs. seeing it in a video).

The Role of Parents and Teachers:

The best results from all technology use for children come accompanied by a skilled adult "coach" who adds language, empathy, and flexibility. The principal rule is not to *tell* the child what to do, but to guide her into the appropriate steps. One way to start cognitive coaching is to show a child how you accomplish something, describing your thinking process as you go. ("When I lay out this spreadsheet, I start by . . ." "See, I'm trying to remember to save my work periodically so I won't lose it.") An even better way, however (and more comfortable for most of us who are not computer experts ourselves), is to put the youngster in charge and learn with him. For example, sit with him, quietly commenting or suggesting with leading questions. Be sure to let him hear you reflect on your own thinking. If you're bewildered (or even if you're not), express your questions, ask for an explanation, and help him develop strategies to find an answer. You might ask such questions as:

"I wonder what that means?"

"Why do you suppose that happened?"

"Let's talk about what steps to take next."

"This seems pretty confusing; how could we figure it out?"

"I wonder what would happen if . . ."

"It seems the programmer put that in for a reason—could it be a clue?"

"I noticed you got that same result every time you did . . . Could that be important?"

"You've worked so hard. Do you really want to blow it all up? What if you saved this and tried again tomorrow . . . ?"

Young children may need to think hard about questions such as these, but with skilled mentors, children of any age can eventually begin to internalize this sort of dialogue, from which they gain self-control and problem-solving skills. As youngsters move through the elementary years, they build on such early foundations and are increasingly able to profit from high-quality technology use.

Now, we should take a multiage look at one of the most promising—and also the most sorely abused and oversold—digital "tools."

The Internet and the Web: Mixed Blessings

"I was spending fourteen hours a day at my computer. I felt my life dribbling away through my modem."

Recovering Internet addict

"The advantage of e-mail is that I don't have to sit in some room to make myself available where students would come and have to wait around for me to get free."
Bob Brown, college physics professor [1]

"Eventually the Internet will grow up, or maybe we will. We will know when this has happened when the Net becomes invisible and we can finally stop talking about it—when it has become a place you wouldn't be ashamed to have your parents visit."
Charles McGrath, editor, *The New York Times Book Review*

Seven-year-old Jordan came home from school with an assignment to make a poster advertising a state so his classmates would want to visit there. From a library book, Jordan had chosen the state of Texas, and he asked his dad if he could look for information on the Internet. Jordan's dad helped him use a search engine, and together they evaluated and chose four sites.

From a site showing all fifty states, Jordan created a large map. Using information from the Texas tourist board, he added ranches, ports, oil wells, and topographic features. He also highlighted the town of Big Spring, where his mother had been born. One of the sites enabled him to leave messages for schoolchildren in Texas, to whom he explained his project and asked them what was "neat" about their town or state. To Jordan's delight, several students sent responses, which he included in his oral report to his class.[2]

■   ■   ■

In New York City, 125 "at-risk" students were given home computers and on-line hookups. Positive outcomes included: withdrawn students conversing on-line, substitution of Internet research for television viewing, and higher enrollment in college preparatory courses.[3]

■   ■   ■

Anyone who assumes that being connected to the Internet*—or any other information source—automatically assures learning is either a fool or a salesman. (This includes politicians, who, like most of us, may

---
* The term "Internet" is used here to denote any on-line communication system or network; the "Web" refers specifically to the World Wide Web.

be a little of both.) Anyone who believes this invention can single-handedly make dummies of the next generation is equally in error. If used thoughtfully, it can be useful for students who are mature enough, or sufficiently well supervised, to eschew the trivia in favor of content. But turning children or adolescents loose with a multiple personality that has barely entered its own adolescence can be risky. Carol Baroudi, one of the authors of the ubiquitous *Internet for Dummies*,[4] states firmly that children below age seven should not have unsupervised computer time. She considers eleven an optimal age for introduction to electronic communications.

The Internet offers two basic educational uses. The first is finding information, by either searching documents "published" on the Web or receiving information through electronic mail (e-mail). The second is sending information or messages, again through "publishing" on a structured Web page or on-line information source, or through informal correspondence. Both uses have advantages, and both have problems.

New Communications: New Challenges

Telecommunications come with built-in challenges. They have tended to impose one language (English) on multinational correspondence, even though the Internet is a democratic forum. So democratic, in fact, that everyone's opinion has equal weight, from seven-year-olds to psychotics to Nobel laureates. Uncritical consumers are ripe victims for innuendo, inaccuracy, and invective. No authority "fact-checks" the information.

A special difficulty—or benefit, depending on your point of view—is its "untidiness," since links have no predetermined organzation. "It's as if the Library of Congress exploded in midair . . . and we haven't arrived yet to sort out the mess," a professional librarian mused. A frustrated businessman commented that his own clicking on the Web reminded him of "a lab rat clicking for more drugs."

Like much of the contemporary social scene, connections abound but are largely meaningless and impermanent, risking a superficial attitude toward research. Plagiarism is more tempting than ever, and harder to monitor. Nevertheless students by middle-school age can profitably learn to use on-line research sources *in addition to* standard texts. One of the few studies looking at this issue gave a "cautious endorsement of on-line learning" with nine- and eleven-year-olds in seven cities. All used printed materials, computer data bases, and CD-ROM encyclopedias, but half the students also used an on-line educational service and the Internet. Researchers felt the on-line group was better at stating different points of view, synthesizing research, and presenting the broad issue. Unfortunately, this study is seriously flawed by the fact that the on-line group was composed of teachers who volunteered—biasing it in favor of more skill and enthusiasm.[5] More research with better controls would be a welcome development.

Naive Excitement vs. Information Literacy

> *"There's all this emphasis on kids having all this information at their fingertips, with this blind naive assumption that they'll know what to do with it."*
>
> High-school teacher, New York

Neophytes in the high-tech world often mistake *downloading* for *thinking*. Not long ago I was interviewed by a reporter who was writing a piece on computers in the schools for a large national newsmagazine. He had just returned from a visit to a high-school classroom where a combined English and history class was making posters on the environment with the help of the World Wide Web. From his comments, it was obvious this fellow had been "snowed" by the technology.

"You should have seen these kids!" he virtually bubbled. "This one pair pulls up a whole page of pictures and information on endangered seals—they even had pictures of bloody cubs! The kids were so turned on—man, was it ever powerful!"

At the risk of seeming hard-hearted I had to ask, "Did their teacher show them how to evaluate the source of this information? Did he insist they gather alternative viewpoints to compare and contrast? How much critical thinking was being taught or required? These are *high-*

school students in an English class; were they being asked to write about the topic or simply paste together a poster? Sorry, but this activity (absent the bloody cubs) is more appropriate for eight-year-olds."

The gentleman acknowledged he had failed to be a critical observer. "I guess I should have thought of that. But this stuff is so visually powerful, it's easy to accept it uncritically."

Indeed.

At this writing, only one World Wide Web is available to students searching for information, and it is increasingly dominated by those organizations with the means to purchase links which will subtly guide consumers toward their products or ideas. For example, if a student is looking up the Zambezi River (the key term is called the "descriptor"), the "search engine" (information-gathering device) might send him to the advertising page of an adventure-travel company. While this trend is lamentable in many ways, and we may hope for a noncommercial alternative, it does offer opportunities for working with young people on "information literacy": critical analysis in evaluating sources of information. Students must learn to ask questions to *distinguish information from opinion or propaganda.*

BECOMING AN "INFO-TECTIVE"

How do we teach kids this skill? Here are some guidelines:

1. Who provided this information? Why?

2. Is someone trying to sell us a product or a point of view?

3. How is the source coded (e.g., ".com" = commercial; ".gov" = government; ".edu" = educational institution, ".org" = nonprofit organization, ".mil" = military, etc.)? How might this influence our evaluation of its accuracy? Can we assume that everything from an educational institution, for example, is necessarily true? How about from a government source?

4. What possible biases may be detected here (e.g., an organization dedicated to environmental protection or a business selling a product)?

5. If quotes or data are provided, are they appropriately referenced?

6. How can we find other information with which to compare and evaluate accuracy (e.g., call sources, check authorized print sources)?

7. Does this information represent theory or evidence? What is the difference between these terms? How can we distinguish one from an-

other? (Even undergraduate university students in the United States have difficulty with this question.)

8. Why might some sources be more accurate than others (e.g., many professional journals are "vetted" or reviewed by experts before publication)?

9. How do the visuals influence the way we receive this information? Is emotion a part of the design? Are sound effects intended to influence our thinking?

10. Do the visuals and the text convey the same message?

With excellent guidance, students even as young as eight can begin to be critical consumers of information.

Media Literacy: A "Critical Lens"

"Since negotiations with media construct our reality, our task must be to give students the skills to analyze those images which lead to ignorance and access and produce that which leads to knowledge."
Bob McCannon, Director of the New Mexico Media Literacy Project

Bob McCannon, director of the New Mexico Media Literacy Project, teaches young people to analyze media messages rather than simply accept them at face value. Across media, he points out, "fact" is increasingly mixed with opinion, with fiction, or with outright marketing. He maintains we must awaken youngsters' critical faculties beyond the simplistic stories and images so prevalent today.

One way is to discuss openly the power of technologies to manipulate thought. Through weighing the advantages, disadvantages, and biases of digital technology against other media, young people will have a better chance of becoming selective consumers rather than digital drones. Gloria DeGaetano, coauthor of *Screen Smarts*,[6] suggests it is never too early to start discussing visual messages. She believes if families regularly evaluate all their media use, children can be inoculated against mindlesssness. She suggests these criteria:

Frequency: How much time do we spend in front of the screen, and how much does screen time subtract from other family activities?

Content: What do we watch and who makes the decisions?
Discussion: Do we regularly talk about and evaluate what we watch?

One other avenue to greater media literacy is having kids create their own multimedia productions. Putting them in the producer's seat—with the help of a knowledgeable coach—enables them to grasp the power of the message inherent in many types of media.

Electronic Communication: My Best Friend

As we saw in Chapter 6, on-line communication may substitute for face-to-face social interactions. Even the handy practice of wiring educational institutions for an *intranet,* through which students, faculty, and sometimes parents at home can communicate in-house, risks this outcome. In one such high school I observed several lonely postings made during the hours on a Saturday night when many teens are (or perhaps would like to be) socializing firsthand with others. Even at the university level, students spend more and more time on-line in their rooms, and student lounges formerly used for "bull sessions" are being carved up into depersonalized computer stations. At Vassar College, in-house communicators are known only by nicknames, and many students spend weekend evenings alone, broadcasting anonymously to anonymous others.

"After a while, it starts to be really unfulfilling," commented one student. "You learn how much of a difference it makes to see someone in person and actually talk to them."[7]

Unless all our assumptions about human nature are incorrect, the novelty of decontextualized relationships will soon diminish. Hopefully, the traditional face-to-face rendezvous will not go the way of other civilities in the contemporary social scene. For those students who are reluctant social learners, however, the situation is troubling.

Bob Matsuoka of the Dalton School in New York City, who has worked with such systems for over fifteen years, recommends four general principles to keep the "virtual school" from subverting the aims of the human one.

1. *Identity: Linking the User to the Community.* Users retain their own names, though their identity (e.g., shy vs.outspoken) may change on-line. Thus everyone is personally accountable to the community for his or her actions.

2. *Relevancy: Building on Local Content.* Matsuoka believes in the 80/20 rule, that is, 80 percent of the content and communication takes place face-to-face between people within the same physical workspace—students, teachers, administrators; 20 percent can then be on-line.

3. *Proximity: Matching Virtual With Real.* On-line contact is reinforced with face-to-face contact, so virtual communication does not replace face-to-face interaction.

4. *Accessibility: The System Is Easily Usable.* The network is set up so people can get on-line easily and workstations are readily available.[8]

On-Line Ambassadors: Good and Bad

"Hi, Kai, Marek and Margaret
"Thank you for responding to my message and telling me what biome your school is in. Could you also let me know what the dominate plants and animals are in your area. [My school] is next to the ocean near Cape Cod in Massachusetts. Although we are in a biome called Middle Latitute Deciduous Forest we enjoy a moderation of our temperature extremes because we are in a maritime environment. We also have a Web page if you would like to learn more about what we do in marine science. Hope to hear from you."
David, middle-school student, Massachusetts, to students in Colorado via e-mail

"Greetings from Eno, Finland! We are building a Webpage about traditional folk music from different schools. . . . At the moment we've received music from Croatia, Czech Republic, Japan, South Korea, and USA. I know your culture is rich when it comes to traditional folk music. So if you have a possibility to play or sing and record some traditional folk music and send a cassette to us, we would be very happy."
Internet posting, April 1997

"It takes a whole lot more work to actually stand back and let students learn on their own, and that's true of networks. . . . You need something more than proximity and ability to communicate. You need to have goals, purpose, and organization, . . . educational support and technical support."

Margaret Riel, Internet teacher-educator

On-line distance communication among students is a powerful educational tool when used well. Unfortunately, it can also be an excuse for nonsense and worse. At a workshop, "Using Computers to Teach Problem-Solving," the leader (who justified most of his recommendations with the phrases, "It's neat because it's electronic," and "You've got to meet them where they're at" [sic]) extolled the virtues of communication with students from other countries to encourage hands-on problem-solving. His students in the United States, communicating with counterparts in Russia, occupied a section of the international ether to discuss the following "meaningful" problems:

    1. How to get the bubble gum, which you were not allowed to chew, out of your hair.

    2. How to get out of playing with a younger brother or sister.

    3. How to get a raise in your allowance without having to do any extra chores.

I am aware that "authenticity" is currently a big buzzword, but surely it can be carried too far (like to Russia?).

It seems reasonable to wait until youngsters can conceptually grasp cultural differences and realize the global import of such conversations. Even young teens require background teaching and discussion before pursuing such an activity (e.g., Where is Russia? What does life in Russia look/feel like? How is their history different from ours? What is really on Russian students' minds? What can we learn from them that might be important to our country, or what can we share that might be important to them? How can we phrase our questions meaningfully and tactfully?).

Teacher educator Margaret Riel (who is employed by one of the large telecommunications companies) reports on successful international "Learning Circles," where students work under trained teachers to discuss problems and interests. Each class picks a topic that fits with the curriculum and then researches, analyzes, and reports on it in written form to groups in other countries. For example, students in India missed their annual class camping trip because of political unrest, so they developed a virtual trip that included native animals, local parks, and environmental threats to wildlife. Students in Saudi Arabia wrote about their reaction to having their country bombed. Electronic messages from students in South Australia explored aboriginal cave art and studies of the southern hemisphere. Students in France wrote for information on the textile industry in other countries. Riel, as a telecommunications spokesperson, claims that by struggling to communicate ideas effectively to others and receiving their critical feedback, students' writing and grammar skills improved more than on standard class assignments.[9]

If homes are wired for the Internet, parents can supplement the school's efforts. Unfortunately, many schools—through inadequate teacher preparation or lack of staff—are still allowing youngsters to surf aimlessly, but you can teach proper procedures at home. Moreover, many Web sites provide useful information on educationally worthwhile sources and activities. Home schoolers and even veteran teachers reach out of their isolated classrooms to exchange curriculum ideas, lesson plans, teaching tips, and generalized support with peers all over the world.

Swimming in the Info-Sea

Valuable suggestions for parents and teachers come from Jamie McKenzie, a longtime enthusiast who left a superintendent's job to become technology coordinator of the Bellingham, Washington, public schools. He soon discovered that turning a school district into a technologically literate community is a long-term (minimum five years), expensive (a $6 million bond issue just for starters), and sometimes frustrating process. He still likes the Internet, but he terms it "the greatest yard sale of information in human history. Poorly organized and dominated by amateurs, hucksters, and marketing gurus, the net offers info-glut, info-garbage, and info-tactics. Schools that plunge students into this info-sea with nothing but mythical or metaphorical surfboards are courting disillusionment, chaos, and what beach folk call 'wipe-out!' " Before schools invest millions of dollars to provide access, he recommends, they would be wise to stop and ask, "Why?"

A survey McKenzie conducted demonstrates the gap between potential and current reality: Most output by students reveals little of interest. Content is amazingly trivial; only 10 percent of sites advertised as being "curriculum-rich" actually are. Students surfing on their own—at home or at school—waste about 95 percent of their time. But McKenzie continues searching for useful models. In one, his students developed a series of "virtual museums" showcasing such topics as "Ellis Island," which featured diversity, national origin, and immigration history of students' own families. Students continue to "curate" their museum sites, keeping them up to date and responding to queries from interested "visitors."

McKenzie reiterates that teaching students to be critical consumers of this glut of information means insisting they constantly probe for meaning. His students work in teams following a format designed to teach specific skills, with the goal being *insight*. Here are the steps they follow:

1. Questioning
2. Planning
3. Gathering
4. Sorting and sifting
5. Synthesizing
6. Evaluating
7. Reporting

Questioning: Most research simply requires students to be "word movers," for example, finding information on Dolly Madison and cutting and pasting it into a report. McKenzie suggests deeper research questions: e.g., How might we restore the salmon harvest? Which New England city should our family move to and why?

Planning: Where can we find the best information most efficiently? How will we divide responsibility? How will we sort and store findings (e.g., data base, word-processing file)?

Gathering: Only relevant information is used. Students must structure findings as they gather them (e.g., summarize and enter in word-processing file). Students must decide whether information will be gathered on-line, from CD-ROMs, or from books or journals.

Sorting and Sifting: Teams scan and organize data according to its usefulness.

Synthesizing: Students analyze findings and select the most important points; they draw relevant conclusions.

Evaluating: Students survey the entire project and decide whether more research is needed. They share and discuss new insights among team members.

Reporting: Teams decide on the most effective means to present their findings (e.g., written report, multimedia presentation).[10]

Bar the Gates When Necessary

Most adults are aware by now that a great deal of inappropriate material is available on the Internet. Teen "chat rooms," especially, where youngsters exchange information, comments, and jokes, may contain smutty, degrading, scary, or biased content. One user likened it to dropping your child off alone in a "bad neighborhood."

On the other hand, Sherry Turkle points out that parents may have a tendency to displace their own fears about teen development onto the Internet. Parental understanding, firm rules, and plenty of conversation about controversial topics are the recipe for a child who ultimately becomes a self-disciplined participant.[11]

Guidelines for Internet Use: (Post Near Computer at Home or School)

&. Give out no personal information about yourself or anyone else to people you don't know—includes full name, hometown, e-mail or postal address, phone number, credit card numbers, hobbies, interests, etc.

&. Be careful that what is "published" contains no names, photos, or personal information that should not be made available to the general public.

❧ No visits to general-interest chat rooms. Family visits to specific interests (e.g., collie fanciers, rock climbers, stamp collectors).

❧ Observe time limits. Twenty minutes should be enough to collect information and not offer temptation to wander.

Parents or teachers will preview sites and post a list of appropriate ones. If you wish, ask your server how to obtain control systems that can block inappropriate material. Make children a part of this decision, however, since youngsters are notoriously good at hacking their way through roadblocks if they feel something is "forbidden." With sufficiently close communication, you can learn to trust each other's judgment.

On-Line Tips From the Experts

❧ Preview sites and select or download those relevant to the assignment. At home, parents can help children with the process of choosing relevant sites.

❧ For elementary-age children, consider investing in software that can simulate use of the Web with preselected sites; although children are not actually on-line, the experience is virtually (oops!) identical.

❧ Help students ask good questions to conduct a productive search and decide on one or two relevant words (descriptors) to narrow the topic.

❧ If your school can afford it, the most effective way to demonstrate on-line research skills for the entire class is with a large overhead display.

❧ Investigate and experiment with the various logic systems (e.g., Boolean logic) used in different search engines. Using categorization skills and identification of main and subordinate ideas, this activity provides good mental exercise for growing minds (e.g., "python *but not* Monty"). The very processs of nesting files and making a folder for each separate topic can also teach categorization and need for precise language use.

❧ Make sure kids read the words rather than simply flipping through the pictures. Require a record of which sites were visited, with critical evaluation of the value of each. Insist on documentation of sources, just as with text material.

❧ Keep abreast of current copyright laws and make clear your expectations for appropriate referencing of sources.

• Advise young people of the hazards of inappropriate e-mail postings. Two boys in a Missouri high school sent a threatening message one morning to the president at the White House. That afternoon, the Secret Service had the boys in custody.

• Teach children that the rule "be careful when you talk to strangers" still holds true in unsupervised cyberspace.

Having laid this groundwork, it is time now to return to a consideration of what, specifically, works and doesn't work for students who are of an age to profit from a wide variety of technology applications.

Primary Years: Good Beginnings

"No, no, a thousand times no. Please dismiss any notion of getting second graders ready for life. . . . Ms. Class entreats you to nurture the children as children, not as miniature stockbrokers and bankers. Life is today, not tomorrow. Primary teachers should concern themselves not with good results but with good beginnings."

Susan Ohanian in *Ask Ms. Class*[12]

"If you're really careful, computers and calculators can help with beginning reading, writing, and math."

Kay Dunlop, first-grade teacher, Shaker Heights, Ohio

If parents or teachers are determined to use computers with this age group, they must choose carefully. Because the brain has a particularly sensitive window of development around ages five to seven, digital forays should be carefully planned.

The "Five to Seven Year Shift"

"Our lower-school teachers feel the computer is a distraction. Kids need more concrete experiences. They can do spreadsheets, with the help of an adult, and hypercard, but they'd be better off fooling around with a piano."

George Burns, Technology Director, Bank Street School, New York

Have you ever noticed the vast differences between most five- and most seven-year-olds? The pronounced changes that take place in the brain around the start of formal schooling are commonly termed the "five to seven year shift." The brain is able to reason more abstractly, outgrow most "stimulus-bound" behavior, understand and enjoy mastering new symbol systems such as written words, math equations, or, finally, computer applications. Contrary to some adult expectations, however, this development doesn't magically arrive with a birthday. Moreover, even a seven-year-old brain still has a long way to go in development of control centers, higher-level association areas, and the important membrane that links the right and left hemispheres for adult attention, memory, abstract creativity and problem-solving.

Many children aged six and seven still tend to focus on one cognitive activity at a time; they may read words out loud without simultaneously thinking about the overall meaning or may have trouble relating numerical equations to real-life problems ("story problems"). Likewise, while they can learn (or figure out) new computer applications, they may be so focused on the mechanics that they fail to learn the desired content.

Even older children may forget the task at hand when confronted by computers. An Internet posting by teacher Tom Woods illustrates how gadgetry fascination is often too much, especially for reluctant readers (who may have a "developmental lag" in language).

"I was recently working with a fourth-grade student who reads at the second-grade level," Woods relates. "I started her out with a marvelous interactive fiction story on the Web called 'The Neverending Tale.' The use of the computer was highly motivating. The student could choose her own pathway through the story and even respond, if she wished, by contributing to the story herself. I found myself getting very frustrated, however, because I could not control where the student went. She was more intent on clicking buttons and highlighting text than she was on actually reading, which is what I wanted her to do. I reverted to more conventional reading material."[13]

Some technophiles would argue that the teacher should respect this child's need to explore; they would find the pathway she crafted more "authentic" because it represented her interests. In this view, her teacher should let her point and click to her heart's content, dropping his own selfish (and obviously verbocentric and controlling) agendas. I vote with Tom Woods, however, who believes his job is to teach this child to read.

Celeste Oakes, first-grade teacher in Henderson, Nevada, stoutly defends the value of two-way telecommunications for her language arts class. "I try to immerse beginning readers and writers in language experiences of all kinds," she says. For Oakes's students, electronic communication is only a small part of a rich mix. With access to only one computer, she started by having selected outside correspondents send messages to the class. Many students were eager to attempt reading the messages themselves, and they helped compose responses as Celeste typed them. As they connected with "key pals" (electronic pen pals) in Alaska, they practiced asking good questions and finding information off-line. They began seeking information about Alaska on an "Ask the Scientist" service, collecting data for graphing activities, and practicing hands-on map skills. Finally, they were able to connect to the computer aboard the space shuttle while it was in orbit, reading daily postings and even asking a question of the astronauts. This teacher gives the new technology high marks for motivating and informing her students. "They have taught me that the only limitations to using telecommunications with young students are those we impose ourselves by failing to empower them," she concludes.[14]

Another example comes from a recent study, in which a specially designed package helped six-year-olds improve "phonological awareness," a prerequisite for reading success. Not only did the children learn to discriminate and sequence the sounds in words, but they also significantly improved in word-reading ability over a comparable group using non-language computer activities.[15] We should keep a close eye out for other developments of this type.

Brain-Appropriate Technology for Elementary-Aged Children

"The tulips emerged through the ground today—add that to the data base!"

Eight-year-old student, St. Louis, Missouri

I have traveled to another technology conference to learn about new methods for teaching with computers, and I am feeling discouraged. In the past two days I have quickly outgrown my initial excitement over presentation software (pedantic outlines look alike—no matter how much they pulsate) and multimedia reports rich with other people's clips and impoverished of language and originality. I am tired of educators who are so dazzled by stamped-on glitz that they lose all critical faculties. I have just come from a talk by two peppy elementary school teachers who explain how to "Build Character with Technology" by creating T-shirt decals printed with uplifting slogans. I am wandering the halls, looking for a session that will answer the question I have just scrawled in the margin of my notes:

"How much intellectual rigor must we sacrifice in order to get kids 'motivated'?"

At this point some benign digital fate leads me to Bob Coulter, who teaches eight-year-olds at the Forsythe Elementary School in St. Louis, Missouri. He actually started his session—to my surprised delight—by discussing the rationale, developmental goals, and critical assessment of technology use in his classroom. Here is a teacher clearly committed to the computer as a vehicle for intellectual challenge as well as for teaching the "basics." In partnership with Joe Walters of TERC (Technology Education and Research Centers) in Boston, Coulter engages his students in Internet projects because he finds that communicating with an external audience "pushes them to think more deeply."

TERC is a pioneer, and Coulter's students use telecommunications for projects spanning the curriculum. One that captured my fancy was a global study of wildlife migration called "Journey North." As spring approaches, students begin tracking the visible signs (e.g., tulips emerging or birds coming to the feeder) and entering them into a global data base; the information is transferred to a computerized world map which graphically displays the season's progress north from the equator as students all over the world enter their sightings. They practice real-life application of geography skills as they record the progress of the bald eagle by latitude and longitude and transfer it to a paper map in the classroom; they also make predictions about weather and length of day. Research takes them to the library as they consult text sources for information on animal species and meteorology. They read both on- and off-line, integrate math and arts projects such as illustrating their maps. They also "talk" on-line with real scientists, of whom they are encouraged to ask intelligent questions.

Needless to say, Coulter's good results didn't come about simply by getting his classroom "connected." When planning units of study, he follows certain important steps:

1. Developing a clear purpose that fits the curriculum
2. Determining what is appropriate for the age group
3. Planning use of a wide variety of supporting materials
4. Working out the logistics of scheduling time for the on-line and classroom activities

He is also careful to observe that his students continue to do well on standardized achievement tests.

Coulter is sufficiently objective to admit that such units are never free of problems. Moreover, he says that trying to graft this type of learning onto a "drill-and-kill" curriculum is doomed to fail. In his classroom, students use the computer to construct knowledge; they see it "as an integral tool for study, used in conjunction with other resources"—not the least of which, I might add, is a hardworking and talented teacher who understands the special needs of elementary-age students.

Ages Eight to Ten: Learning From Many Technologies

"Why are we doing things on computers that we don't need to do on computers? We have to simulate a trip to Africa, but we don't have to simulate playing an African game that involves moving stones around in a certain way. It's scary to me that some kids prefer the simulated on-line game to the real one with the real stones."

Eric Robertson, technology consultant, Minnetonka, Minnesota

"The kids got more excited about the audio and the little buttons than about what I wanted them to be excited about."

Fourth-grade teacher, La Crosse, Wisconsin

Children aged eight to ten are still concrete and literal thinkers: they love mastering routines, data, rules, order, and demonstrating their competency. Generally industrious and product-oriented, they enjoy completing long-term assignments and showing off finished work. Intensely curious, they like to investigate topics such as animals or the environment. By age ten they are generally competent with concrete learning (e.g., mechanics of reading, writing, and math) and need to branch out. This seems an appropriate time for multimedia applications, research skills, and manipulating data bases or spreadsheets. It is also a good time for quality software to review the basics and fill in missing pieces, such as practicing spelling patterns and math "facts." Both at school and at home, preteens still need plenty of adult scaffolding.

Intensely interested in mastering information, they tend to enjoy learning aids such as digitized encyclopedias or guided Internet searches—which may be counterproductive if the reading level is too frustrating. They take special pleasure in research that has value in the eyes of adults and/or some practical use in the real world.

With long-range neural circuits still maturing, elementary-level students must work hard on cross-modal linkages (e.g., imagining visuals while reading a text, focusing on text screens when there are buttons to click on), reasoning about several things at one time (e.g., remembering what you're writing about while struggling to keep your fingers on the correct home keys), and understanding things from different perspectives (e.g., why your mom won't buy you that video game). They are easily distracted from academic tasks by enticing visuals or silliness in software, and they cannot be expected to plan and execute long-range projects without support. They may still be quite hazy on abstract categories, such as the difference among cities, states, countries, and continents; the magnitude of distance around the globe; or cultural differences among countries.

Because most take readily to technology routines, we may overestimate how much they are actually getting from them. Good learning activities for elementary students should include the following: a large component of real-life experience, plenty of integration across learning modes (e.g., text sources, hands-on activities, music, writing, and visual arts), checks on comprehension and use of time, and structured follow-up. Here is a small sampling of interesting projects:

    ❧ Eight- and nine-year-olds followed on-line a real-life recapitulation of Amelia Earhart's flight as part of a study of heroes. They also made a large classroom map of her trip, read related books, and wrote stories about possible reasons for her disappearance.

    ❧ Beginning Spanish students entered selected Spanish-language Web sites, experimented with translation programs, and used vocabulary-building software.

    ❧ One family introduced their ten-year-old daughter to the spreadsheet program by which they keep their tax records. They taught her how to keep track of her allowance by categorizing and entering her expenses. She enjoyed the "grown-up" feeling of mastering an adult skill as well as the improvement in her math grades.

    ❧ Students worldwide participate in "author chats" during on-line interviews with favorite authors. The children type in their questions, and the author attempts to answer as many as possible in a limited time. Needless to say, these interchanges lack something of the personal touch and communication gets somewhat disjointed with thousands of excited kids simultaneously trying to write to one person, but teachers report they spur students' interest in reading. I would like, however, to see more preteaching and screening of questions ("What is the hardest thing about being an author?" vs. "What color is your dog?") before students go on-line.

    ❧ Peggy Oglesby, special education teacher in Anderson, Indiana, took a group of enthusiastic students on a virtual field trip into space for a unit on space travel. They viewed satellite pictures and did research on planets. Oglesby says the added visual information helps the learning disabled grasp concepts more readily than text.

    ❧ Jan Frank, of Bellingham, Washington, took nine- and ten-year-olds on a similar "trip" to "Island Regions of the World." They visited Tahiti and developed original travel brochures. This type of assignment is interesting for students of this age (at least until the novelty wears off) and is educationally useful as long as the teacher sets clear standards for quality and some objective means of assessing learning.

    ❧ Youngsters help their families decide on the destination for trips or outings by making up sample travel brochures from selected information sources. In some cases, children have collected useful data to help with a family move.

🐾 One mom who was learning to use a data base program for her Christmas card list worked along with her daughter to develop a personal address book and enter current data on the girl's friends such as address, hobbies, pets, birthdays, and favorite movies. They had some fun, some major frustrations, and learned some ancillary math skills as they finally triumphed in printing properly sized mailing labels for the daughter's birthday party invitations.

🐾 Some elementary-age children enjoy preparing a regular family newsletter (possibly using desktop publishing software) to be delivered electronically or in hard copy to grandparents or other relatives.

🐾 A technologically adept father told me he had programmed a small computer on top of the television set with challenging math puzzlers and hooked it up so that his son couldn't turn on the TV until a certain number of problems were done. Soon the son began to prefer doing the problems to watching TV.

🐾 Another dad and his seven-year-old daughter played chess together against the computer. "Occasionally, we won!" he beamed.

How Do They Learn to Use It?

"Sometimes we feel we've gone real slow, not having technology available as fast as we should. But we really don't want to 'teach technology'—we want to integrate it into the curriculum that's there. I don't like a lot of busywork and I don't want to see it on the computer."

George Cannon, elementary school principal, Shaker Heights, Ohio

Should we offer direct instruction in computer skills? One point of view insists that "computer lessons" are unnecessary, since children of this age are still experts at playful exploration and old hands at the necessary problem-solving skills. Moreover, many educators object to the decontextualized drills that often accompany "computer lessons." Thus many parents and teachers let the kids learn the technology through demonstration, coaching, and independent exploration. Of course, one of the inevitable thrills is periodic system failure, so plenty of technical assistance is necessary.

For this reason and because some educators believe students will not learn either the proper or most efficient use of applications unless they are directly taught, some schools hire a computer specialist and schedule "computer" as a separate class with a sequential curriculum. Some parents also send children to structured computer lessons. Both sides believe their course is the correct one; to my knowledge we have no research confirming the value of one approach or another. Certainly, if "computer" is taught as a separate subject, it should be done in close collaboration with the classroom teacher and linked to a curriculum.

Brookwood Elementary in Grand Rapids, Michigan, provides direct instruction in word processing, spreadsheets, data bases, desktop publishing, and other applications; like many schools, it has listed a comprehensive set of technology skills and measurable outcomes as students pass from grade to grade.

One of the nicest outcomes of the entire technological revolution has been to see children seriously engaged in teaching adults to use the technology with which their generation seems so attuned. The brain is ever capable of learning new things—including broader conceptions of "education" and lifelong cultivation of the playfulness and curiosity which fuel its own continuing growth!

LOGO and Microworlds

> "The child, even at preschool ages, is in control. . . . And in teaching the computer how to think, children embark on an exploration about how they themselves think. The experience can be heady: Thinking about thinking turns the child into an epistemologist, an experience not even shared by most adults."
>
> Seymour Papert [16]

An entirely different approach to children's computer use is found in the philosophical stance of Seymour Papert's LOGO, which is *programmable,* as opposed to *direct-manipulation,* software. Papert holds that children's best learning comes from open-ended "play" in programming the computer, which he calls the "Children's Machine." Rather than manipulating a program designed by someone else, the child assumes full control.

Overall research on LOGO is inconclusive, and generally more negative than positive as to learning outcomes. Yet because the theory behind LOGO runs so contrary to most institutional conceptions about how children should learn, it has rarely been implemented as Papert intended. Turning children loose to "construct knowledge" without direct instruction and being patient until that event occurs doesn't fit very well into educators' plan books—or perhaps into reality. "But nothing can be more absurd than an experiment in which computers are placed in a classroom where nothing else is changed. The entire point . . . is that the computers serve best when they allow everything to change," argue LOGO supporters.[17]

In her book delightfully entitled *Minds in Play*, Yasmin Kafai describes a long-term study in an inner-city magnet school in Boston as sixteen nine- and ten-year-olds worked in their math class one hour a day for six months designing a video game to teach fractions to younger students.[18] First they were asked to imagine, plan, design, and develop a game scenario (one example was an adventure in which the hero had to solve fraction problems to avoid being "sent flying to the underworld"), keeping a daily journal of their progress. Then each child spent approximately ninety-two hours programming it in LOGO. Next they each developed a marketing package, complete with ads and attractive packaging.

While most of Kafai's students thoroughly enjoyed the experience and produced some original and fanciful programs, they predictably tended to focus more on the visual design and graphics than on the math. In fact, they ended up learning less about fractions than a control group in another classroom where children spent their time using LOGO to design instructional software rather than a video game.

LOGO has spawned not only a corps of enthusiastic acolytes, but also an entire family of software and related activities (e.g., Lego-LOGO), and is still budding with innovative offshoots. The aquatic "Microworld" which we saw in Chapter 6 is only one example of programmable environments where youngsters "construct" rules about complex topics such as systems theory. Work continues at MIT, where innovators like Mitchell Resnick continue to develop "objects to think with" such as small programmable plastic "bricks" which can be assembled to create inventions, robots, or self-propelled toy vehicles.

A cadre of dedicated teachers endorses this approach to learning. Marian Rosen, who heads the technology program at Conway School in St. Louis, Missouri, starts children on simple programming in kindergarten. By age ten or eleven, working in pairs, they create, build, and program their own Lego constructions complete with battery packs, sensors, plastic studs, gears, axles, and miscellaneous "junk."

"In our last session we had a drill, an exercise machine based on a conveyor belt, and an original car wash complete with rotating wheel washers, overhead to-and-fro rag rack, and drying fans. Others accept a challenge such as building a machine that will lift or drag more than thirty pounds or one that can balance on a single wire stretched across the room," she reports.

To accomplish these complex constructions, students must first write many subprograms and combine them sequentially. Even eleven-year-olds still need help, Rosen finds, but they are learning valuable habits of thinking along with math and physics.

Ultimately, "the kids are part of a feedback loop they have created between the [invented] machine and the computer. To be successful at this kind of programming, students have to program their ideas in meaningful chunks. . . . That is a wonderful arena for modeling very important ideas about modular thinking."[19]

Technology and the Middle-School Brain

The image is a little unclear, but the twelve-year-olds surrounding the computer don't complain. They are too busy following the action on the screen where a disheveled-looking young man in bicycling clothes stands amidst a jungle talking earnestly with someone in a bush jacket who appears to be a scientist. They are conversing about some sort of ancient ruin nearby.

One of the students giggles, pokes another, and attempts a whispered comment, but he is rapidly silenced.

"Shush, Damon. Don't be such a jerk. We can't hear!" hisses his neighbor.

What has inspired such serious academic purpose among these kids? They and their teacher are involved in directing (along with others around the globe) a three-month bicycle expedition, manned by a team of cyclists and scientists, through the jungles of Central America in search of lost Mayan civilizations. At the moment, they are debating the possibility of sending the team through a difficult, untraveled jungle track to a special site. How fast can they ride? How far? What obstacles will they encounter? What are the odds of success? What plans must be made?

"MayaQuest" utilizes on-line and satellite phone communications to establish real-time links between students around the world and the adventurers. Because students' votes actually determine the course of the journey, they must problem-solve right along with the scientists. To acquire the necessary knowledge, the class has plunged into a variety of topics: history, archaeology, visual arts, math (e.g., Mayans calculated in base 20), science of flora and fauna, Mayan poetry, building a miniature rain forest, reading the daily journals of the adventurers, researching, developing theories, and debating about why the civilization collapsed. Meanwhile, they are learning teamwork as well as academic skills. Teachers and students are enthusiastic about such possibilities for enhancing classroom work through global adventure.

Technological "Ramps"[20] From Concrete to Abstract Thinking

> *"The goal of computer software should be to help students extend what they know from familiar, concrete contexts to less familiar, abstract contexts by cybernetically linking more familiar representations to less familiar ones."*
>
> James J. Kaput in *Software Goes to School*[21]

Middle school brains are particularly suited for broader experiences.

Starting around age ten new connections prime the brain for more complex thinking. A spurt in frontal areas helps link thought and action, inhibit impulsive responses, facilitate planning ahead, manage motivation, and understand things from a more global perspective. Most youngsters also improve intermodal processing (i.e., being able to combine senses effortlessly),[22] so they can learn content without being quite so distracted by the mechanics of the machine or the software (e.g., reading from a screen and taking notes). In the face of powerful visual displays, however, even adults may have trouble holding a question in mind or resisting an alluring digression.

The intellectual job of the middle-school brain is to start divorcing itself from total dependence on concrete experience, learn to reason about things that can't be seen, touched, or physically manipulated (e.g., a metaphor, a scientific hypothesis, concepts of ratio, proportion, and probability), and deal with abstract symbol systems (e.g., rules of grammar, algebraic formulas). Note, please, that I say "start," as this process takes a number of years. Well-designed technology can help by providing cognitive "ramps" from the concrete to the abstract. "Intelligent tutors" may scaffold understanding in mathematical and scientific principles that are hard to simulate in real life. Cognitive scientist David Perkins and his group in Boston are developing open-ended software for older students exploring difficult notions such as proportion, velocity, volume, and mass, as well as geometric theorems. Teachers and students in Scotland, Norway, and Australia have found these applications productive. "With good pedagogy as the guiding goal," the researchers report, "technologies can be employed selectively to . . . present dynamic visual models of key ideas, to help students gather and display data, to allow them to construct and manipulate screen 'objects' such as graphs or geometric figures, and to give teachers and researchers a window on students' thinking and learning."[23] This latter point is one too infrequently mentioned, since computer use should ultimately provide better understanding of our own learning processes.

The usual caveats apply. Even most high-schoolers are not ready to be plunged totally into virtual learning environments; they still need real-life relevance and physical experience. Learning biology or physics only from a screen might even be dangerous. Neuropsychologist Sid

Segalowitz of Ontario's Brock University, who is enthusiastic about computer applications for young adolescents, explains that because this is the time when frontal lobe maturation is peaking, we must be careful about *overdeveloping cognitive functions at the expense of social behavior.* "A curriculum that divorces cognitive content from the appropriate affective [emotional] load is dangerous business," he reminds us. Witness the aggressive, antisocial statements by computer-intensive people on the Internet.[24]

For teen-aged students, structured opportunities for cooperative group work are especially important. Like all of us, they learn better when they feel some practical purpose or personal relevance in the material. Yet because brain development gives them a more abstract "window on the world," they can also be intrigued by topics transcending their immediate environments and problems to which there is no obvious "right" answer (e.g., discussing the pros and cons of an issue such as whether advertisements should be permitted on the Internet; learning about "media literacy" through examinations of hidden bias in online information sources).

CAUTION: "SCAFFOLDING" STILL NEEDED
Since these youngsters may still be relatively uncritical judges of quality of material, we must teach them to winnow the worthwhile from the foolish. They may tend to put too much faith in anything they see in print or hear from an "authority," so we must teach them to be good, critical questioners.

Some teens still need adult guidance for material they view or download. Offensive or alarming material may cause not only emotional but also cognitive problems. Neuropsychologist Jan van Strien of The Netherlands has shown that hemisphere use is easily altered by negative emotional stimuli, such as unpleasant films or "horrifying" music, which prime the right (more emotional) hemisphere, increasing heart rate and secretion of salivary cortisol (part of the "fight-or-flight" response). On the other hand, nonthreatening verbal tasks prime the left (more logical-linguistic) hemisphere. When academic tasks were given to van Strien's subjects after either positive or negative priming, their hemispheric use and learning strategies were altered, depending on which side had just been stimulated. In other words, students who have recently viewed violent or unpleasant material may have neurophysiological blocks for left-hemisphere tasks such as reading, writing, or math calculation.[25]

"Ramps to the Abstract": Real-Life Applications

Some of the interesting and age-appropriate projects I have come across include:

  ❦ At New York's Mott Hall School for science and math, teams of twelve-year-olds developed independent science projects to form and test a hypothesis related to what they had studied. One group was interested in chemoluminescence, but their experiment ran into problems, and too little information was available to solve them. Finally they located an expert in another state and fired out a desperate query on the Internet. The gentleman took the time to respond in detail, leading them gradually through the steps of the experiment. When, at its conclusion, they discovered that their initial hypothesis had been wrong, they were disheartened—until their new friend informed them that they had behaved exactly as real scientists do.

  ❦ Two brothers living on the East Coast of the United States collaborated with their parents to plan a driving trip for the family through selected national parks. The boys located research and historical information, figured daily mileage, noted potential hazards, listed local wildlife, recommended campsites and nearby restaurants, predicted the probable temperature range, and prepared a booklet of information. The boys learned a great deal and basked in the importance their efforts had in making the trip a success. (Tip: If children use computers for map study, keep a real map and globe nearby.)

  ❦ Ten- and eleven-year-olds took laptop computers outdoors for a geology unit in Kirkwood, Missouri. Having learned to compile data bases, they observed, classified, compared, and contrasted soil types and rock samples and created a hypercard stack. In demonstrating practical application of what they had learned, they had a chance to practice measuring skills and work cooperatively with a partner.

  ❦ At Alexander Dawson School in Boulder, Colorado, middle-school students collaborated via the Internet with the Denver Museum of Natural History in designing a hands-on exhibit on volcanoes and geysers, which drew 10,000 student visitors to the museum. Working in teams, they collected and organized information from a variety of sources, including on-line interviews as far away as Iceland. Armed with this knowledge, they designed and created a plan for the exhibit which they constructed at school with plywood, fiberboard, papier mâché, and random materials including desk seats from their classroom. They produced an accompanying audiotape. When museum personnel complimented the fruits of their labors, the youngsters beamed with pride, and their teacher suspects this lesson is one they will not soon forget.

❧ At Horace Mann Academic Middle School in San Francisco, California, Chinese-American students communicated around the world in Chinese characters, tutoring on-line pen pals who wanted to learn English. Their English skills improved, as did their appreciation of being bilingual and bicultural.[26]

❧ Students in Bisbee, Arizona, converted their hyperstacks related to curriculum units to videotape to produce programs for a local television station. They learned skills in visual composition, lighting, audio, project management, and interviewing techniques.

❧ Marian Rosen's LOGO-centered building curriculum extends into the middle school. Having mastered machines that combine wheels and axles, pulleys, gears, and inclined planes, "They programmed remote-control cars to go in four directions; mix masters that smash cereals with variable speeds; lifters that raise well over twenty pounds; a ski lift that was a triumph of ingenuity; bouncer cars that reversed directions when their sensors were hit; cable cars suspended on twine and controlled by a joystick made of sensors. Science concepts included friction, feedback, mechanical advantage, gear and pulley ratios, tension, electricity, and design."[27]

❧ The well-known (and heavily funded) "Archaeotype" program at Dalton School in New York City puts students in the role of archaeologists on a dig. They work in teams to access and analyze multiple sources of information (electronic, print, and human), and communicate between classrooms to develop questions and solve problems.

❧ Middle school is an ideal time for virtual field trips and real-life adventures that students follow and participate in on-line. In addition to "MayaQuest," many students around the world follow on-line Project Magellan, a real three-year voyage around the world that replicates Magellan's journey. As part of this virtual adventure they receive raw data from which to draw conclusions: pictures, journals, scientific observations, and direct correspondence from the scientists actually taking the journey.

✒ Thirteen- and fourteen-year-old students in a "gifted" class at Twin Groves Junior High School in Buffalo Grove, Illinois, participated in a Virtual Renaissance. They used an annotated listing of Web links and other resources to create a Web site related to their study of Shakespeare and his times. Students practiced skills of project planning, information retrieval, critical evaluation, documentation of sources, and expository writing, as well as demonstrating their understanding in creative skits and presentations for the class. The study was carefully planned and closely directed by their teachers (who refer to themselves as "coaches") and involved the class with Renaissance art, architecture, drama, law, literature, medicine, styles of dress, music and dance, science and math.

✒ Jack McGarvey's students in Westport, Connecticut, use animation to tell a story without words as they study plot, or to make geometric concepts come alive with lines flying together to form colorful twirling cubes, triangles, and trapezoids.

High School and Beyond

"Once upon a time, college libraries were sacred places for research. But now, as cheap, bright and easy electronic information swirls around a youth culture steeped in entertainment values, it is easy to fear that the very purpose of libraries is being torn asunder. Given the weird mix of amusement and genuinely useful information in the Web, it's a nettlesome call for an educator."

Peter Sacks, college professor and author of *Generation X Goes to College*

While the appropriate degree of electronic immersion of high-school and college students—as in the general culture—is still a hot topic for debate, most people agree that new technologies are an important and valuable adjunct in the education of older students. In my opinion, it is ridiculous to be giving computers to young kids when teens, who can profit both practically and intellectually from their use, lack these resources.

At around age sixteen (with wide variation among individuals) the brain is on its way into adulthood. Although significant developments will continue for some time, students by this age should have a broader perspective and a growing ability to ponder trends, issues, and moral dilemmas. These years represent an ideal time to study the history of science and technology as they affect human cultures. Just as our young people embrace new developments, they also need to consider critically the fact that for every technology we add, something is irrevocably lost. Veteran teachers might delight at the prospect of a multidisciplinary course incorporating such questions as how different media affect thought and societal development, the cultural/economic/political implications of technology use, whether our current technologies amplify or restrict knowledge, and how much virtual life will or should supplant the real thing. These conversations could also be very much at home around a family dinner table where adolescents and adults debate and share generational perspectives.

It is, of course, a mistake to overestimate maturation even in the nominally mature. Students of all ages revert to concrete learning when material is difficult or unfamiliar. Even high-school students may have trouble grasping the meaning of the word "yield" if they memorize it for a vocabulary test, but they will learn it readily enough when they have to take the exam for their driver's license. Thus, computer applications providing ramps between concrete and abstract are still important for this age group.

Many of today's teens are disaffected, bored, and impatient to get out into the real world, often because what has passed for "learning" has been far too abstract, passive, and lacking in perceived relevance. New technologies can provide a welcome change. Nevertheless, these are the years when high standards of understanding and precise thinking within a discipline (e.g., history, literature, the sciences) become increasingly important. Working with Howard Gardner at Harvard, Vera Boix Mansilla has looked at media's tendency to blur the boundaries between what might have happened and what has been invented by a writer or director, so that research dependent on visual media (as in film clips or on-line encyclopedias) may block real understanding. When studying history, for example, "visual representations . . . may 'take us to the scene,' but they tell us little about the broader historical interpretations in which these situations must be inscribed."[28] In other words, a student must study all types of input (including written text) *within a specific discipline* to gain critical understanding.

Here are a few examples in which teachers have tried to stimulate critical understanding:

    ❧ Instead of memorizing a disembodied set of facts, students studying American government, economics, or related subjects join a "Virtual Congress," in which the class assumes the role of U.S. representative from their congressional district, makes decisions, communicates via e-mail with "representatives" in other parts of the country, and votes on appropriation bills. They must develop a budget for one of thirteen appropriations subcommittees using reference materials, data bases, questionnaires, and experts. The Virtual Congress is designed as a backup technology for the classroom teacher, who must actively shape it to fit course objectives.[29]

    ❧ Foreign-language students visiting or developing second-language "virtual world" Web sites are immersed in both the language and the culture of the country they are studying.

    ❧ At Emerson High School in Union City, New Jersey, a large grant from industry enabled the school to collaborate with the Center for Children and Technology in New York. Intensive teacher training accompanied installation of two hundred computers (of which, by the way, some thirty are down at any one time, requiring one and one-half full-time technical support people). In the honors U.S. history class, a unit on the Bill of Rights using the Internet required students to research one amendment and related Supreme Court cases. They then interviewed law professors, prepared oral arguments for and against defendant and plaintiff, and analyzed the constitutionality of the Supreme Court's decisions.[30]

    ❧ In studying "Our Ocean Planet," ninth-grade science students in

Denine Morescki's class in Winona, Minnesota, wrote an original piece of interactive learning ware to press onto CD. Each project had to incorporate text sources, scanned pictures, original animations and digitized quick-time movies, statistical graphs, a glossary, and careful documentation.[31]

    At the extravagantly endowed Peddie School in Hightstown, New Jersey, sophomores and juniors—each equipped with a new laptop—pursue a year of rigorous interdisciplinary, globally networked study of a theme which "requires students to think across traditional boundaries." As students pursue projects outside of the classroom both electronically and physically (on organized trips), they learn to think critically about global issues.

    At High School of Technology in Wilmington, Delaware, formerly disaffected students now compete for admission. The school claims a dramatic turnaround from adding a networked system accompanied by bottom-up changes to improve teaching, reach students with different learning styles, increase community involvement, and set higher levels of expectation. Students now use graphing calculators, discover geometry theorems with special computer software, edit their own writing on word processors, and build virtual engines. A rising grade point average and a 50 percent drop in incidents requiring discipline attest to the success of the changes.

It shouldn't take a massive technology budget to show educators and policymakers that students shouldn't be spending their days filling out worksheets, as they previously were at the Wilmington school. Now students feel more interested in and responsible for their learning, and they read and write more, even in technical courses.

Says principal Henry Stenta, "Change is always interesting and challenging. Yet in the educational environment it can be threatening and exhausting. New equipment, new training, new upgrades, new, new, new—you hop on the 'up' escalator and never look back or try to jump off. As long as instructors agree to and even embrace the ride and the administration agrees to pay for it, technology can be the successful instructional tool that we all hoped it would be."[32] Of course, as usual, comparable changes in the teachers' attitudes and methods might well have had similar results, even minus the expense of the new technology.

Assessing Student Work in
the Age of Hypermedia

"Who would fail to be impressed with this display of scholarship? The [student's] report was beautifully printed on a color ink-jet printer, it was longer than the teacher's doctoral thesis, and it included the most up to the minute data available. . . . If only one report was getting an 'A' we might guess it would be the one that looked the nicest, was the heaviest, and had material not found in [usual] news sources.

"In this case, that might be a tragic mistake."

David Thornburg in *Education in the Communication Age* [33]

"Hypermedia" or "metamedia" call for broadening definitions of "literacy" and our methods of evaluating student work. Now that students can "write" with video and graphics, educators must set standards to evaluate new forms of expression. Here are a few preliminary guidelines:

  Hypermedia projects should incorporate all media of concern to the topic at hand.

  To prevent yoking superficial elements together, teach strategies similar to those recommended for on-line research:

1. Gather information from a variety of souces
2. Evaluate quality of information and sources
3. Analyze information to detect general trends and topics
4. Develop a statement of the problem or the hypothesis
5. Select the tools for representing the information
6. Plan the steps to the solution or the finished product

  Students should be required to *elaborate* the knowledge they have gained, rather than simply copying and pasting it or answering multiple-choice questions (e.g., develop an original graphic representation of the topic; apply the information in a new context). After studying the human digestive system, middle-school students created original computer models, drawings, or animations of it and wrote a creative story from the point of view of an organism—real or imaginary—taking a tour through it.

• Ask the students to develop visual concept "maps" or brainstorm all they know about a topic at the beginning of the activity to set a framework for the content to be covered.

• Use the technology to help students visualize and interpret data (e.g., when making science charts or graphs, use a spreadsheet program to create three different types of graphics using the same data).

• With the new ability to cut, paste, and download directly from print sources, firm policies on plagiarism must be articulated for teachers, parents, and students to understand.

• One of the best ways to ensure original work is to ask the student to summarize the entire topic—either orally or in writing. In the electronic era, the "A" reports may be those which do the best job of synthesizing information from various sources.

• Consider setting a *maximum* number of pages for a written report in addition to a *minimum*.

• Try to overcome the natural tendency to judge an assignment by its physical appearance—no longer a guarantee or even an indication of student effort. Some of the fanciest products may represent shallow work.

What Became of Handwriting, Spelling, and Math Facts?

If any single issue divides the new technophiles from the hoary traditionalists, it is the question of how much we should allow electronics to substitute for basic competencies in writing, spelling, and calculation. As usual, the question is not easily answered, but developmental learning needs can guide decisions.

Writing and the Word Processing Wars

"I love computers because for one thing I can get words down faster, but for another reason I have bad handwriting and lousy

spelling and when I type on the computer I don't have to take a long time to work on [them], and there's all the cool things you can do with a computer to make your writing the way that you feel good about."
Middle-school student

"It's hard to believe they spend an hour a day on keyboarding in grade three, and then we have to totally reteach it when they get to grade seven. Something's clearly wrong with our curriculum!"
Middle-school teacher, Colorado

Almost everyone agrees that students should acquire skill at word processing, but almost no one agrees on whether, when, or how keyboarding (touch typing) should be taught. I have been circling through schools, interviewing "experts," questioning teachers, searching out research, and watching kids of every age banging on keys, and I have yet to come up with a completely satisfactory answer. Here are some examples that illustrate the range of opinion I have heard:

"Start teaching keyboarding as early as possible! Forget writing with a pencil!"

"Horrors! Pencils first!!!"

"Forget keyboarding! They will pick it up by themselves."

"Keyboarding will soon be obsolete—we'll be using a stylus or dictating directly into the computer. Teach oral language!"

Somewhat dazed by these clashing opinions, I requested some guidelines from Judy Royer, computer teacher at the Copper Hill Elementary School in Ringoes, New Jersey, who has plenty of real-life experience to back up her colorful opinions. ("I've been teaching since they invented water," she modestly states.)

"Teaching keyboarding? Oh, that's such a bugaboo. Ask me today, I'll tell you one thing, and probably another tomorrow. Maybe best around age eight or nine? But they don't need a $3,000 machine to learn keyboarding. Personally, I don't use children's typing programs because those cutesy graphics take too much time away from the learning. I don't want them watching some bear dancing across the screen when they're supposed to be concentrating on where to put their fingers.

"But they have to learn it sometime. We don't want them in high school saying 'There's no "j" here . . .' "

A Tentative Synthesis

Lacking definitive guidelines, I have attempted to draw up a tentative synthesis of experienced voices, research, and clues from child development.

WRITING ON A COMPUTER VS. WRITING BY HAND: MORE WORDS, BUT HOW'S THE QUALITY?

> "I do not think that computers make you inspired, though it makes you distracted. You get more caught up in what font you should use, how big your title should be, and how big or small your text should be, than what your even going to write about, and how your going to use that stuff."
>
> Kiera, age nine, Colorado

Let's start by discussing the process of writing as opposed to the act of handwriting, which we'll come to shortly. Some children write more words more enthusiastically and are willing to edit more thoroughly on a computer.[34] Computers are invaluable for children with organic handwriting difficulties ("dysgraphia"). "Concept" and pictorial keyboards enable nonreaders to create stories, and voice-synthesized programs help with pronunciation of words. While these latter products are still primitive, they hold intriguing potential for helping with second-language development in minority children and adults, among other uses. In one recent study, nonnative lower-class children in France enjoyed "writing" stories with colorful images which were translated into words they could hear pronounced in French.[35]

Other studies paint a less glowing picture. In one three-year study, eight- and nine-year-olds generated longer and better-quality essays by hand than by computer.[36] It seems fairly clear that good writers readily become good on-screen editors, but poorer writers tend to make editing changes only at the word level (e.g., using a spell-checker) as opposed to substantive changes in content and organization.[37]

Computers will not themselves teach writing skills. Laura Nader, professor of anthropology at UC Berkeley, remarked at a recent conference that she finds college students who have had computers since primary school tend to write papers that read like annotated bibliographies. They have abundant references but lack judgment on how to rank them, how to synthesize a thesis or defend a position.[38] For younger children, however, on-line writing may inspire efforts at clarity, because one can't get by with facial expressions, body language, or the ubiquitous "You know." Thus students must be more explicit in language and learn to consider a message from another's point of view. Because students often take seriously the idea of being "published," they may also put more effort into the finished product. Nevertheless, electronic writing places special demands on teaching. After years of exhorting students to write more, we are now forced to teach them to express more by writing less. Some teachers appreciate the structure that mind-mapping, outlining, or "idea" software brings, but others believe students should learn to organize their own thoughts.

Clearly, no consensus exists. Moreover, writing for hypermedia makes new demands for integrating text and graphics. Eventually, we may have an entire new set of teaching methods and new standards for the old-fashioned process of "writing."

WHETHER TO TEACH KEYBOARDING SKILLS

As the parent of a son who hunt-and-pecked his way through high school, college, and law school with speed and accuracy that rivals that of good touch typists, I find this question difficult. I have seen ten-year-olds who have intuitively mastered the keyboard on their own. Nevertheless, for most students, it is probably useful to follow some structured method of learning keyboarding, but mastery requires maturity and perseverance.

"I worked at it," one girl informed me with a certain degree of satisfaction as she zipped through her assignment. "These other guys goofed off, and now they still have to look to find the keys."

When to Introduce Keyboarding

Efficiency should be our goal in teaching any skill: Strike while the neurological iron is hot—soon enough to forestall bad habits but late enough to have it stick with a minimum of time spent. Somewhere around ages nine and ten, many children are able to coordinate body and brain sufficiently to maintain a hand position and manipulate keys without undue difficulty; prior to that time, many will simply be wasting time and developing bad habits. Experienced teachers tell me that only by age ten do children have the maturity and patience for independent practice. I also hear frequently from middle-school teachers that kids who "learned" it younger still don't know it and need a systematic review at eleven or twelve. Of course, some students may need to await more maturation, and some will be able to achieve proficiency quite early (more girls than boys seem to fall into this latter category).

One of the most neglected points in current practice is that any teaching should be constantly reinforced: If you occupy the instructional time to teach it in fourth grade, make sure they are expected to use it in fifth, sixth, etc. A schoolwide policy is a must, here. Avoid the territorial imperative. ("It belongs in third grade and it's mine!") Some schools adopt reasonable benchmarks for students to meet, such as a certain number of words per minute by the end of eighth grade, or a history report typed in good form.

One trend has administrators purchasing small, durable personal keyboards that children can carry around with them to type stories or reports. Even six-year-olds can use these "child-proof" products at school and at home. Later, they can be connected to a printer for a finished printout. According to several elementary principals with whom I have talked, they are a motivational tool for language and literacy development even when children "hunt and peck" to find the letters on the keyboard. No one I talked to had thought of the implications for children's vision, if there are any.

Should It Replace Handwriting Instruction?

Children below age eight or so should still internalize the muscular and tactile "feel" of forming letters with a pencil, marker, or crayon on paper or chalk on a chalkboard. Children with learning differences and/or kinesthetic learning style particularly profit from extended multisensory experience in forming letters by hand. In one study, eight- and nine-year-olds both with and without learning disabilities practiced their spelling words either on a computer, by writing, or by tracing them. All agreed the computer was more fun but felt that writing or tracing helped them learn better.[39]

How Should We Teach Keyboarding?

A synthesis of opinion and research recommends a structured, straightforward program of learning and practicing hand position on the keys. However, better results are usually achieved more quickly, at least for students up to teen years, if structured teaching supervision accompanies CAI.[40]

The Role of the Home

Here is one area where parents can really help. Many youngsters don't get sufficient practice time at school, so ten or fifteen minutes a day at home can make a difference. You don't need an expensive computer, and you can borrow, buy, or possibly download recommended software and work with the child to set up an organized practice schedule and supervise use. Don't push this on your child too soon, and if you find your youngster simply doesn't have the interest or coordination to persist, drop it and try again later.

One mother who had always wanted to try her hand at story writing learned and practiced keyboarding skills in the evenings along with her son. He was charmed to see her in the unaccustomed role of student, and his own motivation increased as they discussed together their frustrations in mastering the lessons.

New technologies tend to be used initially only in the way that the old ones were (e.g., like a standard typewriter), but imagination offers interesting possibilities.

Spelling and Math Calculation

The same developmental principles apply for spelling and math calculation as for learning letter formation. Learning the muscular and tactile feel of forming spelling patterns in words or writing out equations in math helps children remember them. Even for older students, one of the most powerful remedial techniques for spelling and "math fact" difficulties is a "multisensory" approach: write or trace (feel the shape), see, and say, all at the same time. In math, of course, the tried-and-true manipulatives (cubes, rods, and more complex computational objects) should also have a major place in any curriculum.

SPELL-CHECKERS

Spell-checkers and hand-held spelling aids are useful for everyone and essential for some, but they should not replace basic instruction in word patterns and spelling rules. The best spell-checkers are those that deepen processing by forcing the student into firsthand contact with the word, by having either to type in the correct form or, more frequently, to select from a set of choices.

One serious problem with current spell-checkers is that they don't understand the context in which the word appears and thus mess up royally on homophones (sale:sail; son:sun). Until these tricky little orthographic perversions pass from our language (which is clearly on the way to occurring, if you note the number of errors in any newspaper), we must still teach the words directly, get writers to use a dictionary, or decide two bare the site of fowl-ups.

CALCULATORS VS. CALCULATION

Some very bright people don't seem to be able to learn the multiplication tables. Moreover, the National Council of Teachers of Mathematics has gone on the line (or, possibly, out on a limb) to recommend that calculators be used even for beginning arithmetic. Yet we have legions of middle- and high-school math teachers complaining that kids are too dependent on calculators and lack basic number sense—they punch in numbers and record an answer without analyzing it. The ability to do mental math and to make good estimates is valuable in the real world and seems at risk of being lost. Even some algebra students can't do simple problems in their head or estimate whether an answer is grossly off the mark. (One dozen oranges for $695.00?)

Simply reading or copying an answer off a calculator does not fix learning very firmly into the brain. On the other hand, figuring it out yourself, particularly in writing, moves it more deeply into memory. This fact is known as the "generation effect," for the important difference between *generating* an answer and just *recording* it.[41]

If calculators replace practice in basic skills of pencil-and-paper calculation, they lose the generation effect and thus tend to undermine development of strategies, speed, and understanding of numerical relationships.[42] At the Bank Street School in New York, math teacher Michael Wilkinson's policy is that calculators and computers be used, even for middle-school students, only when the calculations are too laborious to do manually. His students use the computer to develop understanding, as in investigating the relationship of circumference and diameter in many different size circles. After measuring scores of real-life circles, they begin to approximate the concept of pi, and the computer then helps them extend their practice.

In short, optimal learning may take many forms, depending on age, individual needs, type of learning, and available teaching materials. As we become more comfortable with our new technologies, we will doubtless learn that they serve us most effectively as supplements to—rather than replacements for—the time-tested staples of good education.

Digital Scaffolding

Our young people these days can easily intimidate us with their quick digital know-how and their worldly wise demeanor. Yet technological savvy guarantees nothing about basic skills, intellectual prowess, or mature wisdom. Trusting computers—or any other electronic medium—to instill genuine learning is an abdication of our most essential task. This generation continues to need—perhaps even more than any before it—the steady hand, loving collaboration, and proven methods of its elders.

In a way, we now have two younger generations to raise: the human and the digital. In our final chapter, we will look ahead to some of the interesting new conundrums our electronic "children" may present.

Chapter Nine

Computing the Future

"I believe that computers are taking over our world, and they are very helpful, yet frustrating."
Kiera, age nine

"Technology asks only one thing of you: to believe. Believe that it will make the complex simple, the crooked road straight, miraculously transform information into wisdom and easy access into goodness. Believe that the past is marginally relevant, the present fleeting, and the future alone worthy of reverence."
Francis E. Kazemek, St. Cloud State University [1]

With luck and adult supervision, digital technology and today's children may both grow up to the point where they can seamlessly benefit each other. For now, turning youngsters—particularly young ones—loose on computers is somewhat akin to sending them out to play unsupervised in traffic. Educational computer use is in serious disarray, and what the future will bring is a vexed question.

How Ideas Acquire People

In the book *Thought Contagion*, Aaron Lynch describes "the new science of memes: how belief spreads through society."[2] "Memes," he suggests, are ideas or belief systems that attain a life of their own, grow, and reproduce themselves as they gain power in the public consciousness. It's not a question of how people acquire ideas but rather "how ideas acquire people." This theory explains the irrational power of the new meme that computers are beneficial and necessary for our young. Lynch quotes Richard Dawkin, who originated the concept: "When you plant a fertile meme in my mind, you literally parasitize my brain, turning it into a vehicle for the meme's propagation in just the same way that a virus may parasitize the genetic mechanism of a host cell."[3] It seems we don't own this idea; rather, it owns us.

Public debate on the subject of computers in schools tends to be polarized and nonproductive. Either you love educational computing, or you hate it. Ironically, this simplistic dialogue is symptomatic of electronic-visual culture, as emotional sound bites and instant opinion drown out the nuanced argument of intelligent discourse. Instead of discussions, we have talk shows and Internet flaming matches.

As with most questions, however, the truth about children's computing lies somewhere in between. Technology does not have to be the killer whale in the pristine pools of humanism, just as it is not the new incarnation of truth. If we can regain our senses and objectify the situation, we will observe that while most of today's news about educational computer use is not cheerful, the story is still unfolding.

Two relevant themes arise from the miasma of predictions about our children's collective future. The first is the evolution (or demise) of schooling that will be propelled by new electronic thought forms. The second is the challenge that the next generation will face from digital knockoffs of human life and human intelligence. Our children's futures are rapidly merging with those of machines that display traditional forms of intellectual "competence" (i.e., performing the three Rs), simulate human behavior, and even threaten ultimate human control. There is already a change in our traditional notions of "school," and there will doubtless be alterations in the human brain as it interacts with computers. New forms of literacy, virtual reality, and advances in artificial intelligence must all be considered as seminal developments for both education and human cultural evolution.

Digital Evolution in Education:
Where Do We Stand?

"I am pleased to see someone speaking from something other than blind enthusiasm toward computers in education. I am amazed at the potential, and dismayed at the actual lowest common denominator use and the endless cost . . . so often it seems they are going for symbolic gesture instead of focused, self-motivated, and thinking students."

Katie Fisher, computer teacher, Island School, Lihue, Hawaii

Present Realities

Let's start with some summary observations about the current situation.

1. The educational value of today's computers has been vastly oversold to parents, educators, and the general public, primarily by people who benefit financially from adding computers and software to the traditional educational mix.

2. An urgent need exists for better research on fundamental questions related to the physical health of children who use computers.

3. Research is also needed to determine if, when, and how computer applications can actually improve different forms of learning. Far too little attention has been given to either developmental needs or potential effects of human/digital interaction on the growing brain. Good research will also give us a better understanding of how the human mind itself learns and creates.

4. Home use of computers to date consists of far more game-playing than education. Parents, who think computer use is more constructive than television viewing, are relatively uninvolved in most children's home computing and underestimate its potential negative effects. Yet optimal home use depends on informed decisions, reasonable supervision, and on-site support from adults.

5. Objective and well-controlled research on computer effects on learning and motivation is badly needed. (Consensus is lacking even on

basic definitions of "learning," which now depend more on belief systems than on science.)

6. Smaller classes, more active student learning, more attention to individual needs, and more thoughtful curriculum would generally achieve the same or even better results without today's technology. For schools with these ingredients already in place, computers are expensive frosting on the cake. For those schools without such educational attributes, computers represent more of a cop-out than a remedy.

7. New technologies are expensive and drain badly needed funds from proven educational needs.

8. Effective applications of new technologies occur in schools with the following ingredients:

- good teaching
- teachers well-versed in integrating technologies into a strong curriculum
- well-planned utilization of a variety of technologies (including books and paper), guided by which medium can do each job most effectively
- adequate or excellent technical support
- active learning, questioning, and understanding on the part of students rather than passive response to artificially engaging or simple drill-and-practice software
- energetic and thoughtful leadership

9. No critical period exists for computer use; normally developing children do not need computers before elementary-school age, and they may do without them very happily until even later. Too little exposure is far better than too much.

10. Filling children with information does not necessarily constitute learning, and may interfere with their ability to use the information in conceptual ways. Nor will using today's technologies necessarily prepare children for success. Future "haves" and "have-nots" will be separated by the intellectual value of their education, not by their amount of exposure to computers.

Changing Education, Changing Children's Roles

"The key question is not 'What is the role of information technologies in schools?' but rather "What is the role of schools in the age of information technologies?"

Philip J. Bossert, Project Director, Hawaii Education and Research Network

Technology implementation to date has mainly been grafted onto old educational paradigms (as in computer-aided instruction; drill-and-practice programs; lecture courses beamed afar in distance learning), which some observers say is like trying to put an engine in a horse rather than designing an automobile. As it happens, the same trajectory has characterized almost every new educational idea in recent history. In 1986 Larry Cuban of Stanford University surveyed the use of learning technologies to date, including radio, film, television, and computers.[4] He found a similar pattern in each: First, the products were wildly oversold by vendors outside the education business; many educators found them ineffective or were reluctant to take on something unproven, distracting, and often counter to their philosophical beliefs. Soon, disillusionment set in as the technology appeared to be either ineffective or unworkable. And finally the community began to blame the educators. Cuban likens this situation to having nonmedical persons prescribe new surgical tools or techniques. Clearly, such efforts are not only demeaning to the professionals, but also doomed to fail. This pattern still endures as we enter a stage of growing disillusionment with the empty promises of computer gurus. Nevertheless, this technology offers far more varied opportunities than any of the others Cuban surveyed, and sufficient enthusiasm is still being generated from within the teaching profession that we may yet see a different outcome.

A similar cycle is playing out in many homes. Parents, naive about the usage and limitations of digital equipment and anxious to help their children succeed, buy computer products as a result of propaganda that they are "educational." Soon, they find their children (particularly boys) "hooked" on edutainment or video games; disillusionment and anxiety set in, and computer use becomes a bone of contention.

Computer technologies will very likely become the catalyst for throwing out entrenched educational practices and reconsidering the purpose and the manner of—and perhaps even the necessity for—schooling. In *Will We Be Smart Enough?*, Earl Hunt explores new notions of "smart" for tomorrow's workplace, most notable being ready adaptability to change and creative approaches to problem-solving, both of which recast traditional educational goals.[5]

Personally, I believe that the most important potential benefit of technology use is to free the power of children's minds. In one sense, we may be going forward into the past. Throughout much of history, youngsters gained practical skills and self-esteem as they worked and met challenges alongside adults. They exchanged personal effort for a feeling of genuine worth as contributors to family or community needs. More recently, we have isolated youngsters in classrooms, mesmerizing them with memorization rather than calling on ingenuity, perseverance, and curiosity. Now the kids are voting with both their attention and their behavior that they have had enough of this disembodied learning. Well-planned uses of computers can ground education in projects that have intrinsic meaning, while still teaching critical skills of symbolic analysis and a core base of integrated knowledge. But this requires rethinking methods, asking children to tussle with real and intellectually challenging problems, and trusting them to be responsible in new and sometimes unsettling ways.

Far out on the limb of children's digital independence, Jon Katz opined in a recent *Wired* magazine that computers and the Internet are finally empowering our young to escape from centuries of oppressive control by adults. Just as people in autocratic states can now communicate via the Internet beyond their restricted political borders, "so can children for the first time reach past the suffocating boundaries of social convention, past their elders' rigid notions of what is good for them. Children will never be the same; nor will the rest of us." Katz is opposed to any efforts to censor content made available to children. He believes that the core values instilled by the family, not information or images from outside, are what make a youngster into a "Responsible Child."[6]

While my own views differ considerably from Katz's, I believe he identifies the primary tension within digital technology for kids. Although the route, the destination, and even our own children may look unfamiliar in this shifting landscape of new technologies, youngsters still need and want us to accompany them on the journey and to share their challenges, thoughts, and hopes. They may have to guide us into the technology, but it is still our job to guide them into life.

Looking Forward in the Classroom

"The future is always more peculiarly strange than any of our tidy imaginings."

Gregory Rawlings in *Moths to the Flame* [7]

Trying to get a clear fix on the future of technology is like trying to change a tire on a moving truck. Predictions, too, inevitably reflect the agendas of the local crystal ball. In 1996, Dave Morsund predicted in the journal *Learning and Leading with Technology* that certain trends would occur in computer systems within a decade:

- Continuing increases in processor speed
- More power for less money
- Dramatic differences in memory and storage capabilities
- More seamless interface among various software tools
- Better human-machine interface: easier to operate complex programs
- More worldwide connectivity
- Increased digitization of information: dramatic expansion of on-line libraries
- Improvements in and wider use of artificial intelligence (e.g., better voice input; refinement of intelligent agents and expert systems for teaching)
- Merger of media (telecommunications, television, computer)

Since the foundation for which Morsund works is funded by a major software manufacturer, it is not surprising he recommends that families and schools continue to spend increasing amounts of money to keep up with the changes. He offers what is probably a "wish list" for the industry:

297

≈ Every student and teacher with a powerful portable computer and a full range of applications software

≈ Every classroom with a technology infrastructure that includes scanners, printers, camcorders, desktop presentation software, and network connections

≈ Every student and teacher with good access to the full range of technology-enhanced learning (TEL), including computer-assisted instruction and distance education

≈ Maintenance and repair staff and other needed support

≈ Continuing in-service learning and support for teachers

≈ Ongoing curriculum revision and development to keep pace with technological change[8]

For views of the future from someone on the front line of software development, I contacted Ted Hasslebring at Vanderbilt University, who is one of a group pioneering a wide selection of applications grounded in psychology and teaching.

"Computers are going to become a way of life in education," Hasslebring predicts, although so far, he agrees, "it's been very spotty." One reason is the lack of good professional development, but two other reasons are equally important. First, technology to date has not been powerful enough to fulfill expectations placed on it; newer machines have sufficient power, but most schools don't yet have them. Second, we're only now learning how to make and use good software. He cites an intelligent tutoring system for poor readers or nonreaders in middle school which took several years and a lot of field-testing to develop. It was recently tested with two thousand Florida students and achieved "great results" in raising their reading level as much as four years. He predicts that if good voice recognition software becomes a reality, we will get programs that will almost be able to emulate the human teacher-student interaction.

"Does that mean we won't need the teachers anymore?" I asked.

"Absolutely not. The best results we get are when we have a really good teacher along with the software who can monitor and reinforce what the student is learning. I don't think you can ever bypass the teacher."

Of course, Hasslebring's group has the luxury of time and expertise because their funding is not dependent on quick sales or profits. "Our bottom line is: Will kids learn?" he says.

On the opposite side of the fence even some Waldorf schools, which have generally articulated a staunch antitechnology philosophy, now acknowledge that older middle-school students may gain by interacting with computers. Of course, they first take apart and/or build the computers themselves, so there's not much question of the machines taking too much control. The Waldorf schools' recommended high-school technology curriculum includes an in-depth study of the history of technology, its major innovators, and consideration of the philosophical implications of humans interacting with machines.[9]

New (and Some Old) Responsibilities for the Human Brain

New Forms of Literacy

Text literacy traditionally held the driver's seat on the information highway, but it is currently being edged out by some aggressive hitchhikers picked up en route. Cases in point: Image processing and data literacy, newly defined skills of symbolic analysis that may soon be essential for everyone.

IMAGE PROCESSING

> *"If ever there was a way to introduce our students to a useful tool of science and industry and to revitalize classroom presentations, image processing is it."*
>
> Francis Collins, middle-school teacher, Langhorne, Pennsylvania

I felt as if I might have stumbled into the future after my visit to Francis Collins's middle-school science classes in Langhorne, Pennsylvania. If every teacher in the future were as skilled as he at incorporating technology into curricular goals, much of this debate would become moot. On the wall of his classroom, a plaque designating him as a Christa McAuliffe Fellow hangs next to a student-created award: "Francis

Collins, Ultra Energy Man. Always generating and transferring super amounts of energy."

Dealing with twelve- and thirteen-year-olds on a warm May afternoon when flowers and hormones are simultaneously bursting into bloom is not an easy task. Yet the students in Collins's classes were as rapt as I have ever known this age group to be.

The unusual level of attention resulted from good classroom management and a series of lessons based on computer-generated images which plunged students firsthand into the role of scientists. Using image-processing software available in the public domain, Collins and a student aide manipulated digital images on a large TV monitor for whole-class demonstrations; from a computer at his desk Collins was able instantly to choose images, zoom, magnify, move items around, and measure distance and angles. For a first-time observer, such prestidigitation is amazing; even more amazing was the serious intent with which these young teens pursued carefully prescribed follow-up activities, working in small groups to solve assigned problems.

The first class became paleontologists, examining shards of fossils and artifacts, measuring, fitting them together, and drawing conclusions about their origins. Writing a story about what they saw solidified both analytic and summary skills.

"I want them to think like paleontologists," their teacher told me. "I want them involved with the whole idea of geologic time." At this point he demonstrated to the class how to compare to scale the relative size of a tyrannosaurus with a six-foot human. Since understanding proportion is one of the skills made possible (but certainly not inevitable) by adolescent brain maturation, I was struck by how Collins was able to place the abstract notion into concrete perspective with these computer images.

Skills of visual literacy don't necessarily come naturally. Collins starts by teaching students how to analyze closely with a hand lens, only then transferring to computer images. To understand what scientists call "ground truth" as a basis for precision, they must determine the basic measurement unit so that all observations are calibrated. Other lessons require them to analyze environmental events and predict the path of real hurricanes based on past data. Using complex software to "slice" and manipulate images, they predict landfall and list the names of cities that should be warned. Only then do they learn what actually happened so they can check the accuracy of their predictions.

Any image may be analyzed and manipulated, including images from the Hubble space telescope, aerial maps of the students' own neighborhoods for a study of erosion changes, and x-rays of the human body, which they must measure to determine if the angle of the pelvis denotes a male or a female.

As I reluctantly took my leave, twelve-year-olds were "marrying" off a girl and boy in the class; by measuring and analyzing their digitized facial features the class would predict the appearance of their children. I was frankly astonished that neither discussion of male and female pelvises nor this hypothetical union had elicited the slightest amount of nudging, giggling, or terminal embarrassment that I would have expected—perhaps the best possible evidence that these young scholars took their work and their learning seriously.

Such learning tools to augment students' formal reasoning and analytic skills have considerable potential, at least for topics such as science, which lend themselves to this approach. It is likely that "visual literacy" will increasingly infiltrate other disciplines, such as analysis of historical photos or visual effects in films, as the digital age both develops and calls on new forms of intelligence. But simply letting kids look at visuals isn't enough; this skill must be taught and linked to important learning.

"You've got to be right in there with them when they're getting information off a computer monitor," commented another master teacher, Nancy Burton, when I visited her class of nine- to eleven-year-olds the next week. "Otherwise they'll be tempted to amuse themselves rather than ask those rigorous questions. I value children's time highly and I won't take on any of these things lightly." Burton's class at the Jarrow Montessori School in Boulder, Colorado, was finishing the year by collating data from GLOBE, an Internet-based learning project in collaboration with the National Geophysical Data Center. Burton's students were acquiring not only visual literacy, as they worked with on- and offline maps, charts, and graphs, but "data literacy" as well.

DATA LITERACY

It was early in the morning when I arrived at Jarrow's homey-looking school building, but Kyle and Jessica, my student hosts, were already pacing the floor. They wanted me to watch their daily data recording, so we quickly headed to the backyard. Here the children deftly checked temperature boxes to determine the temperature variation (in Celsius) during the past twenty-four hours as well as the liquid equivalent of any precipitation that had fallen. They recorded these observations on data sheets, adding an estimate of the current cloud cover.

"I'd say it's about sixty to seventy percent," Jessica stated confidently.

At this point my husband and I, who have both struggled to teach even older students an understanding of percentage from a textbook, rolled our eyes to each other at her obviously accurate assessment.

"And those are mostly stratocumulus clouds," said Kyle, making quick notes on his clipboard.

"Why do you need to record the type of clouds?" I asked.

"Oh, certain kinds of clouds have more moisture than others, and it might affect the temperature," he responded.

"And what do you do when there's snow in the gauge instead of rain?" I wanted to know.

"Well, we take six measurements and average them, then we use a tube to determine the liquid equivalent."

More rolling of eyes. Cause and effect. Average. Equivalent. More difficult ideas apparently mastered. No time for a pause, however, as we were on our way back to the classroom to enter the data into a world-wide data base collated from students and used by scientists in observing atmospheric and meteorological trends. From it, youngsters are expected to discern patterns, learn about weather, and talk to scientists and other students all over the world about their findings. Most important, they are expected to ask interesting questions. Jessica told me about some of hers.

"We got some e-mail from a school in Eno, Finland, so we were looking at their one-year weather graph. We were really interested in finding out how spring is different from fall there, and whether their seasons are like ours. First we looked up their latitude and longitude and discovered that Finland is right next to Russia! Here, you can see it," she pointed to a large world map posted on the wall by the computer station. "We found out their spring and fall are a lot alike."

"Do you like studying science this way?" I asked.

"I do," volunteered Margaret, who was peering over Kyle's shoulder. The classroom has several older, donated computers, but only one capable of Internet transmission. "It makes you feel like you're part of a bigger project. What I like about GLOBE is they trust children to do work that scientists do."

Later, I talked to Ted Haberman, who is the geophysicist behind GLOBE, as he tried to explain—and show—some entirely new ways of representing and learning information. For younger children, much of the learning is hands-on (measuring and averaging real temperature and precipitation to master math skills) and personal (knowing your data is part of a serious global study). But Haberman's notions about changing education extend into a belief that visuals—icons, pictures, charts, etc.—may sooner or later replace, rather than simply supplement, much written text. For example, we viewed a public-access Web program from which a student can learn to identify different types of cloud formations by simply studying pictures.

Haberman believes a primary task in visual literacy is to become "data literate": Students must learn to "read" data, then create visual representations that make the information easy to understand. They must develop the analytic skills to make sense of a pile of data, no matter what form it comes in.

"You can interpret pictures, charts, and graphs any way, and kids tend to be very strong believers in both visuals and data. Yet most of the data collected about Earth is very noisy—it has lots of errors because there are so many complex interactions. In fact, most real-life data is fraught with problems, and it's very easy to lie with statistics. Even most adults don't really know how to understand visual diagrams like graphs, so it's easy to misrepresent findings."

The only way to counteract this problem, he maintains, is to teach data literacy. The first step is learning to ask good questions. For example, if the data seems to suggest that it's rainier or hotter in one city than another, kids must learn to probe whether the apparent effect is real. Does the data make sense? Did people use the same instruments every time? If we're talking about global warming in Dallas, are the measurements being made over asphalt or over grass? What are the implications of the data?

"It's hard work," says Haberman, "getting kids to ask good questions. But computers have an incredible effect in expanding youngsters' sphere of influence, and they have to learn that the speed at which incorrect things travel electronically is just as fast as the correct. Not only that, but the amount of bad information is going up. You've got to be there to mentor them and make sure they're learning to handle it properly."

One thing a visually educated generation might learn to do better than its elders is to design intelligible, concise, and accurate displays. Bad information design is presently rife and has resulted in serious scientific errors, complains Edward R. Tufte, author of *Visual Explanations*.[10] He also criticizes the design principles of computer displays (as on the Web) that are not only cluttered and unattractive, but also predominantly trivial in information content. He holds that we need an entirely new "information architecture." Here's one for your "visual thinkers" to get their eyeballs into.

Robbie McClintock of Columbia University forsees that in the future "the new technologies [will have] greatly extended the power of multiple representation in the culture. . . . Pictures, icons, sounds, and gestures [will come] to rival written expressions as means of accessing ideas. . . . People will begin to make arguments with them, to explain things through them, discovering how to give images declarative, propositional power."

To avoid giving them too much power, however, the next generation has to start by learning to discern what is real and what is not.

Virtual Reality

"Surrogate experience and surrogate environments have become the American way of life. Distinctions are no longer made, or

*deemed necessary, between the real and the false; the edge usually
goes to the latter, as an improved version with defects corrected—
accessible and user-friendly—although the resonance of history
and art in the authentic artifact is conspicuously lacking."*

Ada Louise Huxtable in *The Unreal America* [11]

Not long ago I accompanied a group of tourists on a trail hike in the
Rocky Mountains. In the group was a young lad of about five who had
thus far spent a well-ordered and privileged life in a large East Coast
city. This child was hopelessly confused by the new experience and delightfully spontaneous in expressing his bewilderment.

"Mom!" he would cry as each rock formation came into view. "Is that
man-made?"

"No, that's natural." His mother's patient explanations did little to
ease his skepticism.

"Well, is that man-made?" pointing to an adjacent mountain. I half-
expected him to inquire about the biological origins of our guide.

Even after two hours of hiking, his bewilderment had not eased. For
a child who had clearly spent more time in Disneyland than in the park,
distinguishing the real from the virtual world was a conceptual challenge, indeed. I wonder if he will eventually decide that the unpre-
dictability and relative discomfort of the real thing isn't worth the effort
compared with the tailor-made cossetting increasingly possible in cyberspace.

The term "cyberspace" was originally coined by William Gibson in
his prescient 1984 novel *Neuromancer*, where he defined it as "a consen-
sual hallucination." As our young folks are increasingly enticed into
some form of digital hallucination, we must ask about the future of real
experience. We must also ask how much supervision they will need as
they wander a medium where, it has been said, bad taste has no bounds
except the imagination.

Gregory Rawlings pondered this question in his book *Moths to the
Flame* and failed to find a simple answer. As we slip ever further into
ego-soothing cyberworlds, he even fears that the question "Is it real?"
might first become irrelevant and then meaningless. "The use of syn-

thetic experience may grow so widespread that some of us will have to make a conscious effort to act as if reality were real." Virtual reality is truly a new world, unknown and unknowable. "We're headed for it at breakneck speed, accelerating as we go. But we don't know where we're going," he comments.[12]

Marvin Minsky, one of the pioneers and farthest-out defenders of artificial intelligence and artificial worlds, believes it doesn't matter. "I don't see a thing wrong with virtual reality," he stated recently to a group of students, "because the real world isn't that good. Things break, there are accidents." In virtual worlds, he points out, we can re-create even ourselves, not being imprisoned in our genes. After all, the fingertips have an extremely rich network of connections to the brain; since they will likely serve as our links into the computer mind, we may be able to experience a richer world, see more colors, rise beyond our human limitations.

"People think this future is scary," he concludes. "But everything new is scary. I love being scared!"[13]

Virtual Hands-On Learning

"VR may transform our understanding of computers from severed heads to extensions of our whole selves."
Brenda Laurel, interactive media designer [14]

The term "virtual reality" is technically used to describe human-computer interfaces that enable users to experience physical sensation through sight, hearing, and touch (and, coming soon to your favorite monitor, smell!), giving a feeling of actual presence and movement in a place where there is none. The images generated by the computer correspond exactly to one's own movements, so you might participate in a virtual game, fly a plane, feel the bonds between molecules, or manipulate surgical instruments in a delicate operation. Ultimately, VR will enable us to explore complex dynamic systems from the inside out, perhaps crawling around through the structures of global economics or hopscotching around the internal patterns of galaxies. Currently, VR requires donning special glasses or helmet and gloves; more sophisticated biological interfaces already promise to make the experience increasingly less cumbersome, with even more verisimilitude.

Virtual reality environments have established a track record in training pilots and surgeons, among others, but the potential has barely been scratched. VR "intelligent" tutors are being developed to guide students through learning situations while simultaneously assessing skill level and calibrating challenges accordingly. These applications are predicated on a rather limited view of human problem-solving as a "trainable" commodity, but at least for routinized tasks they show promise. In a much wider sphere, social scientists are now looking to develop video games which are so immersive and engaging that they can change people's behavior. While violent video environments are compelling enough to induce some people to try to act them out in real life, such tools might also train youngsters in desirable social behavior, like resisting gang pressure or saying no to drugs. Virtual companions could allow children with social difficulties to experiment with personal relationships in a safe, guided therapeutic setting. One question we must surely ask is what controls will be necessary for such powerful "tools."

Experimental projects have studied people learning through biofeedback to control the movement of objects on the screen purely by brain waves, without any overt muscle movement. Among the many possibilities are using brain scanners to control warcraft or teaching children with attention problems to retrain their brain waves to maintain them at optimal frequencies.

Moving farther into the sci-fi realm, if a "biological interface" could connect children to preprogrammed cyber-memories at birth, they would no longer have to attend school to learn data, information, or knowledge. Then parents and teachers could concentrate on teaching them to manage it effectively and wisely. And we continue to speculate. When Manhattan attorneys were asked to describe the inventions they would like someone to make, one gentleman spoke for many members of a digital generation by suggesting it would be ideal if the computer could read a book for you. You would still absorb all the information, he pointed out, as well as have the enjoyment, but it would be instantaneous and save you a lot of time. While many might like to quibble about the notion of instantaneous enjoyment, particularly as it involves reading a book, we must admit that the human imagination holds out few limits on possibilities in cyberspace—or for changes in the "human" experience, whatever that may be.

Very little actual work in virtual worlds has taken place in schools. In one innovative summer program, teenaged students experienced some frustration with the heavy head-mounted helmet, as well as some orientation difficulties. Nevertheless, after one week of creating virtual reality worlds, they stated they would rather "go into" a virtual world than learn about it in other ways.[15]

The actual truth, of course, is never as rosy as virtual imaginings, and psychologists who specialize in perception are beginning to look at adverse effects, suggesting controls are necessary. The brain evolved to deal with one reality, and it may not be ready to jump into another one. As adult participants experience virtual threats, being balanced on the edge of a high ledge or taking fast corners in a car, their bodies and brains react with physical manifestations of fear or car sickness. Even nonthreatening virtual experience may create "the VR pricetag": nausea, dizziness, and lasting changes in perception, described as "the penalty for fooling Mother Nature." The longer the person stays in the virtual world, the worse the symptoms become; five days of rest between immersions is currently recommended.[16]

Other aftereffects include flashbacks, illusory sensations of climbing and turning, difficulties with balance and coordination, and reduced motor control that sometimes last as long as two weeks. States researcher Robert S. Kennedy, "The plasticity of our nervous system is fascinating. It's able to adjust to a new reality rather easily. But the consequence of that is the freedom from symptoms encourages us to stay longer, and the longer we're in that world, the longer it can take to come out and readjust to the real world again."[17]

The more similar the two worlds become, the more difficult it will be to draw distinctions and turn off the perceptual adaptations. Dr. Kennedy believes we should develop a certificate to make sure people leave VR in the same state they went in, to ensure they're ready for real-world tasks like driving a car.

Remember that these effects were found in adult volunteers, and we must be doubly careful about tossing children's developing nervous systems into untried untrue environments. Whatever its potential, and however compelling the experience, VR needs to prove itself in many ways before it becomes a part of the educational scene.

CONTEMPLATION VS. SENSATION

In a fine stroke of (I assume) accidental irony, another article in the professional journal containing Kennedy's remarks described the human need for solitude in the real world.[18] It featured an arresting picture of a young woman gazing out over a lake (not man-made) in an attitude of repose. "It [solitude] gives people a chance to contemplate who they are, what their relationships are to other people, and what their goals will be . . . a kind of settling and self-defining function," stated psychologist Peter Suedfeld of the University of British Columbia, who definitely would not count virtual solitude in the same category. "Downtime" also fosters creativity, although creative solitude is not always a time of particular happiness. Especially for adolescents, spending time alone may be necessary to grapple with unpleasant realities and determine who they really are. In fact, those individuals who possess a reasonable need for solitude are frequently the best adjusted, and even younger children who enjoy playing alone in constructive ways have longer attention spans.

But will our children ever be alone with their thoughts or emotions in an age when we perpetually clog their brains with artificial stimulation? Will contemplation become obsolete? Science fiction writers have long predicted that humankind might come to the point where direct, as opposed to mediated, experience inspires terror, where firsthand contact with nature, one's own mind—or even with other humans—has been eliminated. In the most extreme view, by submitting to such synthetic ease people will end up as info-serfs serving a disembodied Machine Intelligence. Certainly, cramming the young so full of data that they believe they're thinking when they're not, and hooking them into dependence on virtual pleasures, would be a start in this direction. Personally, I have a bit too much faith in human nature to give credence to such predictions. Yet as I watch children fixated on the monitor and dutifully pushing buttons like experimental rats, as I respond serflike to the messages on my Internet server, I sometimes wonder.

Children need a solid psychological and personal perspective from which to cruise phantasmagoric worlds. If we want them to establish strong identities, the best place to start is with the genuine pleasures of firsthand experiences rather than concocted ones where they escape from their own realities, awkward and uncomfortable as they may sometimes be.

Increasingly, all our technologies blur the boundaries between what is real and unreal, human and nonhuman. VR may be the link that brings artificial reality into closer proximity with humanity, with humanity retaining the upper hand. Or it could play out otherwise.

Artificial Intelligence

> "What bothers me about computers? The thought that something SO small is smarter than you."
>
> Shannon, age ten

> "I want to create something that's intelligent and that learns with experience. At the moment, that being is human."
>
> Susan Epstein, researcher in artificial intelligence [19]

Researchers in AI have been distinguished more by their desire to supersede the human brain than by their respect for it. Journalists, too, love their "digital brain bites man" stories; when a computer named Big Blue finally defeated the world's reigning chess champion, Gary Kasparov, in 1997, front-page headlines trumpeted the potential downfall of human intelligence. We love to believe that technology has such mystical power. Perhaps we yearn for something strong enough to solve big problems, such as educating our children while we go out and play.

But Big Blue couldn't possibly tie its shoes, if it had any, or build a block tower (without special human tutoring, AI tends to start at the top). Computers have difficulty mastering other forms of games (e.g., board games) requiring cognitive and perceptual strategies that people use with ease. Experts predict that no computer within a century will be able to beat a skilled human at the deceptively simple game of Go, which requires strategy, understanding of the opponent's motivation, common sense, and intuition. Machines like Big Blue can munch any number in the world but they are singularly lacking in both intuition and common sense—not an ideal prescription for a teacher of children.

During the furor that ensued after the computer's first major chess victory, a high-school class studying the history of technology was presented with a headline lamenting the "Major Defeat for Human Intelligence."

"That's nonsense," commented one thoughtful young man. "The chess champion wasn't competing with the machine; he was only competing with the humans who programmed it!"

For students who have learned to reflect, technology is easily put into perspective.

Possibility and Hubris

It is far beyond the scope of this book to attempt to describe research in the field of AI, as humans work at recasting digital systems (computer circuits) in the role of massive parallel processors (more like human brains). Real progress has been made, not the least of which is developing humility on the part of AI researchers. Even the most ardent AI enthusiasts have been forced to scale down their predictions about its potential to duplicate human intelligence as they find over and over again how far short it falls. Today's computers have particular difficulty because they lack, literally, the ability to engage in "hands-on" learning.

At MIT, AI researchers are devoting years to the design of an artificial two-year-old named "Cog," which can "learn" from its interaction with the environment. This attribute comes automatically with real children, who arrive in the world with several hundred billion neurons waiting to become activated through experience. Since each human brain cell may make connections with a thousand or so others, the potential here (several billion to the thousandth power) is something a computer could easily calculate but even a human has difficulty comprehending. This system would be hard enough to duplicate if we understood it, but some scientists believe it also contains unmeasurable properties that will always defy replication.

At any rate, "Cog" represents a good illustration of either the possibility or the hubris inherent in AI research. It also demonstrates the be-fuddled reaction even sophisticated humans have when they encounter artificial intelligence. Sherry Turkle describes her own reaction upon meeting "Cog" as it navigated around the laboratory on a mobile pedestal:

"Trained to track the largest moving object in its field . . . Cog 'noticed' me soon after I entered its room. Its head turned to follow me and I was embarrassed to note that this made me happy. I found myself competing with another visitor for its attention. . . . Despite myself and despite my continuing skepticism about this research project, I had behaved as though in the presence of another being."[20]

Being a highly trained and skeptical scientist, Turkle reminds us once again that we yet have a lot to learn about the human-AI interface, where even the most informed human can feel that the ground of past assumptions is a rather shaky place.

"JUST ANOTHER COLLEAGUE."

If our children can learn to keep their feet solidly anchored on that shaky ground, and AI in perspective, it may serve them well. Newer computers can do general reasoning that complements and extends the human brain. For example, by solving math problems and doing proofs no human has thus far been able to do, they potentially free tomorrow's human mathematicians to focus on discovering new hypotheses. ("And while I'm sleeping, please water the lawn and prove this new theorem.") Robert Boyer, a computer scientist at the University of Texas in Austin who believes he already sees "clearly a form of computer thinking," adds, nonetheless, "I don't want to make too much of that." We should perhaps think of the computer as "just another colleague, one that is sometimes helpful, but often not."[21]

Yet computers may always lack the most singular ingredient of human intelligence. AI researcher Richard Ten Dyke reminds us that while the computer is a devastating symbol-cruncher, human intelligence is based on reasoning with images, from which it makes original symbols.[22] Computers, being limited to symbols, such as mathematical calculations or chess moves, have much more restricted cognition; until they can learn to create and process original images, they will never be able to think (much less imagine, dream, or create) "like a human." Thus we must be particularly careful not to let them strip our children's minds of their own images by replacing them with formulaic, commercial ones.

Robots and Agents: More Real Than Real Friends

"The limited experiments that researchers have performed thus far only hint at the possibilities now opening up."
Pattie Maes, MIT professor and founder of Agents, Inc.[23]

Picture your child curled up cozily for evening storytime. You are happy, because you know this activity is an important part of reading readiness. Yet you are in the kitchen or downstairs in your office planning a new sales campaign. The patient tutor, who reads aloud in your voice from an electronic book and alerts you to any difficulty, is your handy house robot. Guarding the door is your clean, obedient, and fully house-trained modified pet in the form of an artificial guard dog. Efficient? Yes. A little scary? I hope so. Far in the future? No.

AI research yearly develops more sophisticated "tools" to act as surrogate friends and assistants in our busy lives—made more busy, of course, by our need to attend to the unrelenting demands of their electronic forebears. New developments make it very tempting to trust the machines. With a desperate proliferation of information, humans, hard-pressed to decide what to ingest and what to ignore, seek electronic life preservers in the info-sea. "Push technology" will presumably do most of our surfing for us, bringing information, opinion, and a multitude of products preselected according to our individual preferences and interests. It may be either the greatest step toward efficiency or a crutch for those who don't bother to think.

If some of today's informed predictions hold, useful electronic "agents" will be available by the time your child enters the adult world. Residing inside his computer, they will come to know him, tune in to his needs, and respond to both his verbal and his nonverbal (gesture, facial expression) languages. On the horizon are machines with rudimentary skills of visual perception, which will enable them to observe the user's expression to determine how he is feeling. Cruising instantaneously through the nether regions of cyberspace, agents will gather articles, gossip, statistics, new music, or whatever might interest their owner. As he accepts or rejects their offerings, they will learn, growing sprouts on their data bases to build a neural network of understanding—of him, his tastes, preferences, aberrations, and even personality and moods. ("If it's Monday, bring in cartoons.") While he's off playing virtual tennis, this dutiful slave will be doing his research while one of its counterparts performs secretarial work ("That English teacher is a stickler for run-on sentences; avoid them at all costs") and another one makes shopping decisions and transactions ("Yes, wrap the BMW and send it"). Later, they will report about what they did, accepting suggestions or praise. At some point, his digital proxies may even get together for a gossip session, exchanging information about his idiosyncrasies. They might encounter other people's alter egos out there in cyberspace and share some of the juicier morsels.

With many intelligent agents at his command, your child may well have the choice of living in a totally self-enclosed, self-centered, and self-limited world designed simply to serve his needs, his fancies, and his fantasies. If he wants to avoid other human beings, with their messy emotional agendas, he can probably do so (we see an early analogue in Internet addiction to the imaginary worlds of MUDs and MOOs). Your choices right now, as parent or educator, will play a significant part in determining his attitudes toward real and ersatz experience.

How close are these possibilities? Thus far, developers have failed in attempts to program agents with enough information to do such jobs; they just can't insert the needed common sense. Newer approaches are more promising, however, for autonomous agents who teach themselves, building their own knowledge base by continuously observing a person's actions and automating any regular patterns they detect.[24]

Confronting "Neobiological Civilization"

"[Artificial life is a challenge to] our most fundamental social, moral, philosophical, and religious beliefs. Like the Copernican

model of the solar system, it will force us to reexamine our place in the universe and our role in nature."
Christopher Langdon at First Conference on Artificial Life, 1987

Profound questions arise as we contemplate electronic organisms (sometimes called "biomorphs") that can learn from experience. Unlike many forms of AI, A-life (artificial life) represents a form of "artificial evolution" in which the most effective agents in a system are selected to "breed" an even fitter population for a particular job. Our children may need to cope with new species somewhere between real and artificial life.

Even current developments raise questions. As digital "agents" learn and become more autonomous, for instance, should users be held accountable for their actions? How do we assure they will keep personal information private? Can we "imprison" or kill one if it misbehaves? If an agent detects an owner's bad habit, should it try to teach him a better one—and "better" by whose definition? Could an electronic organism possibly become malevolent? Could a group of them foment a rebellion?

Teaching our children to ask good questions (not simply answer old ones) is not an idle goal. I believe it must be the driving force of educational change. And to give them a basis for finding answers, they need to become philosophers as well as scientists and technicians. (Young children are natural philosophers and questioners, until we or our media teach them otherwise.) There have always been good reasons to study and debate the deeper issues found in history, literature, and the arts, but the particular challenges of this digital future would seem to make the *human*ities more germane than ever.

The Last Stop

The last stop on my journey through learning technologies was an eagerly anticipated meeting with Mitchell Resnick at the MIT Media Lab. It was a nice circular completion, since he is heir-apparent to the theories of Seymour Papert, whose work inspired my enthusiasm so many years ago. Resnick's group occupies one part of the Media Lab, which could be described as a nursery for the future, cradling mind-boggling infant technologies that will probably be routine for our children. Simply the names of departments in the soaring, modern structure are thought-provoking: "Things That Think," "Opera of the Future," "[Artificial] Vision and Modeling," "Machine Understanding." In this building, I have a definite feeling that "machine understanding" means not only humans trying to understanding the machines, but also the other way around!

Children come to Resnick's lab to investigate, construct, and test their own ideas with activities such as programming on-screen microworlds or echelons of miniature robots to see how they will behave with each other. They work on a vast bank of large computers, dimly illuminated with blue and pink ceiling lighting, temperature-controlled, and humming with the eerie drone of billions of electronic handshakes. During my visit no children were present, although evidence of their work was scattered everywhere: building projects and inventions made of plastic bottles, wood, string, Lego blocks, and assorted other materials crowded tabletops and hung from the ceiling.

Resnick believes in tying all learning to concrete experience. In his office he keeps the favorite toy from his youth, a small pair of wheels connected by a shaft which supports a needle pointing downward. A string is tied around the needle and he challenges me to predict which way the needle will move if I pull on the string. It seems obvious to me that it will come forward with the string, but I soon prove myself wrong.

"I was fascinated by this thing all through high school," he tells me. "I spent hours trying to figure out the principles involved and why it worked the way it did. I didn't have a computer, but I had other toys for learning—like this one." The moral? Even grown-ups learn best by doing as well as thinking about it.

Children who come to the lab are currently working with "toys" that become self-organizing systems, massive arrays with many individual elements gradually evolving into a pattern. The idea of self-organizing systems grows out of cutting-edge scientific theory which, in turn, is based on age-old realities in the physical world. Resnick cites a bird flock as an example of a biological self-organizing system. Although we naturally tend to view the V formation as directed by a "leader bird," none of the members of the flock actually have any notion of the overall pattern; each bird simply responds to local cues from the its neighbor. Ultimately, the flock self-organizes into its characteristic shape. Resnick even wants us to believe that traffic jams are self-organizing, and he has demonstrations to prove it! By combining hands-on projects with computer simulations, students in the lab are able to construct and observe such interactions.

Resnick delights in upsetting the applecart of traditional assumptions. In his view, the particular benefit of new technologies—to inspire new kinds of thinking—is mainly ignored in schools. He uses computerized gadgets to help kids "move beyond the centralized mind-set," a skill he deems critical. Technology provides a whole new set of "conceptual building blocks," and even elementary-aged children master concepts—like feedback and rules of systems engineering—that previously took knowledge of advanced algebra.

"We've seen lots of kids working with these materials," he says, "and we've seen startling changes in their perceptions." Among other things, they start to ask different kinds of questions and reflect more deeply on their own thinking.

Naturally, Resnick's ideas are not widely accepted by the educational establishment, since they lack research support, are admittedly difficult to implement, and would require an entire rethinking of the purposes and methods of education. He, in turn, might suggest that the establishment has its own "centralized mind-set."

As I left the surrealistically cool and rarefied atmosphere of the Media Lab, I walked out into a golden late-summer afternoon where a group of young children were holding hands and playing a singing game to the accompaniment of a street-corner guitarist. Somehow the contrast seemed particularly appropriate. While the virtual life incubates in its infancy, children continue to grow, play, and learn in the sunny everyday corners of real experience. The future falls away under our feet like spring snow on a mountainside, but the enduring slope of childhood remains. This, of course, is where our real challenge lies.

Ralph Waldo Emerson said, "Give me insight into today, and you may have the past and the future worlds." Rather than mire our children in the past or abandon them on the brink of an uncertain future, our job is to guide them—here, now, today—to become effective human beings.

Seeking the Dreamers

"Computers are magnificent tools for the realization of our dreams, but they will never replace the dreamers. No machine can replace the human spark: spirit, compassion, love and understanding."

Louis B. Gerstner, Jr., CEO of IBM[25]

The meme that links technology and "progress" in people's minds has taken on the aura of a religion. Human beings have always dreamed of the potential of new machines to improve on the human condition and even to transform civilization. Currently, "information technology" is in the spotlight, but if information alone would do the trick we could simply enlarge the public library system. One of the gravest errors committed in the name of "progress" is to expand young people's heads at the expense of their hearts. We tend to forget that the digital intellect is a mentally impoverished companion for human dreams, emotions, and imagination. Jeffrey Kane, professor at Long Island University, points out that a computer is irrevocably separated from our most essential experience of being human, as it "doesn't have a sense that we live or die— the mortality that shapes us and our value structures. The experience of *being* is antithetical to the experience of *doing* with technology, which is focused on what we can achieve rather than humanly accomplish."[26]

New technology is a voracious infant. Its demands for attention, care, and feeding increase as it grows. Yet we still retain the upper hand. While computers are far more than "*just* tools," they don't independently make decisions (not yet, at any rate). Our wise decisions now can equip our young to master their machines in the service of rich and productive lives. Thoughtful adult models can teach them how to question the vacuous values of those who try to sell them products or promises.

If, on the other hand, we turn youngsters into stimulus-seeking droids able only to follow others' programs, yearn for their products, or click buttons for immediate and trival rewards, we should not be surprised if real minds ultimately become the servants of virtual ones.

The real-life values in the lives we structure for our children will determine the kind of world they, and we, inhabit in the future. Will it be a world dedicated to people or to machines? Will there be space for solitude? For wisdom? For dreams? Will it be one we want to live in?

Suggested Reading

The following references provide follow-up reading to parents and teachers who want to learn more about the topics discussed in this book. Those marked with an asterisk may be of particular interest to parents or readers not specializing in educational issues.

Books

Bruer, J.T. *Schools for Thought: A Science of Learning in the Classroom.* Cambridge, MA: MIT Press, 1993.

*Burstein, Daniel, and Kline, David. *Road Warriors.* New York: Penguin Books, 1996.

Caine, R.N., and Caine, G. *Education on the Edge of Possibility.* Alexandria, VA: ASCD, 1997.

*Capra, Fritjof. *The Web of Life.* New York: Anchor Books, 1996.

*DeGaetano, Gloria, and Bander, Kathleen. *Screen Smarts.* Boston: Houghton Mifflin Co., 1996.

Druin, Allison, and Solomon, Cynthia. *Designing Multimedia Environments for Children.* New York: John Wiley & Sons, 1996.

*Gates, B. *The Road Ahead.* New York: Penguin Books, 1995.

*Goleman, Daniel. *Emotional Intelligence: Why It Can Matter More than I.Q.* New York: Bantam Books, 1995.

*Greenfield, Patricia M., and Cocking, Rodney R. *Interacting with Video.* Norwood, NJ: Ablex Publishing Co., 1996.

*Lacy, Dan. *From Grunts to Gigabytes.* Chicago: University of Illinois Press, 1996.

*Lynch, Aaron. *Thought Contagion: The New Science of Memes.* New York: Basic Books, 1996.

Maddux, C.D., et al. *Educational Computing.* Needham, MA: Allyn & Bacon, 1997.

*Negroponte, Nicholas. *Being Digital.* New York: Vintage Books, 1995.

*Norman, Donald A. *Things that Make Us Smart.* Reading, MA: Addison-Wesley, 1993.

*Papert, Seymour. *The Connected Family.* Marietta, GA: Longstreet Press, 1996.

Papert, Seymour. *Mindstorms: Children, Computers, and Powerful Ideas.* New York: Basic Books, 1980.

Perkins, David N., et al. *Software Goes to School.* New York: Oxford University Press, 1995.

*Postman, Neil. *Technopoly.* New York: Knopf, 1992.

*Rawlings, Gregory J.E. *Moths to the Flame: The Seductions of Computer Technology.* Cambridge, MA: MIT Press, 1996.

*Reeves, B., and Nass, C. *The Media Equation.* Stanford, CA: CSLI Publications: 1996.

Schofield, Janet W. *Computers and Classroom Culture.* Cambridge: Cambridge University Press, 1995.

Salomon, Gavriel. *Interaction of Media, Cognition, and Learning.* San Francisco: Jossey-Bass, 1979.

*Stoll, Clifford. *Silicon Snake Oil.* New York: Anchor Books, 1995.

*Sussman, Martin, and Loewenstein, Ernest. *Total Health at the Computer.* Barrytown, New York: Station Hill Press, 1993.

Teacher's Guide to Cyberspace. New York, The Teacher's Network, Impact II, 1996.

Thornburg, David. *Education in the Communication Age.* San Carlos, CA: Starsong Publications, 1994.

*Turkle, Sherry. *The Second Self.* New York: Simon & Schuster, 1985.

*Turkle, Sherry. *Life on the Screen: Identity in the Age of the Internet.* New York: Simon & Schuster, 1995.

Wright, J.L., and Shade, D. *Young Children: Active Learners in a Technological Age.* Washington: NAEYC, 1993–1994.

Useful Journals

In this fast-changing field, new journals proliferate and old ones change their names. As we go to press, here are just a few possibilities:

ASCD Curriculum/Technology Quarterly

Computers in the Schools

Educational Leadership

Journal of Computing in Childhood Education

Journal of Educational Computing Research

Journal of Research on Computing in Education

Learning and Leading with Technology

Two Articles of Particular Note

Oppenheimer, Todd. The computer delusion. *Atlantic Monthly,* July, 1997, pp. 45–62.

Salomon, Gavriel. Of mind and media. *Phi Delta Kappan,* January, 1997, pp. 375–380

Notes

Chapter 1

[1]Negroponte, Nicholas. *Being Digital*. New York: Vintage Books, 1995, p. 6.

[2]Sava, S.G. Electronic genie. Address delivered at NAESP State Leaders Conference, Arlington, VA, July 25, 1997.

[3]Quoted in Oppenheimer, Todd. The computer delusion. *Atlantic Monthly*, July, 1997, pp. 45–62.

[4]*Wall Street Journal*, November 13, 1995, p. R8.

[5]Sava, S.G. Electronic genie. Address delivered at NAESP State Leaders Conference, Arlington, VA, July 25, 1997.

[6]Special Report: What students must know to succeed in the 21st century. Bethesda, MD: World Future Society, 1996.

[7]*Education Week*, December 11, 1996, p. 5.

[8]Computers in Education: A Critical Look. Invitational Symposium. University of California, Berkeley, June 3–5, 1995.

[9]Sava, S.G. Electronic genie. Address delivered to NAESP State Leaders Conference. Arlington, VA, July 25, 1997.

[10]Sefton-Green, J., and Buckingham, D. Digital visions: Children's creative uses of multimedia technologies. *Convergence*, 2(2), 1996, pp. 47–79.

[11]Papert, Seymour. *Mindstorms: Children, Computers, and Powerful Ideas*. New York: Basic Books, 1980.

[12]See, for example, Kulik, James. Meta-analytic studies of findings on computer-based instruction. In E.L. Baker and H.F. O'Neil, *Technology Assessment in Education and Training*. Hillsdale, NJ: LEA, 1994, p. 21.

[13]Postman, Neil. *Technopoly*. New York: Knopf, 1992, p. xiii.

[14]Greenfield, Patricia. Comments delivered at conference, "Computers and Cognitive Development": University of California, Berkeley, November 17, 1996.

[15]Personal communication, April 14, 1997.

[16]Gates, Bill. *The Road Ahead*. New York: Penguin Books, 1995, p. 276.

[17]Rushkoff, Douglas. *Playing the Future: How Kids' Culture Can Teach Us to Thrive in an Age of Chaos*. New York: HarperCollins, 1996.

[18]Capra, Fritjof. *The Web of Life.* New York: Anchor Books, 1996, p. 69.

[19]Quoted in *New York Times,* January 11, 1998, p. 4.

[20]McKibben, Bill. *The Age of Missing Information.* New York: Plume, 1993.

[21]Personal communication. October 24, 1996.

[22]For extended reading on this fascinating topic, please see: D. deKerckhove and C. Lumsden (eds.). *The Alphabet and the Brain.* New York: Springer-Verlag, 1987, and Logan, R.K. *The Alphabet Effect.* New York: St. Martin's Press, 1986.

[23]*New York Times,* October 20, 1996, p. 37.

[24]Reeves, B., and Nass, C. *The Media Equation.* Stanford, CA: CSLI Publications, 1996.

[25]Stoll, Clifford. *Silicon Snake Oil.* New York: Anchor Books, 1995, p. 45.

[26]Rudnitsky, Al. Personal communication, October 23, 1995.

[27]Business Day, *New York Times.* June 3, 1996, p. D1.

Chapter 2

[1]Walker, Derrick. *Promise, Potential, and Pragmatism: Computers in high school.* Institute for Research in Educational Finance and Governance Policy Notes, 16(5), pp. 3–4, 1984.

[2]Hawkins, Jan. Technology in Education: Transitions. Pre-Summit Briefing Material prepared for National Educational Summit. Palisades, New York: 1996, p. 1.

[3]Wyns-Madison, Peggy. Building bridges from your place to cyberspace. In *Teacher's Guide to Cyberspace.* New York, The Teacher's Network, Impact II, 1996, pp. 27–30.

[4]Harris, Judi. If seeing is believing, is believing doing? Address presented at Midwest Education and Technology Conference, St. Louis, MO, February 25, 1997.

[5]*New York Times,* May 25, 1997, p. 12F.

[6]For one view of this power shift, see: Bly, Robert. *The Sibling Society.* New York, Addison-Wesley, 1996.

[7]Ravitch, Diane. Technology and the curriculum: Promise and peril. In White, M.A. (ed.). *What Curriculum for the Information Age?* Hillsdale, NJ: LEA, 1987.

[8]*Education Life,* January 5, 1997, p. 13.

[9]*Education Life.* November 3, 1996, p. 15.

[10]Buckleitner, Warren. Building brainpower. *Scholastic Parent & Child.* Winter, 1995, p. 26.

[11]Thornburg, David. *Education in the Communication Age.* San Carlos, CA: Starsong Publications, 1994, p. 173.

[12]King, Alison. Effects of training in strategic questioning on children's problem-solving performance. *Journal of Educational Psychology,* 83(3), 1991, pp. 307–317.

[13]Druin, Allison, and Solomon, Cynthia. *Designing Multimedia Environments for Children.* New York: John Wiley & Sons, 1996.

[14]Robler, M. The effectiveness of microcomputers in education: A review of the research from 1980–1987. *T.H.E. Journal,* Sept. 1988, pp. 85–87.

[15]Ramondetta, J. Using computers. Learning from lunchroom trash. *Learning,* 20 (8), 1992, p. 59.

[16]Maddux, C.D., et al. *Educational Computing.* Needham, MA: Allyn & Bacon, 1997.

[17]See, for example, Van Dusen, L., and Worthen, B. Can integrated instructional technology transform the classroom? *Educational Leadership,* October, 1995, pp. 28–33.

[18]Schofield, Janet W. *Computers and Classroom Culture.* Cambridge: Cambridge University Press, 1995.

[19]Mandinach, E.B., and Kline, H.F. Classroom dynamics: The impact of a technology-based curriculum innovation on teaching and learning. *Journal of Educational Computing Research,* 14(1), 1996, pp. 83–102.

[20]Resnick, Mitchell. Internet communication, November 11, 1996.

[21]Breuer, J.T. *Schools for Thought: A Science of Learning in the Classroom.* Cambridge, MA: MIT Press, 1993, p. 291.

[22]Mandinach, E.B., and Kline, H.F. Classroom dynamics: The impact of a technology-based curriculum innovation on teaching and learning. *Journal of Educational Computing Research,* 14(1), 1996, pp. 83–102.

[23]Haughland, S.W. The effect of computer software on preschool children's developmental gains. *Journal of Computing in Childhood Education,* 3(1), 1992, pp. 15–30.

[24]Ibid., p. 76.

[25]Hativa, Nira, and Lesgold, Alan. Situational effects in classroom technology implementation: unfulfilled expectations and unexpected outcomes. In S.T. Kerr (ed.). *Technology and the Future of Schooling.* Chicago: University of Chicago Press, 1996.

[26]See, for example, Liao, Yuen-Kuang. Effects of computer-assisted instruction on cognitive outcomes. *Journal of Research on Computing in Education,* 24(3), 1992, pp. 367–380.

[27]Kulik, James A. Meta-analytic studies of findings on computer-based instruction. In E.L. Baker and H.F. O'Neil (eds.). *Technology Assessment in Education and Training.* Hillsdale, NJ: LEA, 1994, p. 19.

[28]Fletcher-Flynn, C.M., and Gravatt, B. The efficacy of computer assisted instruction (CAI): A meta-analysis. *Journal of Educational Computing Research,* 12(3), 1995, pp. 219–242.

[29]Krendl, K.A., and Broihier, M. Student responses to computers: A longitudinal study. *Journal of Educational Computing Research,* 8(2), 1992, p. 216.

[30]*Los Angeles Times,* June 8, 1997, p. 4.

[31]Foa, L., Schwab, R.L., and Johnson, M. Upgrading school technology. *Education Week,* May 1, 1996, p. 52.

[32]Gooden, Andrea R. *Computers in the Classroom.* New York: Jossey-Bass and Apple Press, 1996, p. 61.

[33]*New York Times Magazine,* February 2, 1997, p. 32.

[34]*Wall Street Journal,* November 13, 1995, p. R31.

[35]Giaquinta, J.B., et al. *Beyond Technology's Promise.* Cambridge: Cambridge University Press, 1993.

Chapter 3

[1]Noble, Douglas. The overselling of educational technology. *Educational Leadership,* November, 1996, p. 20.

[2]Sava, S.G. Electronic genie. Address delivered at NAESP State Leaders Conference, Arlington, VA, July 25, 1997.

[3]Firestone, James A., General Manager of IBM Consumer Division, quoted in *New York Times,* November 13, 1996, p. 8.

[4]Papert, Seymour. *The Connected Family.* Marietta, GA: Longstreet Press, 1996, p. 2.

[5]Burstein, Daniel, and Kline, David. *Road Warriors.* New York: Plume, 1996.

[6]Nickelodeon area, America Online, January 1996. Reported in Montgomery, Kathryn, and Pasnik, Shelley. *Web of Deception: Threats to Children from Online Marketing.* Washington, DC: Center for Media Education, 1996.

[7]*America's Children and the Information Superhighway.* Santa Monica, CA: The Children's Partnership, 1996.

[8]*Los Angeles Times,* Washington Edition, March 22, 1996, p. 1.

[9]Statement issued by American Psychological Association, Washington, DC, March 22, 1996.

[10]Pasnik, Shelley. Personal communication, January 13, 1997.

[11]*Education Week,* June 5, 1996, p. 1.

[12]Computers and the Arts Project. P.S. 19, New York, NY.

[13]Renyi, Judith. The longest reform. *Education Week,* November 13, 1996, p. 34.

[14]Druin, Allison, and Solomon, Cynthia. *Designing Multimedia Environments for Children.* New York: John Wiley & Sons, 1996, p. 103.

[15]*APA Monitor,* January, 1997, p. 30.

[16]*Education Week,* March 13, 1996, p. 22.

[17]Freshmen going for the cash, survey finds. *Honolulu Advertiser,* March 6, 1997, p. 1.

[18]*The Future of Children,* 6(2), 1996, p. 17.

[19]Bracey, G.W. Debunking the myths about money for schools. *Educational Leadership,* November, 1995, pp. 65–69.

[20]Schweinhart, L.J. Making Head Start work. *Education Week,* April 27, 1994, p. 40.

[21]Financing Child Care: Analysis and Recommendations. *The Future of Children,* 6(2), 1996.

[22]*USA Weekend.* February 14–16, 1997, p. 10.

[23]Stoll, Clifford. *New York Times,* Op Ed, May 19, 1996.

[24]*Education Week,* December 12, 1996, p. 3.

[25]*What Matters Most: Teaching for America's Future.* National Commission on Teaching and America's Future. New York: Rockefeller Foundation, 1996.

[26]*Education Week,* November 20, 1996, p. 5.

[27]*Education Week,* July 10, 1996, p. 8.

[28]Tejada, Carlos. Those who can't . . . *Wall Street Journal,* November 13, 1995, p. R6.

[29]Tejada, Carlos. Those who can't . . . *Wall Street Journal,* November 13, 1995, p. R7.

[30]*New York Times,* October 21, 1996, p. D5.

[31]McClintock, Robert. Personal communication, Teachers College, Columbia University, October 2, 1996.

[32]National Geographic Kids' Network. www.edc.org/FSC/NCIP/TC_natlGeographic.HTML.

[33]McClintock, Robert. Personal communication, Teachers College, Columbia University, October 2, 1996.

[34]*Education Week*, February 14, 1996, p. 32.

[35]Burstein, Daniel, and Kline, David. *Road Warriors*. New York: Penguin Books, 1996, p. 176.

[36]Davis, S. and Botkin, J. *The Monster Under the Bed.* New York: Touchstone, 1994.

Chapter 4

[1]Reisberg, Lisa M. Director, Media Matters Campaign. Personal communication, American Academy of Pediatrics, March 25, 1998.

[2]NIOSH Publications on Video Display Terminals (Revised.) U.S. Dept. of Health and Human Services. Cincinnati, OH: Public Health Service, June 1991.

[3]Updegrove, D., and Updegrove, K. Computers and health. *Cause/Effect,* Fall, 1991, pp. 40–45.

[4]Anschel, Jeffrey. Visual ergonomics in the workplace. *p&i,* May/June, 1994, pp. 20–22.

[5]Atencio, R. Eyestrain: The number one complaint of computer users. *Computers in Libraries,* September 1996, pp. 40–43.

[6]Alexander, Melody A. Physical problems associated with computer use and implemented ergonomic measures. *The Delta Pi Epsilon Journal,* XXXVI (4), Fall, 1994, pp. 189–202.

[7]Wilkins, Arnold J. *Visual Stress.* Oxford: Oxford University Press, 1995.

[8]Barber, Ann. Personal communication, December 11, 1996.

[9]Ibid.

[10]Szul, L., and Berry, L. Color variations in screen text: Effects on proofreading. ERIC Document ED397843.

[11]Sussman, Martin, and Loewenstein, Ernest. *Total Health at the Computer.* Barrytown, NY: Station Hill Press, 1993.

[12]Updegrove, D., and Updegrove, K. Computers and health. *Cause/Effect,* Fall, 1991, p. 43.

[13]Miller, Norma L. Are computers dangerous to children's health? *PTA Today,* 17, April, 1992, pp. 5–7.

[14]Neutro, Raymond. Personal communication, August 14, 1997.

[15]Miller, Norma L. Are computers dangerous to children's health? *PTA Today,* 17, April, 1992, pp. 5–7.

[16]*New York Times,* August 25, 1996, p. 14.

[17]*APA Monitor,* July, 1996, p. 18.

[18]*APA Monitor,* July, 1996, p. 24.

[19]Hanson, Victor Davis. *New York Times,* Op Ed, September 2, 1996.

[20]*New York Times,* November 17, 1996, p. 31.

[21]Calvin, W.H. The emergence of intelligence. *Scientific American,* October 1944, pp. 101–107.

[22]Snyder, Janet. Cartoon sickness mystifies Japan TV network. Yahoo News, Reuters, December 17, 1997.

[23]Graf, William D. Video game–related seizures. *Pediatrics,* 93(4), 1994, p. 554.

[24]Kubey, Robert W. Letter to the editor. *New York Times,* December 25, 1997, p. A14.

[25]Schulkin, Jay. *Hormonally Induced Changes in Mind and Brain.* San Diego: Academic Press, 1993.

Chapter 5

[1]Kay, Alan C. Computers, networks, and education. *Scientific American,* September 1991, pp. 138–148.

[2]Pogrow, Stanley. On scripting the classroom. *Education Week,* September 25, 1996, p. 52.

[3]Brown, Jason W. Morphogenesis and mental process. *Development and Psychopathology,* 6, 1994, p. 562.

[4]Goffinet, A.M., et al. Brain glucose utilization under high sensory activation: Hypoactivation of prefrontal cortex. *Aviation, Space, and Environmental Medicine,* 61, 1990, pp. 338–342.

[5]Csikszentmihalyi, Mihaly. *The Evolving Self.* New York: HarperCollins, 1993, p. 136.

[6]National Mental Health Advisory Council. Basic behavioral science research for mental health. *American Psychologist,* 50(10), pp. 838–845.

[7]Pea, Roy D. Integrating Human and Computer Intelligence. *New Directions for Child Development.* 28, June 1985, pp. 75–96.

[8]Sternberg, Robert J. *Successful Intelligence.* New York: Simon & Schuster, 1996.

[9]Salomon, Gavriel. Of mind and media. *Phi Delta Kappan,* January 1997, pp. 375–380.

[10]Quoted in *New York Times,* February 20, 1996, p. B2.

[11]Rochester, J. Martin. The decline of literacy. *Education Week,* May 15, 1996, p. 34.

[12]Salomon, Gavriel. Of mind and media. *Phi Delta Kappan,* January 1997, pp. 375–380.

[13]Ibid.

[14]Salomon, Gavriel. *Interaction of Media, Cognition, and Learning.* San Francisco: Jossey-Bass, 1979, p. 237.

[15]Himmelfarb, Gertrude. A neo-Luddite reflects on the Internet. *Chronicle of Higher Education,* November 1, 1996, p. A56.

[16]Norman, Donald A. *Things That Make Us Smart.* Reading, MA: Addison-Wesley, 1993, pp. 16–17.

[17]Stoll, Clifford. *New York Times,* Op Ed, May 19, 1996.

[18]Birkerts, Sven. *The Gutenberg Elegies: The Fate of Reading in an Electronic Age.* New York: Fawcett Columbine, 1994, pp. 128–130.

[19]Ibid., p. 133.

[20]Sanders, Barry. *A Is for Ox.* New York: Vintage Books, 1995, p. xi.

[21]Ibid., p. xii.

[22]Thornberg, David D. *Education in the Communication Age.* San Carlos, CA: Starsong Publications, 1994, p. 173.

[23]Rouet, Jean-Francois, et al. *Hypertext and Cognition.* Mahwah, NJ: LEA, 1996, p. 32.

[24]Ibid.

[25]Mayer, Richard E. Multimedia learning: Are we asking the right questions? *Educational Psychologist,* 32(1), pp. 1–19, 1997.

[26]Gardner, Howard. *Frames of Mind.* New York: Basic Books, 1983.

[27]*Wall Street Journal,* November 13, 1995, p. R22.

[28]*ASCD Curriculum/Technology Quarterly,* Spring, 1997, p. 5.

[29]Ibid., p. 3.

[30]Giving language skills a boost. *Science,* (271), January 5, 1996, pp. 27–28.

[31]Gibbons, Pamela. A cognitive processing account of individual differences in novice logo programmers' conceptualization and use of recursion. *Journal of Educational Computing Research,* 13(3), 1995, pp. 211–226.

[32]*New York Times Education Life.* August 3, 1997, p. 18.

[33]Elkind, Jerome. Computer-based compensation of adult reading disabilities. *Annals of Dyslexia,* (46), 1996, pp. 159–186.

[34]Greenfield, Patricia M., and Cocking, Rodney R. *Interacting with Video.* Norwood, NJ: Ablex Publishing Co., 1996.

[35]Conference presentation: Computers and Cognitive Development. Berkeley, CA, November 17, 1996.

[36]Greenfield, Patricia M., and Cocking, Rodney R. *Interacting with Video.* Norwood, NJ: Ablex Publishing Co., 1996.

[37]Kafai, Yasmin B. Gender differences in children's constructions of video games. In *Interacting with Video.* Norwood, NJ: Ablex Publishing Co., 1996, pp. 39–66.

[38]Schofield, Janet W. *Computers and Classroom Culture.* Cambridge: Cambridge University Press, 1995.

[39]*CCT Notes.* New York: Education Development Center, 4(1), June, 1996.

[40]*Education Week.* April 2, 1997, p. 6.

[41]Sloan, Douglas (ed.). *The Computer in Education.* New York: Teachers College Press, 1985, p. 6.

[42]Haughland, S.W. The effect of computer software on preschool children's developmental gains. *Journal of Computing in Childhood Education,* 3(1), 1992, pp. 15–30.

[43]Haybron, Ron. Too much emphasis on computers. *Cleveland Plain Dealer,* August 6, 1996, p. 8E.

[44]Wright, J.L. Listen to the children. In Wright, J.L., and Shade, D. *Young Children: Active Learners in a Technological Age.* Washington: NAEYC, 1993–94, p. 10.

[45]Oppenheimer, Todd. The computer delusion. *Atlantic Monthly,* July, 1997, pp. 45–62.

[46]Csikszentmihalyi, Mihaly. *Flow: The Psychology of Optimal Experience.* New York: Harper & Row, 1990.

[47]Csikszentmihalyi, Mihaly. Address delivered at Albuquerque Academy, Albuquerque, NM, October 18, 1996.

[48]Csikszentmihalyi, Mihaly. Personal communication, October 18, 1996.

[49]Gardner, Howard. Personal communication, March 23, 1997.

Chapter 6

[1]Novick, Robert. *The Examined Life.* New York: Simon & Schuster, 1989, p. 15.

[2]*New York Times.* "Technology," June 30, 1997.

[3]Goleman, Daniel. *Emotional Intelligence: Why It Can Matter More Than IQ.* New York: Bantam Books, 1995.

[4]Rich, Dorothy. *MegaSkills: Building Children's Achievement for the Information Age.* New York: Houghton Mifflin Co., 1997.

[5]O'Neil, John. On emotional intelligence. A conversation with Daniel Goleman. *Educational Leadership,* September, 1996, p. 11.

[6]Halpern, Samuel. School-to-work, employers, and personal values. *Education Week,* March 12, 1997, p. 52.

[7]Coles, Robert. *The Moral Intelligence of Children.* New York: Random House, 1997.

[8]Spreen, Ottfried, et al. *Developmental Neuropsychology.* New York: Oxford University Press, 1995, p. 150.

[9]Goleman, Daniel. Early violence leaves its mark on the brain. *New York Times,* October 3, 1995, p. C10.

[10]DeFrancesco, J.J. Conduct disorder: the crisis continues. *APA Monitor,* August, 1995, p. 4.

[11]See, for example: Damasio, Antonio R. *Descartes' Error.* New York: Avon Books, 1994.

[12]Environment is key to serotonin levels. *APA Monitor,* April, 1997, p. 26.

[13]Sylwester, Robert. The neurobiology of self-esteem and aggression. *Educational Leadership,* February, 1997, pp. 75–79.

[14]Diamond, Marian. Computers and Cognitive Development. Invitational workshop, UC Berkeley, November 17, 1996.

[15]Oades, R.D., et al. A test of conditioned blocking and its development in relation to childhood and adolescence. *Developmental Neuropsychology,* 12(2), 1996, pp. 207–230.

[16]Sylwester, Robert. Finding and following the grain of our brain. Unpublished manuscript, p. 10.

[17]Ibid., p. 19.

[18]O'Boyle, M.W., Benbow, C.P., and Alexander, J.E. Sex differences, hemispheric laterality, and associated brain activity in the intellectually gifted. *Developmental Neuropsychology,* 11(4), 1995, pp. 415–443.

[19]*America's Children and the Information Superhighway.* Santa Monica, CA: The Children's Partnership, 1996.

[20]See, for example, Greenfield, P.M. Language, tools, and brain. *Behavioral and Brain Sciences,* 14, 1991, pp. 531–551.

[21]McKay, K., et al. Developmental analysis of three aspects of information processing. *Developmental Neuropsychology,* 10(2), 1994, pp. 121–132.

[22]Rimm, Sylvia B. An underachievement epidemic. *Educational Leadership,* April, 1997, p. 18.

[23]Caine, R.N., and Caine, G. *Education on the Edge of Possibility.* Alexandria, VA: ASCD, 1997.

[24]Miserandino, Marianne. Children who do well in school. *Journal of Educational Psychology,* 88(2), 1996, p. 203.

[25]Ibid.

[26]*APA Monitor.* October, 1994, p. 4.

[27]National Mental Health Advisory Council. Basic behavioral science research for mental health. *American Psychologist,* 50(10), 1995, p. 843.

[28]Cordova, D.I., and Lepper, M.R. Intrinsic motivation and the process of learning. *Journal of Educational Psychology,* 88(4), 1996, pp. 715–730.

[29]O'Boyle, M.W., Benbow, C.P., and Alexander, J.E. Sex differences, hemispheric laterality, and associated brain activity in the intellectually gifted. *Developmental Neuropsychology,* 11(4), 1995, pp. 415–443.

[30]Teasley, S.D. The role of talk in children's peer collaborations. *Developmental Psychology,* 31(2), 1995, pp. 207–220.

[31]Denby, David. Buried alive. *The New Yorker,* July 15, 1996, p. 50.

[32]Reeves, Byron, and Nass, Clifford. *The Media Equation.* Stanford University: CSLI Publications, 1996.

[33]Goleman, Daniel. Laugh and your computer will laugh with you, someday. *New York Times,* January 7, 1997, p. B9.

[34]Rawlings, Gregory J.E. *Moths to the Flame: The Seductions of Computer Technology.* Cambridge, MA: MIT Press, 1996, p. 27.

[35]Easterbrook, G. The heart of a new machine. In J. Zerzan and A. Carnes, *Questioning Technology.* Philadelphia: New Society Publishers, 1991, p. 138.

[36]Quoted in Turkle, Sherry. *Life on the Screen: Identity in the Age of the Internet.* New York: Simon & Schuster, 1995, p. 105.

[37]Turkle, Sherry. *Life on the Screen: Identity in the Age of the Internet.* New York: Simon & Schuster, 1995.

[38]Ibid., p. 185.

[39]Ibid., p. 232.

[40]Murray, Bridget. Computer addictions entangle students. June, 1996, p. 38.

[41]Mobility, freedom, can foster alienation. *APA Monitor,* September, 1995, p. 46.

[42]Angier, Natalie. The importance of being social. *International Herald Tribune,* May 2, 1996, p. 19.

[43]Smith, M. Brewster. Selfhood at risk. *American Psychologist,* May, 1994, p. 407.

[44]Birkerts, Sven. Subjectivity and the changing face of time. *Lapis* (four), 1997, p. 69.

[45]Smith, M. Brewster. Selfhood at risk. *American Psychologist,* May, 1994, p. 409.

[46]Miller, P., et al. Relations of moral reasoning and vicarious emotion to young chil-

dren's prosocial behavior toward peers and adults. *Developmental Psychology*, 32(2), 1996, pp. 210–219.

Chapter 7

[1]Stress, depression, and hormones are linked. *APA Monitor,* June, 1996, p. 6.

[2]*Education Week,* December 11, 1996, p. 5.

[3]Thatcher, R.W. Psychopathology of early frontal lobe damage. In D. Cicchetti, ed. *Development and Psychopathology*, 6, 1994, pp. 565–596.

[4]See, for example, Denham, S. Maternal emotional responsiveness and toddlers' social-emotional competence. *Journal of Child Psychology and Psychiatry and Allied Disciplines*, 34(5), 1993, pp. 715–728.

[5]Radell, P.L., and Gottlieb, G. Developmental intersensory interference. *Developmental Psychology*, 28(5), 1992, pp. 794–803.

[6]Turkle, Sherry. *The Second Self.* New York: Simon & Schuster, 1985.

[7]*New York Times,* April 5, 1997, p. 10.

[8]Fox, N., et al. Frontal activation asymmetry and social competence at four years of age. *Child Development*, 66(6), 1995, pp. 1770–1784.

[9]Mariani, M., and Barkley, R.A. Neuropsychological and academic function in preschool boys with attention deficit hyperactivity disorder. *Developmental Neuropsychology*, 13(1), 1997, pp. 111–119.

[10]Bjorklund, D.F., and Harnishfeger, K.K. The resources construct in cognitive development. *Developmental Review*, 10, 1990, pp. 48–71.

[11]Frye, D., et al. Inference and action in early causal reasoning. *Developmental Psychology*, 32(1), 1996, pp. 120–131.

[12]*Education Week,* January 12, 1994, p. 33.

[13]Bowman, Barbara T., and Beyer, Elizabeth R. Thoughts on technology and early childhood education. In Wright, J.L., and Shade, D.D. (eds.) *Young Children: Active Learners in a Technological Age.* Washington: NAEYC, 1993–1994, p. 23.

[14]Wright, J.C., et al. Young children's perceptions of television reality. *Developmental Psychology*, 30 (2), 1994, pp. 229–239.

[15]Mandl, H., Gruber, H., and Renkl, A. Learning to apply. In Vosnaidou, S., et al. (eds.) *International Perspectives on the Design of Technology-Supported Learning Environments.* Mahway, NJ: LEA, 1996.

[16]Case, Robbie. Some thoughts about cognitive development. Computers and Cognitive Development: Invitational Workshop, UC Berkeley, November 16–17, 1996.

[17]For a summary of Siegel's work, please see Ellsworth, P.C., and Sindt, V.G. Helping "Aha" to happen. *Educational Leadership*, February 1994, pp. 40–44.

[18]For a complete review of this topic, please see Thelen, Esther. Motor development. *American Psychologist,* February, 1995, pp. 79–95.

[19]Calvin, W.H. The emergence of intelligence. *Scientific American,* October, 1994, pp. 101–107.

[20]Turvey, M.T. Dynamic touch. *American Psychologist,* 51(11), 1996, pp. 1134–1152.

[21]Brosterman, Norman. *Inventing Kindergarten.* New York: Abrams, 1997.

[22]Weikart, Phyllis S. Purposeful movement: Have we overlooked the base? *Early Childhood Connections,* Fall, 1995, pp. 6–15.

[23]*Early Childhood Today,* January, 1997, p. 4.

[24]Quoted in Wright, J.L., and Shade, D.D. (eds.) *Young Children: Active Learners in a Technological Age.* Washington: NAEYC, 1993–1994.

[25]Angier, Natalie. The purpose of playful frolics: Training for adulthood. *New York Times,* October 20, 1992, pp. C1, C8.

[26]Ibid., p. C1.

[27]See, for example, M.H. Bornstein and A.W. O'Reilley (eds.) *The Role of Play in the Development of Thought.* San Francisco: Jossey-Bass, 1993, or Doris Bergen (ed.) *Play as a Medium for Learning and Development.* Portsmouth, NH: Heinemann, 1988.

[28]Computers in Education: A Critical Look. Invitational symposium, University of California, Berkeley, June 3–5, 1995.

[29]Stoll, Clifford. *Silicon Snake Oil.* New York: Doubleday, 1995, p. 138.

[30]*Wall Street Journal.* November 13, 1995, p. R10.

[31]Gates, B. *The Road Ahead.* New York: Penguin Books, 1995, p. 191.

[32]Bergen, Doris (ed.) *Play as a Medium for Learning and Development.* Portsmouth, NH: Heinemann, 1988.

[33]Cohen, D. and MacKeith, S. *The Development of Imagination.* London: Routledge, 1992.

[34]Singer, D.J., and Singer, J.L. *Partners in Play.* New York: Harper & Row, 1977.

[35]Wright, J.L. Listen to the children. In Wright, J.L., and Shade, D. *Young Children: Active Learners in a Technological Age.* Washington: NAEYC, 1993–1994, p. 10.

[36]Buckleitner, Warren. Behind the scenes. *Scholastic Parent and Child,* Spring, 1996, p. 29–30.

[37]*Education Week,* March, 12, 1997, p. 6.

[38]Gilpatrick, Liz. Personal communication, April 28, 1997.

[39]Petry, M., et al. The effect of language on visual spatial attention. Paper presented at Annual Meeting of the International Neuropsychological Society, February, 1996.

[40]Pellegrini, A.D., and Galda, L. Ten years after: A reexamination of symbolic play and literacy research. *Reading Research Quarterly,* 28(2), 1993, pp. 163–175.

[41]Arnold, D.H. Accelerating language development through picture book reading. *Journal of Educational Psychology,* 86(2), 1994, pp. 235–243.

[42]See, for example, Diaz, R.M., and Berk, L.E. *Private Speech.* Hillsdale, NJ: LEA, 1992.

[43]Berk, Laura E. Why children talk to themselves. *Scientific American,* November, 1994, pp. 78–83.

[44]Haughland, S.W. The effect of computer software on preschool children's developmental gains. *Journal of Computing in Childhood Education,* 3(1), 1992, pp. 15–30.

[45]Labbo, Linda D. A semiotic analysis of young children's symbol making in a classroom computer center. *Reading Research Quarterly,* 31(4), 1996, pp. 356–385.

[46]Clements, D., et al. Young children and computers. *Young Children,* January, 1993, pp. 56–64.

[47]Patton, M.M., and Kokoski, T.M. How good is your early childhood science, mathematics, and technology program? *Young Children,* July, 1996, pp. 38–44.

[48]The Haughland/Shade Developmental Scale, Revised Edition. In Haughland, S.W., and Wright, J.L. *Young Children and Technology.* Boston: Allyn & Bacon (A Viacom Company), 1997, p. 27.

[49]Ucci, Mary. Personal communication, April 14, 1997.

[50]Elkind, David. Conference Paper. Education for the 21st Century: Toward the renewal of thinking. New York: Teachers College, Columbia University, February 10–11, 1994.

[51]Computers in Education: A Critical Look. Invitational symposium, University of California, Berkeley, June 3–5, 1995.

[52]Quoted in Wright, J.L., and Shade, D.D. (eds.) *Young Children: Active Learners in a Technological Age.* Washington: NAEYC, 1993–1994.

Chapter 8

[1]Quoted in Wilson, K.G., and Daviss, B. *Redesigning Education.* New York: Teachers College Press, 1994.

[2]Reported in Haughland, S.W., and Wright, J.L. *Young Children and Technology.* Boston: Allyn & Bacon, 1997, p. 107.

[3]Editorial: *New York Times.* December 28, 1995.

[4]Levine, J., Baroudi, C., and Levine, M. *Internet for Dummies.* Boston: Harper Audio, 1996.

[5]*Education Week.* October 23, 1996, p. 11.

[6]DeGaetano, Gloria, and Bander, Kathleen. *Screen Smarts.* Boston: Houghton Mifflin Co., 1996.

[7]*New York Times,* November 11, 1996, p. C10.

[8]Matsuoka, Bob. Virtual schools, virtual communities: A primer. *Technology in Education* 1(1), 1996, p. 8.

[9]Riel, Margaret. Lecture taped at Simon Frazer University, Vancouver, British Columbia, June 30, 1991. Internet posting.

[10]McKenzie, Jamie. Making WEB meaning. *Educational Leadership,* November, 1996, pp. 30–32.

[11]Turkle, Sherry. *Life on the Screen.* New York: Simon & Schuster, 1995.

[12]Ohanian, Susan. *Ask Ms. Class.* York, Maine: Stenhouse Publishers, 1996

[13]Internet posting, February 7, 1997.

[14]Oakes, Celeste. First grade online. *Learning and Leading with Technology.* September, 1996, pp. 37–39.

[15]Barker, T., and Torgesen, J. An evaluation of computer-assisted instruction in phonological awareness with below average readers. *Journal of Educational Computing Research,* 13(1), 1995, pp. 89–103.

[16]Papert, Seymour. *Mindstorms.* New York: Basic Books, 1980, p. 19.

[17]Papert, Seymour. *The Children's Machine.* New York: Basic Books, 1993, p. 149.

[18]Kafai, Yasmin. *Minds in Play.* LEA: Hillsdale, NJ, 1995.

[19]Rosen, Marian. Internet communication. February, 1997.

[20]Thanks to David Perkins and his group for this concept.

[21]Perkins, David N., et al. *Software Goes to School.* New York: Oxford University Press, 1995, p. 132.

[22]Charvin, Heidi, and Proteau, Luc. Developmental differences in the processing of afferent information for motor control. *Developmental Neuropsychology,* 12(4), 1996, pp. 387–407.

[23]Perkins, David N., et al. *Software Goes to School.* New York: Oxford University Press, 1995, p. xvi.

[24]Segalowitz, Sid. Parallels between cognitive development and brain growth. Paper delivered at Invitational Workshop: Computers and Cognitive Development. UC Berkeley, November 16–17, 1997.

[25]van Strien, J.W. Hemisphere-specific priming and interference effects of stimuli with positive or negative emotional valences. Nineteenth Annual International Neuropsychological Society Conference, June, 1996, Veldhoven, Netherlands.

[26]Fang, Fan. Traveling the Internet in Chinese. *Education Week,* November, 1996, pp. 27–30.

[27]Rosen, Marian. Personal communication, March, 1997.

[28]Mansilla, V.B., and Gardner, H. Of kinds of disciplines and kinds of understandings. *Phi Delta Kappan,* January, 1997, pp. 381–386.

[29]*ASCD Curriculum/Technology Quarterly.* Fall, 1996, p. 10.

[30]Center for Children and Technology. New York: 1993–1994 Summary Report.

[31]Presented at METC: St. Louis, MO, February 24–26, 1997.

[32]ASCD *Curriculum/Technology Quarterly.* Spring, 1996, p. 2.

[33]Thornburg, David. *Education in the Communication Age.* San Carlos, CA: Starsong Publications, 1994.

[34]See, for example, Boone, Randy, ed. *Teaching Process Writing with Computers.* Revised Edition. Eugene, OR: International Society for Technology in Education, 1991.

[35]Cohen, Rachel. Do new technologies modify the learning process of young children? Paper presented at the European Conference on the Quality of Early Childhood Education, Paris, France, September 7–9, 1995.

[36]Shaw, E.L. Comparison of spontaneous and word processed compositions in elementary classrooms. *Journal of Computing in Childhood Education:* 5(3–4), 1994, pp. 319–327.

[37]See, for example, Wolf, Dennis. Flexible texts: computer editing in the study of writing. *New Directions for Child Development,* 28, 1985, pp. 37–53.

[38]Computers in Education: A Critical Look. Invitational symposium, University of California, Berkeley, June 3–5, 1995.

[39]Vaughn, Sharon, et al. Which motoric condition is most effective for teaching spelling to students with and without learning disabilities? *Journal of Learning Disabilities,* 26(3), 1993, pp. 191–198.

[40]Nichols, L.M. A comparison of two methods of teaching keyboarding in the elementary school. *Computers in the Schools,* 11(4), 1995, pp. 15–25.

[41]See, for example, Healy, A.F., and Bjork, R.A. Long-term retention of training and

knowledge. In E. Bjork and R. Bjork (eds.) *The Handbook of Perception and Cognition,* Vol. 10. New York: Academic Press, 1996.

[42]McNamara, D.S. Effects of prior knowledge on the generation advantage: calculators vs calculation to learn simple multiplication. *Journal of Educational Psychology,* 87(2), 1995, pp. 307–318.

Chapter 9

[1]Kazemak, F.E. Losing wisdom for information. *Education Week,* December 4, 1996, p. 40.

[2]Lynch, Aaron. *Thought Contagion.* New York: Basic Books, 1996.

[3]Ibid., p. 27.

[4]Cuban, Larry. *Teachers and Machines.* New York: Teachers College Press, 1986.

[5]Hunt, Earl. *Will We Be Smart Enough?* New York: Russell Sage Foundation, 1995.

[6]Katz, Jon. The rights of kids in the digital age. *Wired,* July, 1996, pp. 121–123.

[7]Rawlings, Gregory J.E. *Moths to the Flame.* Cambridge, MA: MIT Press, 1996, p. 111.

[8]Morsund, Dave. Effective practices: the future. *Learning and Leading with Technology,* April, 1996, pp. 5–6.

[9]Sloan, Douglas. Personal communication. May, 1997.

[10]Tufte, E.R. *Visual Explanations.* Cheshire, CT: Graphics Press, 1997.

[11]Huxtable, A.L. *The Unreal America.* New York: The New Press, 1997.

[12]Rawlings, Gregory J.E. *Moths to the Flame.* Cambridge, MA: MIT Press, 1996, p. 41.

[13]Minsky, Marvin, on Arts and Entertainment Network, August 26, 1997.

[14]Laurel, Brenda. Virtual reality. *Scientific American,* September, 1995, p. 90.

[15]Bricken, M., and Byrne, C. Summer students in virtual reality. In A. Wexelblat (ed.), *Virtual Reality: Applications and Explorations.* New York: Academic Press, pp. 199–218.

[16]Azar, Beth. The VR pricetag. *APA Monitor,* March, 1996, p. 25.

[17]Ibid.

[18]Solitude provides an emotional tune-up. *APA Monitor,* March, 1996, p. 1.

[19]Quoted in *APA Monitor,* 28(3), 1007, p. 1.

[20]Turkle, Sherry. *Life on the Screen.* New York: Simon & Schuster, 1995, p. 266.

[21]Kolata, Gina. With major math proof, brute computers show flash of reasoning power. *New York Times,* December 10, 1996, p. B5.

[22]Ten Dyke, Richard. Opinions expressed in letter to the editor, *New York Times,* May 11, 1997.

[23]Maes, Pattie. Intelligent software. *Scientific American,* September, 1995, pp. 84–86.

[24]Ibid.

[25]In commencement speech at Wake Forest University, May, 1997.

[26]Kane, Jeffrey. Personal communication, May 9, 1997.

Index

Failure To Connect

1. According to your own experience, what is the general public perception of computer learning for kids? What factors contribute to people's attitudes on this issue? How did you personally feel about computers before reading Chapter 1?

2. Respond to Patricia Greenfield's idea that we increasingly esteem technological intelligence and devalue the social and emotional. Is this a new trend? Can you describe any examples of computers either helping people connect socially or isolating them from others? As an employer, which skills would you value more: social/emotional, intellectual, or technical?

3. What will really be important if kids are to "win" the race to the future? What would you consider the three most critical qualities or skills to teach to today's kids?

4. Have you seen any evidence that education is becoming "an adjunct to the technology business, a sort of training school for the hi-tech world?" Is such a trend desirable or undesirable?

5. How could computer use be more hazardous than TV for youngsters' minds?

6. The author seems to feel that our society does not understand young people's real needs and too often ignores them. Can you cite examples to either support or dispute this notion?

7. Is it possible that the growing use of digital technology might actually influence the evolution of the human brain? Will electronic media make us more or less creative?

8. Have you observed any gender differences either in attitudes toward or usage of various technologies? Why do you think these differences occur?

9. React to the proposal by Reeves and Nass that even sophisticated adults have a social relationship with their computers. Do you? Is anyone you know "addicted" to computer use?

10. The author wonders if "our passion for the fruits of technology has caused us to separate intellectual and moral values, mind and soul." Comment on this statement.

11. Chapter 7 takes a strong position that normally developing children under age seven are better off without computers. Do you believe the author has successfully made her point? Would you purchase software for toddlers? What criteria would you use for selecting them?

12. What do you believe should be the first priorities for young children at home and at school? Who should be responsible to see that they are met?

13. Describe your own experiences with the Internet and World Wide Web. On the whole, have they improved the quality of your life or your teaching? At what age do you believe youngsters should be allowed unsupervised time on-line? Should material available to children be censored by some regulatory body?

14. Could humans be lulled into preferring "tailor-made cosseting" from virtual "agents" in cyberspace to the ups and downs of a real environment? What would you particularly want for your own virtual world? What would you miss?

15. Explain your personal beliefs about whether artificial intelligence represents a threat to human intelligence.